SUNSET
IN THE EAST

CONTENTS

DEDICATION

To my dearest wife,
our children and grandchildren.

GLOSSARY

ALFSEA	Allied Land Forces South East Asia
Aloon aloon (Java)	Grassy area in town
Ayo Gurkhali!	War cry of the Gurkhas
Babu	Clerk
Bahadur	Courageous, brave
Banana Boat	Troopship
Banda log	Monkey folk
Barathea	Fine woollen cloth
Basha	Bamboo and grass hut
Betel Nut	Chewing drug
Bidi	Native cigarette
Bowunja	Punjabi for '52'
Bund	Earth bank
Butty	Hurricane lamp
Charpoy	String bed frame
Chai	Tea
Chapatti	Dry pancake
Chitthi	Note, memo.
Chota peg	Short drink
Chindit	Burmese dragon
Chowkidar	Door keeper
Dacoit	Thief, brigand
Dhal	Lentils
Dushman	Enemy
ECO	Emergency Commissioned Officer
EPIP	Square tent
Fifti	Red under-pugri
Force 136	Malayan Maquis
G.S.M.	General Service Medal
Ghi	Cooking fat
Halal	Muslim butchering
Havildar, L/Havildar	Sergeant, L/Sgt
Hurribomber	Hurricane bomber
Jawan	Young man, soldier
Jeepable	Road that takes Jeeps
Jemadar	Lowest V.C.O.

Jhatka	Sikh butchering
Ji	Term of respect
Ji	Yes
Jungly	Wild
Kachcha	Shorts
Kanga	Comb
Kara	Bangle (quoit)
Kes	Uncut hair
Khana	Evening meal
Khud	Edge of cutting
Kukri	Traditional Gurkha knife.
Kirpan	Dagger
Kismet	Fate
Koi-hai	Blimp-like old officer
Krait	Large venomous snake
Laager	Night defensive position
LCT	Landing Craft Tank
Long John Collins	Gin and lime
Lota	Pewter water pot
LST	Landing Ship Tank
M.S.	Mile Stone
Mahrattha	Hindhus Bombay area
Merdeka (Java)	Freedom
N.I.C.A (Java)	Nederlandsch-Indie Civil Administration
NICA's (Java)	Dutch Indies money
Naik, Lance Naik	Corporal, L/corporal
Nullah	Stream bed
Pagri, puggree	Head dress
Pasar (Java)	Indonesian Bazaar
Pathans	N.W. Frontier race
Phanek (Manipur)	Woman's dress
Pi-dogs	Feral dogs
Pongo	Navy name for soldier
Punjabi Mussulman/PM	Muslims from Punjab
Punji	Bamboo spear
Quad	Gun limber
Ram Ram	Hindhu greeting
Roti	Midday meal
Sahib	Sir
Sathi (Gurkhali)	Chum, mate
Sat Sri Akal	Sikh Greeting
Shabash!	Hooray!
Shikari	Hunting
Sikhs	Soldier race (Punjab)
Stand-to	Dawn/dusk alert
Subedar	Senior V.C.O.

Sweepers – dry	Clean up everywhere
Sweepers – wet	Deal with excreta
Tail-end Charlie	Last man in a patrol
Thik Hai!	O.K.
Tokyo Rose	Japanese Broadcaster
Topi, topee	Sun helmet
Turd-fith	3/5th Gurkha Bn
Turd-tenth	3/10th Gurkha Bn
Turd-turd	3/3rd Gurkha Bn
Urdu	Lingua Franca of Indian languages
V.C.O.	Viceroy's Commissioned Officer
Wallah	Fellow
Wavy Navy	Naval Reserve personnel
Williwaw	Small whirlwind
Yakdans	Mule boxes
Zakhmi	Wounded

PLACE NAMES

1943	Now
Ambarawa	Surakarta
Bandoeng	Bandung
Batavia	Jakarta
Buitenzorg	Bogor
BURMA	MYANMAR
East Bengal	Bangladesh
Port Dickson	Tanjung Senebui
Port Swettenham	Klang
Rangoon	Yangon
Soerbaja	Surabaya

FOREWORD

I have written this book in the idiom of the time and used the phrase-ology and portrayed the attitudes that were normal to us then. The Second World War was a desperate time for us and, rightly or wrongly, we had a very real hatred of our enemies. Fear induces hatred. To see one's loved ones slaughtered by bombing, to see little children torn from their families, to see all the things you have always treasured smashed before your eyes is very frightening. Young men were obliged to exchange domestic security for distant battlefields and to live with death.

We were brought up by strict Victorian parents and given a very high code of ethics which affected the way we behaved man to man, how we regarded women, kept a 'stiff upper lip' and tried to behave with probity. I had no thought of a military career until it was thrust upon me. After a good schooling in the idyllic pre-war days I was pitched into the coarseness and unpredictability of soldiering. I was then flung half way round the world, to become a bilingual Indian Army Officer, commanding Sikhs and fighting alongside Gurkhas against the most frightening enemy of all. When we went to war we went for years and could not see any end to it, neither could our loved ones.

Writing about a foreign life in a foreign language can lead to italics everywhere. Especially when those languages were formerly written in scripts other than the Roman alphabet. For example the word pagri, a headdress, may be spelt pugri, puggaree, pugree depending upon who is writing it, and it is pronounced pugg-ree. After the war Eastern countries changed old colonial names for national ones. I sailed into Batavia which is now Jakarta.

John Hudson
Cornwall
2001

IMPHAL 1944.

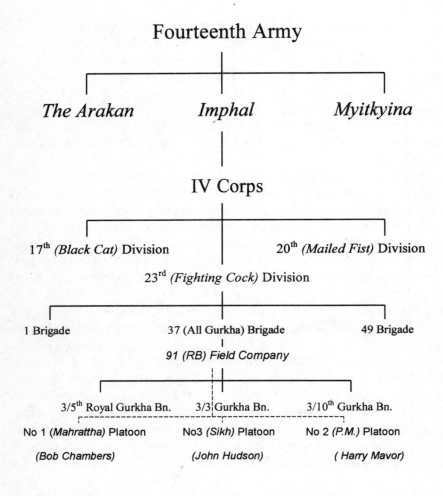

Fourteenth Army

The Arakan   Imphal   Myitkyina

IV Corps

17th *(Black Cat)* Division   20th *(Mailed Fist)* Division

23rd *(Fighting Cock)* Division

1 Brigade   37 (All Gurkha) Brigade   49 Brigade

91 (RB) Field Company

3/5th Royal Gurkha Bn.   3/3 Gurkha Bn.   3/10th Gurkha Bn.

No 1 *(Mahrattha)* Platoon   No3 *(Sikh)* Platoon   No 2 *(P.M.)* Platoon

(Bob Chambers)   *(John Hudson)*   *(Harry Mavor)*

The Sapper Field Company Commander reports to Brigade HQ and the three platoon
subalterns work for each of the three infantry battalions

Chapter 1

CURTAIN UP

When first under fire an' you're wishful to duck
Don't look nor take 'eed at the man that is struck.

The pink dust below the roadside was as fine as face powder. I snuggled my body down into it and caressed the walnut stock of my Lee Enfield rifle. The drill we had been taught so long ago on the firing ranges echoed in my mind:-

"Legs spread-eagled – heels touching the ground – take aim – *sque-ee-eze* (don't pull, lad!) – rapid fire!"

A Japanese officer brandished his naked sword and swaggered about the paddy fields to goad his crouching men forward. I knew that it was my bullet that threw him down, and the words of the recruiting sergeant in a freezing school hall in Derby came back to me:

"There are three things you never forget, Laddie!"

He leered like a Rottweiler at my goose-pimpled nakedness.

"Your army number, your first woman, and your first 'Un!" Little did I know at that time that my first would be a Jap and not a 'Un

My *havildar* (sergeant) Surajbahn Singh eased himself down beside me and spoke into my ear above the percussive noise of gunfire:-

"*Teja Singh zakhmi hogaya, Sahib.*" (Teja Singh's wounded, Sir!)

This was the first casualty in my platoon, and I crawled along behind the *bund* (mud bank) that edged the paddy field to where the wounded man lay.

Teja Singh had stiff-waxed mustachios that gave him the nickname 'Moochoo'. Sikhs all carry the same last name Singh, meaning lion, and they have less than a hundred available forenames so they are adept at inventing sobriquets.

He lay in the dust with blood oozing across his ebony hide, and as I stooped over him he received me with a look of unquestioning trust.

1

A mortar splinter had torn into his left thigh and the injury yawned crimson, like a cut on a butcher's slab. The horror of it dismayed me. My lads always believed that I was much cleverer than I am and their belief in my powers was humbling. He was relaxed in his fatalistic conviction that Sahib *Bahadur* (complimentary title 'the brave') would quickly put things right, but I approached the injury with trepidation. I knew too little about First Aid, and I had nothing with which to treat him, apart from his own First Field Dressing which was useless to staunch such a flow of blood. The *pugri* (headdress) that all Sikhs wear upon their head supplied me with enough material to contrive a tourniquet, which I tightened about his groin using his own bayonet.

A Sikh on parade, with his crisply wound pugri, rolled beard and coiled hair, is as smart a soldier as you will ever see, but this dishevelled warrior with his waist-length tresses cascading over the dirt looked absurdly like a ravished woman. His spaniel eyes gazed up at me like those of a faithful pet, but I had no medical resources and could only give him the solace of spiritual healing. I held him close and concentrated on the awfulness of his situation, and allowed my own energy to seep into him. I could do no more and the noise of battle racketed about us as enemy bullets kicked up dust spurts on every side. Two Gurkha stretcher-bearers took him to a more sheltered place and I returned to the fight. A month or so later he was back with the platoon, cockily displaying his wound stripe, an inverted chevron on the lower sleeve.

It was mid-March 1944 and the battle of the Tiddim Road on the Manipur front was at its height. I was twenty-three years old, a sub-altern commanding an engineer platoon of sixty Sikhs, and we were working in support of an all-Gurkha infantry brigade. We were sandwiched between two fierce Japanese attacks.

As they carried Moochoo away the infantry commander called me over and said, "Sapper! Have you got any explosives with you? I think we'll have to get out of here before we're overrun!"

What a question! You would be more likely to find a Gurkha without his kukri (knife) than a sapper without explosives! I had a 3-ton truck full.

He asked me to destroy a bridge over a deep nullah and demolish all the vehicles incarcerated on our short stretch of road by the encircling enemy. This was my sort of thing; I loved to blow things up.

I was determined that the Japanese were not going to win any of our stores or vehicles. I drove my lorry off the road, manoeuvred it under the bridge and laid the charge. The crude log structure could easily have been demolished with a box of gelignite and my three tons was enough to blow Sydney Harbour Bridge, but I did not intend to leave any for them.

I organized my men into parties to destroy the line of stationary vehicles. The first team removed all the sump plugs and drained the black engine oil out into the dust; the second party started each motor and jammed open the throttles until the engines screamed to a seize-up; the rotor arm man followed; the carburettor man with a sledge hammer; the tyre slasher, and finally an arsonist to fire the fuel tanks. No resourceful Jap was going to cannibalize one single roadworthy vehicle out of this lot!

I reported to the colonel that the trucks were completely destroyed and that I was ready to demolish the bridge on his command. When he gave the order my lorry load of Ammonal and Gelignite made such a bang that it was heard 85 miles away in Imphal, and the vast conical crater would have held a temple.

General Mutaguchi commanded the Japanese Fifteenth Army in Burma, a force of about 100,000 men. His name still trickles like ice water down my spine and he was reputed to have such an ugly temper that his subordinates were afraid to give him bad news. This was often to our advantage because he was not always aware of the real situation. The Japanese had rolled up country after country in a few months and, to his way of thinking, too much time and face was being lost in the delay over getting into India. Unable to force the swampy southern coastal belt in Arakan or drive past Stilwell's Chinese army round the mountainous frontier up north, he saw the central front as the only way ahead. In his determination to be first to seize the next parcel of our commonwealth he threw a three-pronged attack into Manipur. He hit us first with his crack 33rd Division. Through dense jungle and over precipitous mountain slopes they swarmed across the Imphal Plain, taking us unawares and cutting off one-third of our defence force at a stroke.

Our 17th (Black Cat) Division was in position 150 miles south of Imphal at Tiddim in the Chin Hills and totally dependent upon a road that was little more than a cart track. The Japanese seized the Manipur River bridge at Tonzang on the first day of their assault and set up a road block at milestone 130 on the Tiddim Road. Road builders from pre-war days had marked each hard-won mile with whitewashed milestones, which were often the only reference points in that wild country. I was with the 23rd (Fighting Cock) Division and we pelted helter-skelter across the plain and roared down the road to tackle the threat.

The battle that ensued was unlike anything seen before or since. The enemy forces ranged freely across country, coming out of the mountains and across the paddy fields from every direction. We were strung out in single file with our vehicles and could not alter the order of march we had adopted when we first took to the narrow road. We were at that time very committed to our lines of communication and the road had to be held open long enough for our boys to come back from Tiddim. The enemy strategy was to chop up our column, like garden worm segments beneath the spade, and eradicate us piece by piece.

This was the first time they encountered the aggressive spirit of our Gurkhas, fresh and lusting for action, and neither had they seen our ability to regroup into defensive boxes. Our Fourteenth Army Commander, Lieutenant-General Sir William (Bill) Slim, had imbued his forces with a new mental and tactical attitude. No longer did we surrender or panic when surrounded but faced outwards from our boxes and fired back. Our column was like a thread of mercury and as they fragmented it so we fought back and forced the globules to coalesce together again into longer beads. At times it was impossible to say who was surrounding whom.

In the savage fighting our small box had shrunk under pressure from all sides. The enemy took no heed of danger and their officers bravely led them on. The sight of my one wounded soldier had been deeply disturbing to me and yet the enemy appeared to welcome death. How could we conquer such fanaticism?

I snuggled down beside my Sikhs and pumped my rifle bolt for dear life. I had come to my first real battle like an actor on opening night, with butterflies in the stomach and the dread of not being up to the part. The adrenalin kicked in as soon as the show started and all the previous months of rehearsal and training took over and I began to glory in it. I looked around me during a lull and took stock of my bearded sepoys. They too were in their element, flaunting a bright-eyed excitement to match my own. They bantered coarse remarks

4

about, boastfully swapping stories and openly including me in their allusions. I need worry no longer about being accepted by them and knew that I had arrived. Another attack came in.

Before this first encounter we had been in awe of Japanese soldiers, not only because of the speed of their advances but also their indomitable courage and resourcefulness. Unlike us they did not rely upon supply lines because each soldier carried a looted bag of rice at his waist, that was replenished as they took new villages and left a starving population in their wake. They were indoctrinated with a religious fervour to die honourably for Emperor and country, never to surrender and to keep advancing at all costs. Not a bad set of rules for winning a war and it made them a cruel and remorseless enemy. Their men crossed terrain that we had thought impenetrable and they had no regard for personal safety or losses as their hordes swept relentlessly on.

I always carried a rifle or sub-machine gun in place of the officer's puny revolver. The Short Lee Enfield rifle was fast, accurate and lethal, and the practised drill of our well-oiled bolts snicking rhythmically had a devastating effect upon the advancing knots of ochre-clad men. By late afternoon we were almost back-to-back and the fierce little Gurkhas were reaching for their kukri knives and whooping their battle cry *"Ayo Gurkhali!*

We fought our way out and circled around our attackers to join the next box back. The Japs were left facing each other across a few burnt-out trucks and a very large crater and we now surrounded them. A few days later the ebb and flow of battle brought us back to the same place and we recaptured a much longer section of the road. The finality of my extensive demolitions was laid bare, and one or two wits asked me when they could have their trucks back? None of those vehicles ever moved again and they eventually rusted away in the rains. When the withdrawing troops of 17 Div reached the place their sappers cut a new road around my crater and filled in the dry bed of the stream.

We advanced and withdrew with the rhythm of a dance formation. We lost a lot, regained a lot and even captured some of their stuff. They had very little and what they had was rubbish, but souvenirs like badges, documents and photos of Japanese girls gave us our first thrill of looting. One day perhaps we would display our trophies back at home – if we ever got home.

I entered a Japanese position for the first time. It was deserted and a fire smouldered in a pit with a tin of rice bubbling over it. For the first time I inhaled the pungent odour of our enemy, a stench that I grew to detest and can still smell to this day. Their dead sprawled in grotesque poses about the rim. War had now come very close to me and its actuality hit me hard. I wondered if next time we made a fire to heat some chow our enemies would storm in, kick our mess tins about and rob our corpses.

We were fighting against elite troops, in the peak of condition, who were inspired by their own invincibility and brooked no impediment to their advance. The Gurkhas were not impressed and fought back stolidly. The withdrawing troops from Tiddim came up from the south, attacking along the road at full divisional strength, and as their progress absorbed our boxes the whole road was reopened. We let them pass through our positions and fell back ourselves to the strong points in front of Imphal. We had lost our southern fortress but had become a much tighter ring of defence.

Chapter 2

OVERTURE AND BEGINNERS

I did no more than others did,
I don't know where the change began.
I started as a average kid,
I finished as a thinkin' man.

I wore nothing but a trilby hat as I queued among the flaccid forms
of embarrassed strangers in a hall that smelled of disinfectant and a
thousand unwashed bodies. I was enlisting in the Royal Engineers and
that is where it all began.

The veterans of the Great War came home and spawned the generation that would fight the Second World War. We were that
generation. Our fathers, uncles and schoolmasters were scarred men;
they were grim, gassed and afraid of laughter; they had lost limbs,
eyes and their sense of fun in the trenches. My boyhood was coloured
with their stories. In bitter tones they chanted monotonously:

"Little do you know, Son! Little do you know!"

My childish fantasies were pre-packaged, oven-ready, and it was
not long before I was enlisted as a sapper in the Royal Engineers in
the stiff woolly khaki that stank of chloride of lime (believed to be a
protection against mustard gas) and became a pongo, a 'brown job'
with big boots and a rifle.

I invented a senior officer called Colonel Strongbottom, S.O.C.C.
(Staff Officer for Cock-ups and Confusion). He was very real and
never far away from soldiers at war and throughout my military
career his bungling bureaucracy dominated my life. It was through his
influence that this innocent middle class boy from a good Christian
home ended up in the battle dust of the Tiddim road.

After two years in the ranks I was commissioned and almost immediately sent home on embarkation leave. It was as though I was

doing everything for the last time. I had never seen Mount's Bay in Cornwall looking lovelier as spring burgeoned in the countryside. The hedges around the tiny fields were dressed red, white and blue with pink campion, lady's bedstraw and bluebells. I waved the last goodbye to my parents through the steam of the departing train and joined my embarkation draft in Halifax.

The folk of this northern town were accustomed to seeing soldiers leave for foreign battlefields and they regarded us with pitying eyes. We had been cut out of the herd to be shooed towards the slaughterhouse door, whilst others stayed behind knee-deep in English daisies.

ATS girls issued our tropical kit. They had seen the men of the Eighth and Fourteenth Armies file before them. Had the retinas of their eyes been film they might have collected likenesses of Corporal Green M.M. (Tobruk), Private White V.C. (posthumous), Lieutenant Brown (died of wounds, Toungoo). Now their pretty eyes flashed my image on the screen. They gave us an outfit that should have been in a museum. It was the stuff of earlier wars – solar topees, puttees, spine pads and bleached khaki uniforms that a Fuzzy-Wuzzy would have recognized. Local shopkeepers cajoled us into buying a lot of trash. They produced small copies of *The Holy Bible* with a steel plate in the cover ("Could save your life, Chum!") and similar gadgets that had been on their back shelves since 1918.

We stared out through the grimy windows of our billet, across the sad Yorkshire landscape to where the white plumes of smoke from trains presaged that final journey to the port. On a dark morning we assembled in a thin drizzle and watched our train pull in. Troop trains are not like other trains. They are stark, uncomfortable and over-crowded. They do not stop at stations, but wait for hours in gritty sidings whilst regular trains roar through. We gazed longingly through the sooty windows, absorbing our last glimpses of England; trees, valleys, sheep, buses, shoppers, women, canal barges, cinemas and little railside houses. Our lives were on the line, but these people were busy with their daily routines and never gave us a glance or a goodbye wave. We felt very sad.

The train steamed right inside the cathedral of a freight shed on Liverpool's Gladstone Dock. Doors flew open, Movement Control officials harried and shouted at the troops as they fell out of the carriages on to the dirt below. A ray of sunshine shafted through the smoky air from a roof-light and illuminated the silent ranks. We humped our kit and shuffled out on to the wharf.

Suddenly it was all bustle and light. Sunshine sparkled across the waters of the Mersey, boats fussed about the river, horns tooted, dockworkers shouted and there, towering above us, reared the sheer sides of our ship RMS *Highland Brigade.*

Tense occasions inspire bonhomie. High above us the ship's rails were lined with troops. They were ensconced aboard, quarters allocated, kit stowed and beyond harassment and they were free to enjoy the sport of taunting the heavily burdened new arrivals that were filing towards the gangplank below. Petty officials herded us along whilst coarse comments and nicknames of accurate cruelty rained down upon the heads of the scrawny, the stout, the lanky and the sad.

"They've caught up with you at last, Lofty!"

At least someone was noting our passing.

My feet left English soil and began to climb the ribbed gangway.

A last taunt from above as I ducked into the shadow of the promenade deck:

"If yer muvver could see yer now, Shortarse!!"

Tugs drew the troopship out into the Mersey, darkness fell and the city slipped into total blackout. The nightly blitz, the firebombs and the Luftwaffe had turned this happy city into a grim fortress.

I stayed aloft. I looked wistfully back at the silhouette of the skyline. Would I ever see those old Liver Birds again and did they really look down when a virgin walked underneath? Homesickness washed over me.

We crossed the boom and the first lift of the bows lifted my spirits, almost to the point of exhilaration. This had to be the experience of a lifetime. I gloried in the throbbing power of the diesels roaring defiance to all U-boats from the funnel above me and we headed out into the black waters.

It took three months and two ships to sail right around Africa and across the Indian Ocean. Bombay smote us with the impact of a fireworks display. After weeks of monotonous sea and sky it was like stepping out of a Sunday morning Church service into a mad fairground. The extravagant colours and the cacophony of sound bludgeoned our senses and shafts of hot sunshine pierced the pungent air.

Thankfully we threw the spine pads, shin-length shorts and solar topees into Bombay harbour and obediently bought outfits that the native shopkeepers vowed were correct for 'English Officer Sahibs'.

I was sent to join The Royal Bombay Sappers and Miners (RBS&M). I realized that I was now Indian Army and that Poona was a real place and not a music hall joke.

The monsoon swept the deserted platforms of Poona station in the small hours, there was nobody to greet us and we spoke no word of the language. Eventually a wild, bearded Sikh in a crooked pugree rushed into the station and began to carry our mountain of steel trunks and other kit outside to a Chevrolet truck. He wore a uniform of sorts and obviously knew what he was doing. His friendly grin shone like a mouthful of piano keys and his beard glistened with raindrops.

He drove out of town on to a rutted muddy track and kept the accelerator hard to the floor, wrestling with the steering wheel and bottoming the springs through each enormous pothole. We were flung about in the back as he ploughed through tropical lightning and driving rain until he lost control and the Chevvie plunged her long nose into a flooded yellow ditch. Half-cursing and half-weeping, we slurped about in the liquid mud as the first watery light of dawn lit our misery. The driver had disappeared and we felt helplessly lost in the vastness of India.

We had reached the depot and soon a pack of half-naked long-haired savages splashed up to us through the rain. They were shouting and laughing and led by our man. For the first time I met the noisy exuberance, the wild night appearance and the cheerful strength of Sikh soldiers and our truck was soon back on the road.

The RBS&M depot at Kirki was a place of great charm and antiquity. The red stone buildings were draped with Virginia creeper, wisteria and ivy, and there were gardens, tennis courts, squash courts, polo pitches, swimming baths and every possible recreational facility. We had stepped out of wartime Britain, out of danger, out of black-outs and deprivation straight into an opulent and cloistered peacetime retreat. I had to buy another new outfit, to conform to the Poona cut, and gave my Bombay purchases to the sweeper.

The palatial officer's mess was bedecked with tiger skins, silver plate and trophies, and inhabited by a hard core of pre-war regular staff officers who looked down on us. We had upset their tranquil lives and they called us 'Bloody ECOs' (Emergency Commissioned

Officers). If they found us intrusive we found them incomprehensible. We had moved a long way east and a long way back in time and, although we were highly trained in Western warfare, we did not know what a *chota-peg* was. (a short drink) The old boys glared balefully at us as they chanted repetitively "*Koi hai?*" (Anybody there?) to the silent mess waiters and downed another Long John Collins (gin and lime). We had to weather their contempt as the conveyor belt carried us past them to distant battlefields.

Only the best people were allowed into Poona Race Course, where events such as gymkhana, polo tournaments and dog shows also took place.

At the annual dog show Madame Olga, the doyenne of the most famous Officer's brothel in the world and one of the wealthiest and best known ladies in India, was showing her prize Pekingese. A newly arrived second lieutenant, who was also an Honourable, went over to her and praised her dogs. Delighted by his shared interest she asked if he would walk them round the judging ring for her. Her dogs won handsomely and she was so delighted that she told him to come and see her at Number 6, Grant Road, next time he was in Bombay. What an offer – a hand-picked girl and free drinks all night! A few weeks later he was in Bombay with his fiancée, an English nurse and decided to take her along to meet his new friend. A very surprised chowkidar opened the heavy door, but announced them formally to Madame. She behaved impeccably, gave them biscuits and tea from bone china in her private salon and saw them away in a taxi. Neither knew that they had spent the afternoon in a whorehouse.

We came under instruction from the new generation of Indian Army Officers, real veterans, men who had been in the retreat from Burma. They taught us to love the dark-skinned *jawans* (young recruits) as they made us into real Indian Army officers. I learned respect for these splendid mercenaries and I never felt worthy of their inherent deference.

The Viceroy's Commissioned Officers (VCOs), were unique to the Indian Army. They stood between the men and us and acted as confidants, advisors and trouble-shooters. It would have been easy for us to commit a ghastly solecism in speech, or over a religious scruple, or a caste problem, or any other deep-rooted Indian tradition. These mature warriors with their campaign medals had worked their way up from village youth to an impressive seniority. They were gentlemen who, despite my newness, treated me as a young man of good British stock. They assumed implicitly that once I had learned the language and rudiments of Indian Army procedure I would go off to war and probably win a gallantry medal or two. That is not fanciful. These mature warriors had seen many a red-necked subaltern falter and stumble, and they had seen many a young Sahib do things well beyond the reasonable call of duty. They gave us the dignity of our calling before we had earned it and they inspired us to succeed.

At first the language barrier was a deformity, a paralysis, and I could not speak to the lower ranks at all. I studied Urdu (the lingua franca of the military) for hours a day. Most VCOs and a few senior NCOs spoke perfect Urdu and some had a smattering of English. They were diffident about using English to me because, with characteristic sensitivity, they did not wish to imply a tacit criticism of my inability to master their tongue.

As soon as I was deemed to have grasped the rudiments of being an Indian Army Officer, and had passed my language examination my posting came through. At last I was going on active service. I was told to report to 91 (Royal Bombay) Indian Field Company, RIE, without having the foggiest idea what part of the world they were in or what they were doing. RBS&M companies were in the Western Desert, Paiforce (Persia and Iran) and, of course, Burma.

Before I could leave Poona I had to pay my mess bill. I had received no pay since being commissioned in Britain nine months before and the extravagant Indian peacetime way of life had reduced me to penury. We had existed on handouts that we had cadged from Strongbottom on the journey so far. My wet sweeper probably had more cash than I did. I had to mortgage my future pay on active service by giving the mess officer a post-dated cheque. It was a relief to know that I would soon be experiencing 'the bullets kickin' dust spots on the green' instead of sinking deeper into the red in that expensive retreat.

From the outset I did not know where I was going. It was the start of a mad game of chance and I drew my first card – 'Go to Movement Control, Bombay'. Once there I had to wait my turn until the next move. My next card was 'Go to Gaya. Take The Calcutta Mail.' There were no train seats for ten days and I was soon reduced to poverty again. Our lives depended on this strange game of chance, but at last I knew that my die was cast for the Burma Front.

No.1 Platform, Victoria Station was a vast and exciting temple to steam power. It was noisy and crowded in the late afternoon, with luminous darts of sunlight shafting through the vapours exhaled from the powerful locomotives. Filthy coolies in red loincloths and pugri's shouted and spat red *betel* (stimulant chewing nut) juice as they fought over my luggage.

Two days later I reached Gaya, in Bihar Province, three-quarters of the way to Calcutta, and a place that Gandhi complained was the dirtiest he had ever seen. This transit camp sweltered on a dusty plain and was the one and only pipe through which the whole of India's defence against the flames of Japanese aggression had to pour. It had an evil reputation for unpleasantness, bureaucratic chaos and suffering. Officers, British troops and Indian soldiers were segregated in barbed wire cages and lived in rows of *E.P.I.P.* (Egyptian Patent Indian Pattern) square tents containing bug-infested *charpoys* (string beds) and stained mosquito nets.

It was a turnstile between two different ways of life. Streaming up from the Indian continent came a motley crowd of travellers, wearing every shade of khaki, from broken white to muddy ochre, with head-gear of every shape and size, and each identifiable from the badges they wore. There were infantrymen, cavalrymen, gunners, sappers, signallers, medics, and drivers, all with their own distinctive flashes, shoulder tabs, badges and insignia. We could categorize each man at a glance. I was a lieutenant (two pips) of Indian Army Engineers (badge and flashes) Bombay Sappers (blue lanyard), and obviously a greenhorn (Poona khaki). Going the other way, travelling west against the flow, was a trickle of experienced soldiers returning from the front for transfer or promotion. In contrast their uniforms were threadbare jungle green and they wore bush hats, soft jungle boots and a hard man look on their gaunt yellow faces.

My game suddenly changed and I drew a winning card. At the bar I noticed that the veteran next to me wore a sapper cap badge in his jungle hat and the RBS&M blue lanyard. Nervously I approached him:

"I see you're a Bombay Sapper!"

Dragging hard on his cigarette he turned and looked me over. He was a Major, and very thin, but quite agreeable and I learned that his name was Jim.

"Where're you heading, lad?"

13

"91 Field Company — but God knows where that is!"

"Christ man! Where the bloody hell have you been all this time?" He exploded.

I was his replacement!

He had been adjutant (captain rank) in 91 Company and was now promoted to Major to take over a new company being formed back in the Poona depot. I was posted to take the place of the lieutenant who had been promoted captain in his place. It only took a few moments to learn that they were on the central front in Manipur and how to get there! Jim had the innate contempt that all front line soldiers have for bureaucracy and soon put me right about kit, wangled a train ticket and put me on the next Calcutta Mail. I left obstructive ineptitude behind and made my own way up the line. I was exposing myself to the risk of being labelled a deserter for slipping away without official sanction, but I did not care. I was getting out of Gaya.

Under Strongbottom's benevolent guidance I had equipped myself with everything a British officer should have for active service in India. I had a green canvas hand washbasin on folding criss-cross sticks that would neither hold water nor stand up. There was a diabolical tangle of battens, clips, hinges and heavy canvas, called an officer's camp bed, that could easily amputate a finger and which I prefer to forget. A square canvas tray, laughingly known as an officer's bath, was too small for even a second lieutenant's bum and always collapsed in use. My green canvas bedroll, or valise, with hand-sewn leather work was the design of a lunatic. You may laugh, but I actually had a collapsible metal cup which, when filled with whisky and water, concertina'd and shot the drink over your boots. It did the same for gin-and-lime. There were other oddments like my steel-backed bible and an ivory cigarette holder. It was all very North-west Frontier.

At Howringhee Station, Calcutta, I made a bold move. I dodged the Military Police and marched straight into the RTO's Office where I found a pleasant Indian clerk and told him that I had to get to Imphal urgently. Using my newly acquired Urdu, I soon had him in the palm of my hand. He issued passes, warrants and other documents to take me on the next difficult leg of my journey. He even booked me into The Grand Hotel.

It was said that 'The Hooghly River is the arsehole of the world and Calcutta is a hundred miles up it!' In those days of famine, with dead bodies lying in the streets and floating down the river, it was a steamy pit of vice and crime. There was a sharp divide between the very wealthy and the utterly destitute and it was full of Fourteenth Army men.

In the past year I had worn five different outfits. I had begun in the khaki of a common soldier, followed by the fine barathea cloth of an officer in Europe, Victorian tropical, Bombay shopkeepers tropical, formal Poonah tropical and now I had to find the correct outfit in which to meet the Japanese.

Because of the leeches, mosquitoes and tearing thorns of the forest shorts were never worn and I bought jungle green long trousers, bush jacket, cocky jungle hat and a sweat rag. I began to look the part. Out went all the ridiculous tackle to be replaced by a small cloche-like mosquito net, a spring-steel cot and an all round reduction in size and weight. I felt that I was getting there. Little did I know that the day would come when I would think this frugal outfit outrageously sybaritic.

I sat on the slatted wooden train seats as we headed into the wild mountains of Assam and saw through the louvred openings azalea and rhododendron clothing steep mountain sides. We chugged smuttily through the heat to Parbatipur, where hordes of yelling coolies hit us in the middle of the night to hustle our belongings and us across the platform on to the narrow gauge train.

We crawled along the Brahmaputra valley to a ferry where more shouting coolies manhandled the tiny train on to river barges and we sailed up the vast magnificence of that giant amongst rivers in the golden glow of the setting sun. The train was disembarked at Gauhati and puffed along the last leg to the Dimapur railhead.

We had taken more than two days to cover the 600 miles north-west from Calcutta. We had reached the last fire hydrant through which the whole flow of men and armament had to pass to quench the creeping flames of Japanese aggression on the central front. The hardest part still lay ahead, 130 miles of narrow mountain track to Imphal, the capital of Manipur State.

We entered an entirely different kind of transit camp. In place of stuffy red tape and confusion it had the relaxed air that one always finds near the front line. The troops called it 'The Valley of The Pricks' because it was set in a sacred garden of enormous stone phallic symbols. It was shady and cool, busy mountain streams

15

chuckled through the undergrowth and the mountain air was sweet.

We had travelled a long way north of Imphal and now had to go south-east again along the only road through the passes over the north–south ridges that guarded The Plain. The morning convoy assembled on the narrow dirt track. The lofty mountains to the east of us made sunrise very late in the cool gorge and the forest trees lanced shafts of sunlight through the thick lorry smoke. A motley crowd of strangers, men of all ranks and colours, herded into the dark caverns beneath the canvas tilts, all travelling into the unknown. It was late December, between the monsoons, and the air was like wine as the column trundled along the valley bottom and took to the narrow rock-cut shelf of mountain road that snaked up into the mountains.

Single-track working meant that the up and down streams of traffic had to pass at special staging places. A convoy moves at the pace of the slowest driver. A puncture or a boiling engine stopped all the vehicles behind until the fault was put right. In three days we never covered more than ten miles in any single hour.

The procession wound its way upwards like a serpent and the packed travellers were spun first one way and then the other at every hairpin corner. The open rectangle at the rear was a cinema screen, with the picture veering crazily from side to side, as though shot by a hosepiping cameraman. Engine fumes, red dust, tobacco smoke, noise and the increasing heat soon induced Burma Road Sickness. Gut-wrenching potholes, crashing gears, overheated engines and the spinning backward view tortured the travellers throughout the hot day. Man after man vomited over the stern gate and collapsed into stupor. An opening was forced through the front canvas and men took turns to stand and face forwards into clean air.

We reached Kohima late in the day, set like a jewel on the rim between Assam and Manipur. Whitewashed buildings gleamed amongst rich foliage, the red splash of the corrugated tin roof over the Mission Chapel and the mown precision of the tennis court contrasted with the tumbled savagery of the blue-green mountain backdrop. This was the country of the head-hunting Naga tribe, who had chosen to be our friends and allies.

No wonder the defence of this frontier had never been taken seriously. Impenetrable jungle-covered ranges soared to the skyline in every direction, barring any passage between Burma and India. The ability of the Japanese to cross any terrain had changed all that. As we stood like tourists gazing eastwards across the Naga Hills our enemy were probably less than seventy miles away. I shivered at the thought that one of their long-range patrols might at that very moment be gazing slit-eyed through binoculars at our awkward newness. On this high oasis a terrible battle would shortly be fought. That green rectangle of tennis court, sleeping in the sun, would be soaked red with blood to mark the high-water mark of Japanese aggression in the Far East.

After a cold night on the ridge we crossed the Maram saddle to plunge south through awesome country into the State of Manipur. Now we swung giddily on the over-run, with stabbing brakes and low gear, and there was no backward view over the tailgate. Through gorges, under beetling jungle slopes, skirting sheer drops of wet oblivion the milestones ticked past.

Were men expected to move and fight in this country? The gradients became less steep, the mountains drew back and we stopped at Kangpokpi rest halt, MS 107 from Dimapur, and spent the second night in bamboo *bashas* (grass-walled huts). On the third day the valleys opened out, there were cultivated terraces and the road levelled off for the final run into the township of Imphal.

To my dismay 91 Field Company was still another 40 miles further south and I sent a radio signal to them for transport. To my surprise the vehicle that arrived was a pale yellow, long-nosed Ford V8, a half-truck conversion of a softly sprung American limousine and obviously designed for the Western Desert. The driver was a Mahrattha and I could not understand a word of his ceaseless chatter, but his welcome was a joy. The truck carried the red rampant fighting cock of 23rd Indian Division, and the white 51 on a blue square for 91 Field Company.

Night was falling but the driver did not use lights. Perhaps they did not work? Or he did not know where the switch was? Or were we already under the eyes of the enemy? He tore along the dusty track across the paddy, skirting deep nullahs and plunging through potholes the size of craters. In pitch darkness he found our camp at Shuganu and my week of travelling from Calcutta was over. My eyelashes and hair were pink-frosted with road dust and I reported, shaky and tired, to my new Commanding Officer, Major Beddowes, by the light of a paraffin lamp.

17

"And where the bloody hell have you been all this time? We'd just about given you up!" I would become accustomed to such caustic welcomes from him, but the other officers in the mess soon made me feel at home.

Instead of 'The Green Hell' of the media, I found myself in 'a garden eastward in Eden'. Imphal was tranquil and beautiful on a rich alluvial plain where villages dozed in the brilliant air surrounded by palm groves, paddy fields, banana, mango and bamboo. This last frontier between India and Burma is still remote and mysterious. The people had Mongolian features and the pretty women floated along in colourful *phaneks* (ankle-lengthcotton sheaths) that hung from their plump breasts and exposed smooth golden shoulders. Some carried a baby on their back, some a basket on their head and many wore little green velvet jackets or yellow shawls. The men dressed soberly in white loin cloth, white shirt, black jacket and umbrella; it was their uniform. From time to time they squatted under the umbrella to urinate at the roadside. They took great pride in their bicycles and it was said that they joined us against the Japanese because our bicycles were the best in the world.

The Imphal Plain is about the size of the Isle of Wight and it is cradled in the arms of precipitous jungle-covered north-south ridges that are criss-crossed with the tracks of head-hunting tribes. In this tranquil paradise we hung, dependent on the vulnerable thread of that one crude road back to Dimapur, like a fisherman's bait before the hungry jaws of Nippon.

I had arrived in the front row of the stalls, in time for 'Curtain Up!' The whole continent of India lay behind me, and the Japanese army threatened from Burma to the east. There was an eerie peacefulness in the air as we prepared for their arrival.

I was the newcomer, the rookie, the new kid at school. I knew nothing about jungle and very little about the men I had to command. Ted Allison, promoted to Captain, was struggling with his new adjutant duties and gladly handed the Sikh platoon over to me. On my first morning he took me to where they were practising pontoon bridging across the Manipur River. On the narrow path a snake whipped in front of us. He stopped so quickly that I bumped into his back.

"Gosh!" I exclaimed "Wasn't that a snake? I bet you get lots of them out here?"

"Hundreds!" Ted sounded bored "They're everywhere!"

We ploughed on, stamping our feet to frighten them away. Some weeks later, when I had not seen any more snakes, I dared to remark on the fact and Ted admitted that it was his first too, but he didn't want to disappoint me on my first day in the jungle. I guessed that Ted was reporting back to the OC each day on how the new chap was shaping up, and probably saying, "He's a bit green. Nearly shat himself when we saw a *krait* (venomous snake) down by the river. Doesn't seem to know much of the lingo either!"

The RBS&M recruited Mahratthas, Punjabi Mussulmans (PMs) and Sikhs in equal proportions. The Mahratthas (always No.1 Platoon) are strict Hindus from the Bombay area, short and dark-skinned with a happy nature, who smoke and drink. The proud PMs (No.2 Platoon) are Mohammedan, tall, fair-skinned, teetotal and do not eat pork. They smoke through their hands so that tobacco does not touch their lips. The Sikhs (No.3 Platoon) never cut their hair, nor smoke, but drink alcohol. Thus the platoons were three completely different ethnic units, although headquarters staff (clerks, cooks, drivers, etc.) were mixed. The handling of three different religions, castes, tongues and customs in one small company was an amazing feat that we officers had to master.

My platoon had relatively low caste Mazbhi and Ramdasia Sikhs, who had, at one period in their history, been spurned to such an extent by higher caste Sikhs that they turned to brigandry and other villainous pursuits. It was said that if you wanted a throat slit in the Punjab these were the men for the job, which may have been a calumny, but not unbelievable.

They had very dark skins, a wicked and swashbuckling air and spoke a coarse Punjabi, in contrast to the higher caste soldiers of the crack Sikh infantry regiments. My recently acquired Urdu was a foreign tongue to all the lower ranks.

My first impressions of Jemadar Narinjan Singh (one pip, lowest VCO rank) filled me with dismay. He was self-effacing, untidily dressed, with wispy tails of black hair escaping from under his loose pugree, and was unlike other Sikhs. He flustered easily and had the embarrassing habit of rubbing one boot up and down the back of his other leg whilst talking. He spoke no word of English and not much Urdu. His promotion was almost certainly because of his higher caste. The next most important man in the platoon, Havildar Surajbahn

Singh, was the very opposite. He was exactly what I expected a Sikh soldier to be. His immaculately tied pugree, with the red *fifti* (head band) showing brightly at his forehead, his accurately rolled beard and whole demeanour impressed me. He spoke perfect Urdu, some English and he was smart and quick to react. He was backed by dapper lance-havildar Dalip Singh, a little treasure of a man.

Down by the river the naiks (corporals), lance naiks and the sappers were noisily making a show of great activity to impress their new sahib. I was lost in a great pit of loneliness. This was my longest day. The pontoon bridge they were trying to build was not a difficult task, and it had grass walls each side to make sure that mules did not stampede with fright when crossing the running water. Although I knew far more than they did about the job I could not instruct them, nor even talk to anybody. I stood about awkwardly under their searching scrutiny, tapping my leg with my swagger stick, not knowing what to do until the Jemadar Sahib came up and saluted deferentially:

"Permission to break off, Sahib Bahadur?"

It was Christmas Eve. I trudged back through the blazing heat and wondered if Mum had found enough out of her wartime rations to make a pudding this year.

The nearer you get to the enemy the less base-wallahs, military police and staff officers there are. The warmth and camaraderie between real fighting men rinses away all the gritty irritations of life further back. Dress becomes individualistic, even raffish. Ways of getting things done become brutally direct. Humour is highly pitched and often macabre. Men are judged by what they do and not what they purport to be. Life is more intense, as though it is nearly over, and for many it is.

Christmas Day was a watchful holiday for the division. The Brigadier, commanding 37 Gurkha Brigade, turned up with a live duck under his arm. Sensing my awkwardness he drew me into the circle and enquired about the way of things back in India. Because of his exalted rank he had been issued with this bird for his Christmas dinner, and now it was his pet. I was allowed to give it a sip of my gin. The blazing heat, the inebriated duck, the Japanese army just over the hill and the false Christmas spirit was unreal to me, like a comedy film.

It was the warm season before the monsoon and Shuganu was beautiful. The forest slept in the sparkling air and it was the Sherwood

Forest life of Robin Hood. We lived on a knoll around which we had trodden paths and dug foxholes, latrine holes and bunkers. I slept in a pit covered with a piece of canvas raised on bamboo walls.

We were close to the first wooded escarpments where wild game abounded. The sharp cough of the barking deer was so human that it made you go for your gun. The Gurkha infantry honed their rifle skills and jungle craft as they hunted the wild boar, deer and jungle fowl. We had so much fresh meat that we threw away lorry loads of issue bully beef and army biscuits. The time would come when the destructive noise of modern warfare would drive the wild life out of the mountains and we would be half-starved and longing for what we were now discarding.

In the Indian Army there were only a few British officers amongst large numbers of native troops. There were five of us to about 300 Indian ranks in our Company, the OC (Major), Adjutant (Captain) and three platoon subalterns. The officer's mess cook was a very black-skinned rascal whose speciality was curried bully beef and little else, and he always put the mess crockery outside for *pi-dogs* (wild dogs) to lick clean. As they were known to carry rabies and other ghastly diseases we were not too keen on this economy.

I was frequently away from HQ on detachment with my Sikhs, working in support of 3/3rd Gurkha battalion, that my platoon served. It was a very lonely existence, one white man amongst sixty or more Sikhs and nobody to talk to in English. I had no cook and received one tin of bully beef and a packet of hard biscuits from time to time, so I always ate the hot spicy food of the men. Indian Army officers were expected to eat one meal a week with their men in order to monitor the food. Men took turns at cooking and Sikhs, more than any other, tried to outdo each other at making their curries fiercer and hotter. It was braggart behaviour; the hotter the curry you could eat the more manly you were, and the more you could eat the greater your kudos. This was a constant worry to me, because I am a small eater, but they would insist:

"Give our Sahib Bahadur another plateful . . ."

And they would pile more cardboard-dry *chapattis* (pancakes), greasy gobbets of goat's meat and ladles full of *dhal* (lentils) on my plate. Smiling bravely I have been known to stuff chapattis down my socks, up my shirt and fling them surreptitiously into the jungle.

To avoid meat going rotten in the heat goats came up as 'Fresh meat

21

on the hoof'. The troops killed them as the need arose according to their own religious customs. The animals roaming about the lines were always a nuisance. The men insisted that they were fattening them, awaiting a feast day, or an increase (many were pregnant) but in fact it was just the soldier's natural yearning for a pet, something to love. I never got over the problem and it was always a relief when we suddenly received a movement order. Hurriedly goats and kids were rounded up, slaughtered and thrown into the pot. For half a day everyone stuffed handfuls of hot dripping curried goat into their mouths with both hands and belched like foghorns. What we could not eat we could not keep and it was always gorge and go.

Officers were supposed to be issued with one bottle of spirits a month and sometimes a bottle of something else (like sherry) and a tobacco ration. There were no canteens. Our cigarettes came up with the live goats and were moistly stained on arrival. We dried them in the sun before lighting and called them 'Foul fags under hoof'. We all smoked in those days and survived on parcels from home. Some made bamboo pipes to smoke and use up their *doofers* (fag ends, 'do-fer-another-time').

Then one day an unexpected stroke of good fortune came my way. A deep penetration patrol into Burma was going to float down the Manipur River and I was detailed to accompany it. It was to be led by a sapper officer, an experienced jungle man called 'Nipper' from Divisional Intelligence, supported by a section of Gurkhas and transported in six flat-bottomed army boats with three outboard engines. It was always the practice when small detachments went out for me to take the havildar and leave the jemadar with the rest of the platoon. This not only meant that we shared responsibilities but, for my part, I preferred Surajbahn's company.

Chapter 3

DOWN THE RIVER

Scent of smoke in the evening,
Smell of rain in the night—

The dawn chorus woke me. Not the sweet trilling of little English song birds but the raucous hawking and spitting of sixty Sikhs. As soon as they left their bed they always cleared the phlegm from their tubes with noisy abandon and it continued right through washing, cleaning teeth, voiding waste and tying up their long black hair. At first light this din could be heard from the mountain tops, and the first principle of jungle warfare is silence. I spent months trying to persuade them to get up quietly.

I took Havildar Surajbahn Singh and a dozen men to go on the river patrol. Nipper arrived from Divisional Intelligence to take command; he was my senior and had survived the long retreat and fighting in Burma the year before. He was easy company and I listened to him attentively as he put me right about many things. He recommended the Thompson 0.45 sub-machine gun (Tommy gun) and I drew one from the guard room. We took plenty of ammunition, grenades, a Gurkha kukri and little else. We carried nothing that could identify us if caught. We had a load of food stores and a pack of iron rations per man.

Although we were so far from the ocean, the Manipur River was about the same size as the Thames at Reading, and it would grow in size as we went downstream into Burma. It was looking its best that sunny morning flowing between red banks and on the far side the elephant grass and yellow-green bamboo jungle stood out against the backdrop of forested mountains towering into the blue sky.

Gurkhas come from the greatest mountain range on earth. At home they were accustomed to descending deep into the valleys for a pot of

23

water and carrying it all the way back. This explained their incredibly muscular legs, but it also meant that they were strangers to navigable waters. We had six folding boats and three outboard engines and my sappers set about making things ready, loading stores and embarking the clumsy infantry. As the first Gurkha soldier entered the second boat some idiot let go of the painter and he drifted rapidly away on the current.

"Throw the rope!!" we bellowed after him in Gurkhali, Urdu, Punjabi and English.

"No need!" he called back. "I can easily push this little thing back to shore!"

We watched helplessly as he pushed, heaved and strained with both hands against the gunwale of the disappearing boat. One of our six boats, one of our men and a load of stores were on their way to the Chindwin and it looked as though he would be in Burma before we set out. Nipper and Surajbahn Singh were away in a flash with an outboard engine to overtake him and drag him back.

We got away by mid-morning and headed into virgin country where no white man, or probably any man at all, had trod before and I was thrilled. We soon discovered what a capricious bitch the river could be – all sweetness and beauty one moment and a virago the next. We were swanning along a broad smooth reach between the jungle walls, outboard motors puttering away in their blue clouds of smoke when we saw our first rapids foaming ahead.

Within an hour we had lost our first boat. We had arranged our flotilla so that Nipper, Surajbahn and I, each with an engine, towed a stores boat. A boat under tow, loaded with rations, went the wrong side of a boulder in that first stretch of white water. Because we had not divided our supplies carefully throughout the fleet we had lost all our flour and grenades and one of our six boats in a single stroke, but there could be no thought of turning back. The very idea of fighting our way home up the rapids and against the current and, worst of all, admitting our incompetence was unthinkable.

Below the rapids we gathered by a quiet pool and held a council of war to work out future strategy. We would try to find the deepest channel on the outside of bends, have one sapper steersman in each towed boat with a paddle, and cast off tows as soon as rapids were seen. We made a wiser distribution of stores between the remaining five boats and set forth again.

24

Steep rocky rapids punctuated the tranquil lengths. Before we arrived at the next rapids we entered a stagnant zone of dense floating waterweed that clogged our propellers, and we had to hack and paddle our way through the dragging growth. The unpredictable river, with a sudden change of heart, gave us back the boat that she had so wickedly snatched in the rapids. There it was entangled in the green weed, undamaged apart from water in some of the rations.

Nipper was leading the flotilla when we hit the next white water stretch. The man in the stern of one boat fumbled with the towline knot as they accelerated into the cataract and failed to cast off. The lead boat dodged a big rock into the left channel and the tow went to the right of it. The resulting crash stop tore the stern out of the boat and as I swept past I saw both boats roll broadside, throwing men and stores into the raging water.

At the foot of rapids there is always a tranquil basin with pleasant sandy beaches, and as I jumped ashore to pull in my boat I saw the gleam of Surajbahn's white teeth as he came grinning in behind me. We plunged together into the water to gather the towed boats and flotsam from the pool. I assessed the damage – in a few short hours the score was three to the river goddess and only one to us! With three hours of daylight left it did not look as though we were going to win this contest; we had lost our leader, several men, a lot of rations and two boats. The river had carried us well down into the Chin Hills, beyond any tracks that would take us home and we were in the middle of untrodden country.

Surajbahn and I took a few of our own men with ropes and we half-waded, half-swam back up the inside of the bend, where the water was shallowest, to the place where we had last seen Nipper. We left the Gurkha infantry behind at the pool to guard our stuff knowing that they would be no help in the river. Dense jungle grew right down to and even into the river and we forged the rapids by keeping to the edge and picking out the shallow places. We found Nipper and the others in midstream clinging to boulders. Wisely he had awaited our return and was bolstering up the spirits of the frightened men about him. That afternoon I met the inborn courage of the Gurkha soldier. They were so terrifyingly out of their element in the swirling spate and yet they remained steadfast and cheerful as they watched us working to bring them to safety.

Rapids are where the river goes over shallow rocky weirs but there are deep runnels everywhere and they are treacherous and difficult to traverse. It took a lot of skill and hard work with the ropes to get the men ashore. We rescued a boat from a cleft in the rocks so that we still had five left, but we only found pieces of the smashed one. Eventually we assembled back at the pool.

Our reduced fleet swam along the next calm reach, motoring between the high jungle walls in warm sunshine and the total peace of uninhabited country. It was like a Sunday afternoon trip on the river and our spirits soon lifted. Tropical birds wheeled colourfully over the green water and monkeys chattered from the trees as they watched our passing. On one sandy beach a magnificent tiger dripped crystal drops from his beard as he lifted his head to gaze curiously after us. We had to keep repeating to our trigger-happy lads, "*Shikar nahin!* " (Don't shoot!)

We did not want to alert any patrolling enemy to our presence and we could not retrieve any game that they killed. The native creatures of the forest had never seen man before and were exceptionally tame.

Our orders were to run south-east with the Manipur River until we came to the Myittha River in the Kale Valley. I wondered how Nipper would know when we had gone far enough in this unmapped territory. We were well south of 17th Division, the last outpost at Tiddim, and moving beyond Kalmyo into country where, it was thought, Japanese troops might be massing for their next push. As we emerged into more open country we might easily be spotted, or caught, and our purpose was to see and record all we could without them knowing of our visit. We were alert for river crossings where they might be moving forward and signs of large troop movements. If we failed to return the Corps Intelligence Staff would guess that we had probably been caught and that there might be enemy activity somewhere down there. We had been given the usual vague orders from above that many a soldier before me had carried to his death.

Nipper's jungle-craft was invaluable. When the sun touched the rim of the high wall of mountains there was about an hour and a half of daylight remaining and he pulled us into a sandy beach. We stretched our legs, emptied our bladders, lit a tiny fire, brewed up and ate our dried rations. Birds sang and monkeys chittered in the forest and we lay on the warm sand as though enjoying a picnic. The fire was placed against the bole of a tall tree to dissipate the smoke through the branches. We ate well that first night, reasoning that the food was

26

better in our bellies than in the next day's rapids. Because of our inexperienced loading we had lost more of some things than others and our diet was completely out of balance.

Nipper was not given to panic and had seen worse than this many times before. He told me that the jungle was full of edible roots, fruit and nuts, as well as game.

Immediately after eating we doused the fire, covered the ashes and all other traces of our sojourn and slipped back on to the river for another short run to a beach further down. Another lesson learned! Always move on after the evening meal so that, if the enemy has spotted your smoke or activity, you are elsewhere before he can find you. The boats were hidden in the undergrowth, the Gurkhas quietly set their night guards and we scratched out sleeping holes in the soft sand to fall asleep to the music of the river. I slept the sleep of utter exhaustion and good fresh air, but awoke in alarm. My pit was full of water and I thought the river had risen suddenly, but it was only a flash tropical rainstorm and dawn was spilling a thin light over the camp. I prepared to face the rigours and adventures of the new day.

Getting soaked went with jungle life. We were often so wet, night and day, that our whole bodies became white and crinkled like an old washerwoman's hands. This would be the rule later when the monsoon rains hit us. I thought of my mother's horror of damp sheets. To her any bed that was not crisp and cracklingly dry was a death trap that ended in pneumonia, rheumatic fever and what else.

"You'll catch your death!" She used to cry whenever I got wet. She wrote in one airgraph letter, "and make sure that your orderly airs your bedding every day!"

After cruelly testing us our lady river became more benign on the second day and she had grown large from tributaries out of the mountains. We cruised along broad reaches between the green walls, negotiated rafts of floating weed and found that the rapids were much less aggressive. We smoked and joked together and even the Gurkhas were picking up the rudiments of boat handling. At an open place we heard elephant moving behind the wall of elephant grass, which took its name from the razor-edged fronds that only they could move through. This was worrying because we did not know if they were a wild herd or working beasts from a Japanese encampment. The enemy had requisitioned the Burmese forestry elephants, but, unlike our Elephant Bill, the Fourteenth Army expert, they never understood how to manage them correctly. Elephant can place a plank in a bridge with the precision of a carpenter, but they are clock-watchers and at six in the evening they 'down trunks' and refuse to do another stroke. Nobody disobeys orders in the Japanese army and the poor beasts were made to suffer much cruelty.

We were well down into Burma and had to be very much more cautious as the country opened out into the foothills beyond the tall mountain ranges. Enemy forces were congregating in this area in large numbers. We knew that we were crossing their approach routes to Imphal and without maps it was guesswork. Nipper had the skills that all jungle men develop and used mental dead reckoning and orientation to make an appreciation of our position. We spent another night following our stealthy routine with even more care and he would not allow any fires so we ate dry rations and drank river water.

On the fourth day the country opened out. Nipper took a foot patrol of Gurkhas to an eminence from which he could overlook the Kale Valley. My men and I stayed nervously with the boats and even the ebullient Surajbahn was taut and spoke in whispers.

I was not ready for a brush with the Japanese. Only a few weeks before I had been sipping my Long John Collins in the The Grand in Calcutta and trying on my new jungle green. Now my bush jacket was stained and torn, I was somewhere opposite Mandalay and well beyond our most forward positions, almost in the valley of the mighty Chindwin River. I felt very exposed. I had no idea how I would cope if Nipper were killed. With Gurkha and Sikh soldiers to look after me I would probably have acquitted myself tolerably well, but I was too green to know that.

At the confluence of the two rivers we turned back. We had obeyed orders and now had to get home. It was Nipper's show and if he was satisfied that was good enough for me. Gratefully we turned our faces north-west and for the first time I felt the good feeling of coming home from a long patrol. We had proved the territory, we knew the river, and could now relax our wariness as we made our way back. The fast-flowing river had given us at least thirty miles a day coming down, but it was now unwilling to allow us even eight as we fought our way back against the current.

Our little motors were tired and short of fuel and even the placid reaches were slow going as they chugged hotly away against the current. We came to know each rapid, rock by rock. What had been a swift blur going down was now a gut-wrenching struggle with ropes and brute strength. We could not porter round them because the lush valley jungle was at its most impenetrable along the river banks and the razor-sharp teeth of elephant grass and thorn bushes could rip the pants off a man. We worked the inside of the bends where the water was slowest over the sandbars. Time after time we pursued a promising channel to find that it petered out in muddy swamp.

A cordiality grew between us, born of mutual suffering. The colour of your skin no longer mattered, nor whether you were officer or man. Character was more important than rank. One man turned out to be a comic, one a strong guy, one a grumbler and another the quickest at lighting fires. Everybody contributed in personal ways to the joint effort. We waded through fierce thunderstorms and we were wet above, wet below, wet all day and wet all night. Food spoiled, weapons rusted, clothes rotted and boots as well. Leeches and mosquitoes bit into exposed flesh and it was not always easy to stay optimistic and wear a brave face.

I awoke one morning on a flat beach and saw, to my horror, that enormous tiger pug-marks were crisply impressed into the sand between Nipper's sleeping hollow and mine. One very large cat had strolled between us in the night, had a drink and walked back into the jungle again. His footprints were so large that a clenched fist would not fill the hollow of a single pad. A striped, golden-eyed maneater had passed within a pace of my sleeping form. I imagined its enormous claws, the smell of its breath, its dripping jaws and my knees went watery.

"Ye Gods!" (or the equivalent in my poor Urdu) I yelled angrily at the sentry "Didn't you see that bloody great cat? It must have been as big as a bullock!"

"Ji, sahib!" He answered calmly "I saw it all right! I got up into the fork of that tree over there and kept quiet until he had finished his drink!"

"Why didn't you shout a warning or shoot him?"

"What, with this?" He held up his small bore army rifle and smiled knowledgeably.

How right he was. Had he frightened or wounded the beast with his pop-gun we would all have been in peril. As it was, he watched the contented cat, with a belly full of deer taking his after-dinner drink before retiring for the night. The phlegmatism of that little Gurkha

29

was another lesson I learned; he had not even bothered to report it.

Our wonderful Indian soldiers could make a fire and be calling *"Garam chai, sahib!"* (Tea up!) in no time at all, even though water was flooding over the forest floor. They found dry tinder in the very heart of a bamboo clump, and one Gurkha always carried a little tin of smouldering punk to light their *biddies* (Indian cigarettes). As non-smokers the Sikhs were not so well equipped, and later I carried my own matches or a lighter in a condom to make fire. (Paradoxically, in this womanless place we were issued with rubber protectives to keep our matches, lighters and watches dry.)

One afternoon, when we were nearly back to the Imphal plain, we landed on a beach in a tropical storm. We were worn thin, almost out of food, wet, cold and exhausted. Spirits were not too high when we came ashore, but at least we knew that the Japs were well behind us. A Gurkha bagged a barking deer, the rain stopped, our fire roared up into the night sky in spiralling twists of sparks and smoke, and the orange full moon hung over the distant mountain tops. Nipper produced a bottle of rum that he had been hoarding against a dire emergency. Neither Sikh nor Gurkha were too concerned about the religious niceties of butchering the meat, and soon there were spit-roast slabs of venison being passed round on bamboo skewers. We glowed with hot food, strong rum, the blazing camp fire and good companionship. Loudly we boasted how we'd beaten the bloody river and how we were going to thrash the bloody Nips as well! We sang songs, told braggart tales and fell happily asleep in a drunken heap. A wonderful, unforgettable evening.

In those few short weeks, at the very beginning of my time on the Burma front, I had been given the best jungle training in the world. Nipper's expertise, the natural abilities of my Indian troops in this environment, the wildness and freedom of that vast country made all my previous training pale into nothing. I had changed almost over-night from a twentieth century white European into a jungle-wallah.

We dragged what was left of our boats on to the river bank at Shuganu. We had lost our razors in the rapids and had taken a boyish pride in letting our beards grow. We felt and looked like real *Chindits* (Wingate's Force).

I never found Major Beddowes to be either likeable or competent. He always looked as though he had dyspepsia and nobody ever called him by his first name. We behaved circumspectly toward him more in respect of his rank than the man. When he entered the mess bunker we stiffened and stopped our bantering. He was often sickeningly obsequious as he attempted to become one of us, but he never understood our hidden jokes.

When I reported back he eyed me up and down and said caustically, "And where the bloody hell have you been all this time? And what's that bloody fuzz on your face? Go and get cleaned up before anybody sees you!"

My new CO frequently nit-picked but he never handed out praise.

My little canvas-covered hole in the ground seemed very civilized when I crawled back into it. I now felt that I had earned my colours as a member of the team and could take my proper place in the company as a man amongst men.

Chapter 4

FIRST NIGHT

No easy hope or lies
Shall bring us to our goal,
But iron sacrifice
Of body, will and soul.

The first months of 1944 gave me a chance to settle down and get into the routine of handling the No.3 (Sikh) platoon. They taught me the music of their coarse Punjabi tongue and I began to enjoy their rumbustious ways. My first contact with them was through my orderly, who the jemadar had chosen without consulting me. Perhaps he disliked the man, or me, but I ended up with the most clumsy and useless servant an officer could have.

Achchha Singh was uncouth and had filthy ways. Sleeping in my canvas- covered hole with thin bamboo walls I could easily have heard the rustle of a passing snake. He arrived before daybreak each morning, hawking, spitting, coughing and singing tunelessly to himself as he started to light a fire, right by my head. He chopped sticks, banged tins together, dropped things, gargled phlegm, belched and farted noisily. He blew gustily at the fire and frequently crashed against the fragile walls of my shelter. After half an hour he wrenched open the canvas, nearly falling on top of me as he shook my shoulder vigorously and whispered hoarsely:

"*Sahib! Chai, sahib bahadur*" (Tea up, sir) and I had to feign a surprised awakening.

The other officers had superb orderlies who turned them out immaculately. To my way of thinking it was embarrassing to ask a fighting man from this militant race to be my lackey, and I was frustrated by my raw newness and inability to speak the coarse dialect. I had an inspiration; I told the jemadar that he was not the sort of man

I wanted to be at my side in battle. I did not want to hurt the man's feelings, but I needed a quick and accurate shot, a good man on the trail and a real soldier.

I got Sarwan Singh, nickname *Bowunja*, (Fifty-two, his last two numbers) and he became my guardian, friend, mother-and-father. He was homely to have around and he saved me from many a hazard; we were together for more than three years.

The militant Sikh religion is a breakaway from Hinduism. The tenth and last Guru, Govind Singh, laid down that all Sikhs were brothers and he gave them the common title Singh. He also ordained that each Sikh should wear the five Ks:– *Kes* (uncut hair), *Kanga* (comb) *Kara* (iron quoit or bangle), *Kachha* (shorts), and *Kirpan* (steel dagger). Under British rule carrying a dagger was illegal so they wore miniature silver knives hanging from their comb. Similarly the steel quoit, a razor-sharp disc that was flicked at the enemy like a frisbee, was discouraged and they wore the iron bangle on their wrists instead. They believed that cutting hair sapped a man's strength, that nudity was vulnerability, that smoking impairs the wind and one should always have a sword to hand. It was part of their creed to give military training to every Sikh. The British benefited greatly from our liaison with them and like the Gurkhas they were superb warriors. They stayed loyal to us through the Indian Mutiny.

It was strange commanding a platoon of men who all had the same surname and a limited number of forenames; if I called "Teja Singh!" five men answered. For roll call we had to add the last two digits of their army number. Their nicknames were cruelly accurate and everybody had one, including me. Later I discovered that they called me *Chha-Chha* or Uncle, a childish diminutive meaning someone they could trust.

I learned to call the roll entirely in sobriquets which in English would have been:- "Old 'Un – Goat – Moustachios – Fifty-two – Clumsy – Beanpole . . ."

We all had to take one anti-malarial Mepacrine tablet a day. On evening parade the jemadar handed each man a pill, the havildar checked that he put it on his tongue and gave him a drink of water and finally the lance havildar made him recite his name, rank and number as proof of swallowing. It was like trying to give an unwilling pet a worm pill. It was the ideal occasion for Sikh humour, as Surajbahn called, "Give The Goat his pill! It might cure his stupidity!"

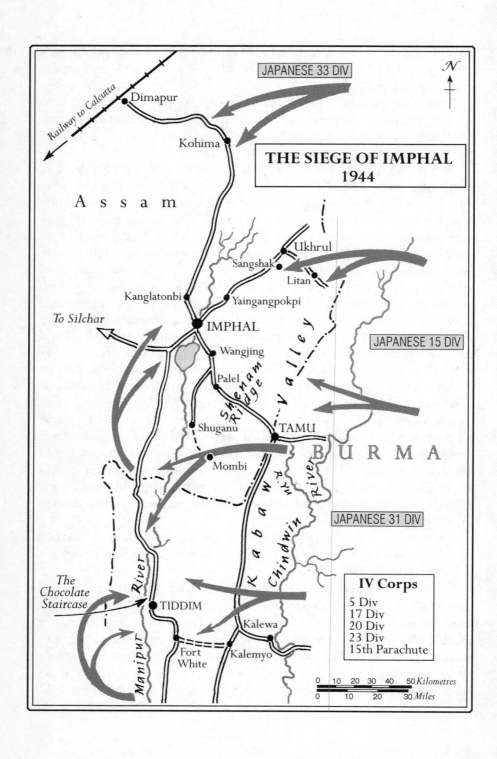

THE SIEGE OF IMPHAL
1944

JAPANESE 33 DIV

JAPANESE 15 DIV

JAPANESE 31 DIV

N

Railway to Calcutta

Dimapur

Kohima

A s s a m

Ukhrul

Sangshak

Litan

Kanglatonbi

Yaingangpokpi

To Silchar

IMPHAL

Wangjing

Palel

Shenam Ridge

Valley

TAMU

B U R M A

Shuganu

Mombi

Kabaw

Chindwin River

The
Chocolate
Staircase

Manipur River

TIDDIM

Kalewa

Fort
White

Kalemyo

IV Corps

5 Div
17 Div
20 Div
23 Div
15th Parachute

0 10 20 30 40 50 *Kilometres*

0   10   20   30 *Miles*

"Swallow, Goat, then bleat!" followed up Dalip. Teja Singh *Bukra* grinned and muttered vulgarly that he was a better hung ram than either of them; Surajbahn good-humouredly flicked water at him. Life could be fun with the Sikhs!

Anti-mosquito cream and an oily insecticide (against scrub typhus) were particularly unpleasant for the bearded men, but by daily use the Fourteenth Army gradually overcame the inroads made by jungle diseases, which had accounted for most of our losses so far. For years after the war I still banged out my boots to get rid of scorpions or centipedes.

Apprehension was in the air. The Japanese were massing in the Chindwin Valley, only one valley to the east of the Kabaw Valley, and we were very thin on the ground. We had brigades here, there and everywhere and the whole of the 'Black Cat' Division isolated down south at Tiddim. The main thrust against Imphal was expected to come up the Kabaw and over the Shenam Ridge from Tamu, but they were masters of surprise and we did not know what to expect. The monsoon was only weeks away and their time was getting short.

Outposts were pulled in and our division was concentrated in the Imphal Plain. We were pulled back from Shuganu and settled on the Tamu road near the airstrip at Palel.

Bill Slim transmitted to all of us his staunch determination to win this fight: "There will be no monsoon this year!" he said, killing the old idea that rain stopped play. The Japanese stopped for nothing and he imbued us with the determination that neither would we. Everywhere about the Imphal Plain there were stockpiles, transit camps, store depots, ammunition dumps, tented field hospitals and headquarters establishments. The military presence completely dominated this quiet little State.

The monsoon was expected about the middle of May and The Plain was tranquil and pleasant. Purple flags of marsh iris bloomed in damp corners, jasmine and wild rose abounded, the orange-red of the dried earth contrasted with green paddy and blue waterways. In every direction the horizon was bounded by the forest-green backdrop of jungle-clad mountains against the lapis lazuli sky. This paradise would become a muddy lake when the rains began.

Our soldiers were quick to make contacts in the villages and bazaars and Surajbahn arranged *nautches* (dances) for our entertainment. Beautiful young Manipuri girls came to our lines and performed their ancient ritual dances. The *Shikari* dance was a vivid portrayal of the chase as they mimed the hunter, the flying arrow and the startled deer in rotation. They performed sword dances and other native ballets of integrity and charm that were authentic and unsullied by commercialism. The girls were under the watchful eyes of their fathers, brothers and uncles, who were also the orchestra, and their mothers and aunts took charge of the money. Payment was simple. The dancing girls swirled about the seated circle of troops who held rupee notes out over the heads of other men. As the girl plucked the note she struck, quite hard, the head or face of the man beneath the note. The men loved this sport and the sly chance to have their NCOs and officers assaulted by the saucy maidens, and the money rolled in!

I developed a life-long friendship with the other two platoon officers. Bob Chambers was a tall, sandy-haired Irishman who stood prominently above the tiny dark Mahratthas of No.1 Platoon. He was outstanding as a man and outstanding as a target. (I was small and white and just as conspicuous alongside the massive bearded Sikhs) He could be bitingly rude and autocratic when he thought something was wrong or second rate, and he was always at loggerheads with authority. I think Beddowes feared him. He taught me to strip down to essentials, to throw away, and throw away, and throw away again, until I carried no more than a Naga tribesman – a blanket, a knife and a gun. I settled for a rifle, the Tommy gun was too heavy and full of faults, and we usually added a few grenades on our belt.

Harry Mavor, a Scotsman, commanded No.2 (P.M.) Platoon and was the perfect foil for Bob and me. He was another of God's gentlemen, a man to trust your life with and the possessor of a dry humour that could defuse the most ghastly situations. When I was uptight, or Bob was bitter and angry, Harry remained relaxed and smiling:

"Just wait, now!" he would say in his cultured Scottish manner "Let's sit on this log a moment and have a cigarette before we rush about and do something silly!"

He was a very good person to have around when the shot and shell were flying.

It was a sapper's war and we were always in demand. The engineers help the infantry to hold and capture ground with mines, booby traps, demolitions, revetments, bridges, wire and a lot of ingenuity. In

Imphal we were lifted from the part of stage hands to a key role and as Harry said, "There's a Sapper-spotter up there somewhere and as soon as he sees us stop for a smoke he finds another job to make sure we get no rest!"

One morning a Royal Indian Army Service Corps (RIASC) officer flagged my Jeep down on a steep muddy track:

"I say, Sapper! I've got a spot of bother up the mountain there. Would you help?"

Taking Surajbahn and Fauji 'Beanpole' I drove my Jeep up the rutted track, climbing a thousand feet or more in less than a mile, until we reached his 'spot of bother'. His Jeep had gone off the road and come to rest against a massive tree way below us. It was the sort of work I loved and with ropes, tackle and some skill I winched it back up to the track again.

When I was not out with *Turd-turd* (3/3rd Gurkha Battalion) I worked from Company HQ. When the infantry were in action we were always on detachment with them, but at other times we had to do any other dogsbody of a job that Beddowes could think up. Bob always worked with 3/10 Gurkhas and Harry with 3/5 (Royal) Gurkhas.

"Right, Johnnie!" Beddowes bustled into the Mess with his usual harassed look. "You're off on detachment tomorrow. Come round to the office and I'll fill you in!"

I had to bring back a flotilla of boats from the Manipur River near Shuganu to a safer place, a distance of about 40 miles. It was great fun wading along the narrow waterways towing strings of boats through shallow channels and each night we bivouacked on the paddy.

Outside a Manipuri village one evening I saw a tight-faced deputation with black umbrellas approaching. Language was a serious obstacle but Surajbahn, a born mimic, had already picked up a smattering of their tongue (pillow talk perhaps?). The headman pushed a small boy forward with a dead duck hanging from his fist, adding that a pig was also missing and one or more ladies of the village had been sexually assaulted. Gravely I presided over this kangaroo court, using Surajbahn as a biased translator. The defence claimed that the duck had died of shock whilst Fauji Beanpole was trying to rescue it from being crushed beneath an oncoming boat. The pig was nowhere to be found and could not be produced as evidence and the ladies' honour

37

did not appear to be too badly dented. I awarded the villagers ten rupees costs, which I paid out of my own pocket and it all ended most amicably.

In the dark that evening great cooking fires roared up. I was told that I would have to eat the duck myself because it had not been killed by *jhatka* (Sikh method of slaughter). Obviously the piglet had received the correct treatment because there was an appetising aroma coming from the lines. After this unfortunate case the Judge went to bed amply rewarded – his belly bloated with roast duck and curried pork. Well, I had been warned that life with a Sikh platoon was always eventful!

The proximity of the enemy was brought home to me one day. I took my platoon over the Shenam ridge and into the Kabaw Valley to make a pendulum ferry. This was a square raft floating by a hawser from a tree that could be made to swing back and forth across the river by adjusting its angle to the current. It was a silent ferry and used no power. All of a sudden we were attacked by three British Hurribombers (Hurricane fighters with bomb racks). They plastered the ferry with machine-gun bullets and cannon, dropped their bombs and vanished over the mountains. We took cover behind an enormous tree that was shredded and riddled by their shells. Nobody was hurt, but I was furious! I complained to Div HQ and a few days later the Air Force sent a special car out to collect me for a formal apology. At Palel airfield they showed me aerial photographs of the corrugated country, which looked like a piece of dark green rucked carpet and there were the Japanese in the next valley to mine doing an identical ferry. It was easy to see how the pilots had picked the wrong place.

The weather grew hotter before the rains and, between sweat-soaked periods, we were struck by williwaws (mini-tornadoes) that presaged tropical thunderstorms. The Plain was a grill pan waiting for the monsoon to quench it.

Beddowes sent me off on a long-range patrol, south to Mombi in the Chin Hills. I sometimes felt that he did not love me, nor my Sikhs, as much as he should, and sought ways to get rid of us. It was an infantry task that the Gurkhas could have done much better, but they were busy with their own patrols.

Surajbahn and I, with twelve men, drove along the old familiar road to Shuganu and continued as far beyond as it was 'jeepable'. We picked up the daily mule train and climbed towards a remote mountain peak outpost that was manned by a small and courageous bunch of Pathans (NW Frontier tribesmen). These men of The Frontier Field Force were led by a belligerent officer with a huge curled moustache and as fighting men they were far superior to anything the enemy could produce. They were monitoring Japanese preparations and movement.

We climbed a muddy gutter of a track, deeply scoured by rain, with a sheer drop over the *khud* (precipice) to our right and the steep wall of mountain on the left. I had always treated mules with respect – and a little loathing. Bill Slim had wisely put the whole army on a mule basis and we had to pack everything into the leather boxes called yakdans, that hung by rings from the harness. This meant that if vehicles or roads were not available we could use mule trains. The yakdans could be slung into the backs of lorries or even into waiting transport aircraft at a moments notice. It gave us the fluidity of movement that would be one of the decisive factors in the ultimate victory. Company Office became a stack of leather boxes instead of filing cabinets, water was carried in galvanised tanks and there were special ammunition yakdans.

> *When the cartridges ran out, You could hear the front-ranks shout,*
> *'Hi! ammunition-mules an' Gunga Din!'*

We were inspired by the gospel according to Orde Wingate and it was only a matter of time before we became mobile jungle men and this was very different from the trenches and tanks of the Western Front.

I trekked up the Mombi track behind my first mule train, with a trepidation born of ignorance, and reached the summit full of admiration for them. The muleteers were seasoned professionals in grubby rags of clothing; I had never seen such wild, unkempt soldiers, but they were masters of their craft. They toiled uncomplainingly up that punishing slope through flies and heat, hour after hour, coaxing their beasts with firmness and limitless patience.

A mule turned suddenly and bolted back down the track, hooves flying, crashing crazily past the climbing train, yakdans awry and flailing other loads, until it vanished into the distance below. With timeless resignation and no rancour the muleteer went down after it. That evening, four hours after we had reached the sanctuary of the mountain top, and in pitch darkness, he came into the lines with his loaded animal and made no complaint. That was the muleteer's life, up one day and down the next, week after week in sunshine or rain and always vulnerable to enemy attack.

I spent a wild night in the Pathan fortress, drinking whisky out of enamelled mugs and listening to their blood-curdling tales. They spoke clearly, in a tongue that was probably based on Persian and sufficiently like academic Urdu that I could understand all they said. Next morning they walked us along the ridgetiles of the roof between India and Burma and set us on our way. We were high above the timber line on bare rock, in dried grass and thin scrub, following the well-worn trails of the Kuki, who were the tribe to the East of the Nagas.

From a bluff we looked across the green sea of rain forest to a silver thread of river far below. Through field glasses I saw my first Japanese soldiers. Tiny figures, clockwork soldiers in baggy yellow-ochre uniforms, moved puppet-like about their tasks. It was a forward camp mustering assault troops for their coming attack on us. It looked peaceful enough and there were one or two working elephants moving about. The hated rising sun flag, the red disc on a white background, flew from a bamboo pole. They were oblivious of our gaze and it occurred to me that I, too, had probably been watched by their patrols from the mountains that ringed the plain.

I was sorry to leave the comforting protection of the Pathans and reluctantly pressed on with the patrol. We moved north cautiously, along the ridge, in correct jungle fighting patrol order. The two leading men fifty paces ahead scanned the track left and right, ready for ambush. I led the body of the patrol and about fifty paces to our rear 'Tail-end Charlie' followed. He was the get-away man and supposed to run back and raise the alarm if we were ambushed. We had our safety catches off and 'one up the spout' as we advanced warily.

We reached a Kuki village and it was apparent that we were the first visitors from the rest of the world that they had ever encountered. There was a stockade of bamboo and elephant grass hurdles, with a ring of *punjis* round the perimeter. These lengths of split bamboo, with razor-sharp fire-hardened points, were pushed into the ground at such an angle that they would pierce the groin of an approaching runner. They were invisible in the yellow grass and such an effective defence that we ourselves adopted them in lieu of barbed wire on many occasions.

They knew we were coming long before we found the village and our reception was cautiously non-committal rather than hostile. Beddowes had written in his orders: "Contact native hill tribesmen to ascertain if they know anything about Japanese activities!"

We had certainly contacted them, but even Surajbahn could not speak to them, their tongue was probably closer to Burmese than Indian.

They were very jungly (wild). They were naked apart from a deer-skin apron ornamented with teeth and feathers and the long hair of the men fell to their waists. We saw no women and the men led or carried the smallest children. Apart from child-minding and fighting the men did no domestic chores, but they were obviously talented head-hunters. The largest building in the village had a steeply pitched roof that reached to the ground and was adorned with hundreds of skulls. They were graded by size from mouse at the ridge down to barking deer at the eaves and halfway down, below monkey, were the human skulls.

We managed to establish by sign language that they knew of the little yellow soldiers and detested them. The enemy had not visited the village up to that time and we moved on. Along the tree line the travelling was easiest and there was always cover to drop down into. After much wild country, steep gullies and jungle we found another couple of villages but still no signs of enemy movement and our time and supplies were running out. I turned west off the ridge and descended into the valley to join the track back to the Imphal Plain. This time I made sure that I had a quick shave before reporting in my tattered sweat-stained uniform to Beddowes. I knew I was home when I heard his usual greeting: "Where the bloody hell have you been all this time – China?"

I must have done reasonably well because he made no other snide remarks over my report, drawing hard on his cigarette, before saying curtly: "OK! Dismiss! Go and make yourself a bit more presentable!"

Later Ted told me that the OC had been congratulated by Div HQ on my patrol, but he never mentioned it to me. Although the enemy were so close to Imphal that I had looked down upon them, battle had not been joined. On the other side of the mountains General Kawabe Masakazu (GOC Burma) also knew that time was running out if he was going to seize Imphal and win the war before the rains came.

91 Company HQ was on a hillock near the Palel airstrip close to the main road that led eastwards over the Shenam saddle into the Kabaw Valley. It was a temporary position and we lived in bamboo bashas. Mine was the size of a garden shed and always filled with whirling dust, flying bugs and small creatures. If a whirlwind flattened a basha it was quickly replaced. I bathed by sloshing water from a bully beef tin over my body and the suds ran out under the wall, but because nakedness was offensive to Sikhs I skulked in a corner to take my bath. Even in remote river valleys I never stripped off in front of the men and they respected me for it.

We knew that fresh Japanese divisions were in our vicinity as information about their battle plans began to trickle in from Frontier Force. They were often careless to the point of stupidity about security; it was an arrogant assumption that they were going to conquer whether we knew about their plans or not.

Intelligence had discovered that Mutaguchi intended to drive his crack 33rd Division across the Imphal Plain and isolate 17 Div at Tiddim and that this thrust would probably be in the south and cross the Shuganu valley. Beddowes was always at his nonchalant best when sending me to my death and he said casually, "Take a few men out to Shuganu, Johnnie, and report back as soon as you see anything happening!"

I took Surajbahn and a few men in a couple of trucks and bummed off down the long dusty road that I knew so well, into the flat salient of open country that ran south-eastwards into the mountains. One of the trucks had a puncture as night was approaching and I felt nakedly exposed under the beetling hills. A quick repair was vital and that meant doing it myself. British officers with native troops soon learned that they were much better equipped to correct mechanical faults in vehicles than their men. In the 1930s my father had taught me how to mend punctures and do minor repairs on our family saloon, whereas the Sikhs had probably never seen a car before the day they enlisted. I disposed the men on a small knoll to cover me as I worked.

We piled back into the trucks and moved on. When I arrived at the old place where I had first joined 91 it was ominously quiet and deserted.

In my imagination I felt like another lieutenant of Engineers, John

Chard, who had waited in the peaceful valley at Rorke's Drift 65 years earlier for the Zulu hordes to sweep down from the hills. In this quiet spot I was sitting directly in the path of thousands of fierce Japanese warriors.

We concealed the trucks in a dry nullah as best we could and took up a defensive position on a small hill, using some of the old 91 Company trenches that we had dug months before. I had no idea, now that the time was so near, how I would conduct myself in real battle. I had bayonetted a few sacks of straw, hit some bullseyes on the rifle ranges, but what would it be like when a pack of flesh and blood devils poured out of the mountains on top of us? Was I expected to stand firm and win a posthumous VC or was it my duty, like Tail-end Charlie, to turn and run back as fast as possible to report their approach? I did not think that a dozen men under my callow leader-ship could hold back the 33rd Japanese Division for long, but they shot you for cowardice, didn't they? The word coward frightened me more at that time than the word enemy! A proper infantry patrol would never have been sent out with such loose instructions as Beddowes had given me, but I was not infantry and neither was he. I was a very inexperienced young man and I really did not know what I should do, but I was determined to do my best and try to win the respect and confidence of my men.

We obliterated all traces of our night's sojourn and set out before dawn to search the Manipur River banks for traces of enemy cross-ings. How I pined for Nipper's experienced leadership. We explored mountain tracks towards the direction from which the enemy might approach. After two days' bumbling about I made a quick recon-naissance up and down the road with the trucks and decided it was time to return and report what I had not seen.

When I reached the junction with the main road, near the Palel airstrip I encountered another small convoy coming out. It was under the command of a bumptious artillery captain and he had with him a few soldiers from the RAF Regiment. These British lads in pale blue uniforms were airfield defence and not front line infantry. He commanded me to join him and turn back up the Shuganu track.

I did not like it at all. Was he empowered to give me orders? He was senior to me in rank, but he was not even from my division and he was a stupid gunner to boot! I would have had no qualms about obeying any senior infantry officer, but I did not know if this fellow knew what he was doing. He was brash and domineering in his manner, from a British Artillery unit, and he gave me no confidence. He had no written orders, but hinted darkly that his orders came from 'very high up' and had been given 'at a later date' than mine. He began to use blackmail to dragoon me into his little command by implying that I was yellow. He used emotive phrases like 'fleeing in the face of the enemy' and he warped my common-sense judgement.

I can see now how stupid I was to let him bully me into going along. I believe that, like me, he had been volunteered by some over-keen senior officer seeking a bit of personal kudos. The whole of our Corps was in a state of flux and nobody's left hand knew what their right was doing.

As soon as I submitted to my new boss he became even more insufferable. It was obvious that he was far less competent in the field than me, especially after my training and recent patrolling experiences. Even Surajbahn Singh muttered, in his Punjabi vernacular, that the Gunner-officer-sahib did not seem to know his arse from his elbow, which was an unwonted breach of the code from a regular Indian Army soldier to a British officer, but true for all that.

Open disagreement broke out between us the next morning when he ordered pompously, "Take your Indians up that mountain track over there!"

It was a northbound track and I patiently explained that my orders were to reconnoitre east-west tracks for a Japanese breakout and not go swanning off up any jungle path. Again he threatened to report my blatant insubordination and refusal to obey orders when we got back.

It all sounds a bit silly now, but it was very stressful at the time. The Sikhs and I trudged dejectedly over ground we had already covered. Just as I had decided to ditch the man and report back to base, my luck changed dramatically. My crazy old Pathan chums of Frontier Force came streaming down out of the hills; they had abandoned Mombi and not without reason.

"Christ! Johnnie!" The officer's dark face split into a wide white grin "What the hell are you doing out here? The Japs are breaking through everywhere!"

He told me that their 33 Div had been crossing the mountains somewhere between Mombi and us all through the night.

"Let's get out of here as quickly as possible!" He twisted his mustachios dramatically. "We must warn Corps!" His delight was unbounded when I told him I had transport and I was overjoyed to put myself under orders from this crack jungle warrior. I leapt to do his bidding. They piled into my trucks and we sped back towards Imphal.

At this point my memory fails me. Did I just bum off and leave the puffed-up gunner to his fate? Or did he follow us because the Pathan officer was senior and to be obeyed? I no longer cared what happened to him and neither was I shot for cowardice, but after being so close to thousands of Japanese throughout the night I had still not made contact with one of them.

Beddowes was shaky and rattled when I got back to Wangjing and for once he forgot to ask me where the hell I had been. He did not even want to hear my report. The Japs were swarming into the Imphal Plain in great numbers and the whole of 23 Div swung into action to join the fray. The three Gurkha battalions of our 37 Brigade were speeding away down the Tiddim road to meet the threat from the Japanese 33rd Division and there was bitter fighting beyond Bishenpur. My Jemadar had already taken the rest of the platoon to join 3/3rd Gurkhas and Surajbahn and I rushed off to catch up with them.

It is easy to get lost in the fog of war. Nobody ever knows what is really happening. Officers and men follow orders blindly on their own narrow band without seeing the whole spectrum. Things happen so quickly that the Army generals probably do not know precisely what is going on, but at least they are far enough away to take a broader view. Looking back a lot later and after reading a few reports, it is possible to make a guess at what probably occurred in the mud and the noise.

One thing was certain. Mutaguchi had a bold and typically Japanese plan and he fully expected the rapid collapse of our forces before the monsoon. He wanted Manipur with all our stores, transport and good roads before the rains came.

The vulnerability of 17 Div so far south at the end of a narrow track was a worry and Corps HQ gave the order to withdraw immediately. In the weeks before this attack they had sloughed off all their non-combatant troops and were ready to go. They were a tough fighting force of about 16,000 men, with vehicles and stores, and they were needed now for the defence of the Imphal garrison.

This was it! The battle for the gateway to India was on. On the central front IV Corps had only three divisions in the plain. They pulled 20 Div back from the Kabaw Valley to defend the road to Tamu and secure the heights of the Shenam ridge. 23 Div had the Gurkha Brigade down the Tiddim Road assisting the 17 Div withdrawal, another brigade guarding the only LOC (line of communication) from Dimapur and the third brigade north of Imphal up the Ukhrul road. We were very thinly spread on a long perimeter.

For Mutaguchi the battle was not going according to plan. He expected that we would fold or flee, as we had done thirteen months before in Singapore and everywhere else on the long retreat. The cocky resistance of our Gurkhas and the way they held out and fought back from their boxes must have maddened him. His men only had what they could carry or capture, whereas we had supplies and a strong base in Imphal.

There could no longer be any doubt that the Japanese were hellbent on breaking through on the central front. The whole of the 15th Japanese Army (comprising 15, 31 and 33 Divisions) was swarming out of Burma and making for India. They did not come up the road through Tamu but moved through dense jungle and along mountain tracks, which gave them the element of surprise. Their 15 Div crossed the River Chindwin and hooked round from the north to attack Imphal and our LOC, whilst further north their 31 Div struck cross-country to attack Kohima in a final thrust to seize the Dimapur railhead and open the way into India.

To our relief the 15th Indian Parachute Brigade dropped in by air to reinforce us and, within a couple of hours, fired their first shots as they attacked enemy columns of the Japanese 15 Div to the north. They killed almost a thousand enemy troops in the first few days. We were suitably impressed and delighted to welcome their Snarling Tiger emblem to our garrison.

The encircling enemy columns cut the main supply road and on April Fool's day 1944 we were surrounded and the siege of Imphal had begun, with a substantial part of Slim's XIVth Army completely cut off from India. At least our General had got himself a really big box now! We felt very isolated as we faced a future where every round we fired, every bite we swallowed and every fag we smoked would have to come in by air, if that were possible. It was difficult to believe that our little airstrip at Palel could cope with a fleet of Dakota

46

transports, especially as the forthcoming rains would soon turn it back into flooded paddy.

As the brigades of 17 Div threw their weight back up the road they forced their way north, passing through 37 Gurkha Brigade, and we followed them back past the prepared defences at Bishenpur, which were held by 49 Brigade of 23 Div. There were now three divisions of IV Corps and the Parachute Brigade, cut off but consolidated, around the Imphal Plain and we were ready for the next battle.

Harry had been with 3/5th Gurkhas, further forward down the Tiddim road than we other two, and was last to return to base. He had such hair-raising stories to tell of his adventures in battle that Bob and I gave him best, at least for one whole evening. He told us how the enemy had captured his new Jeep and a few days later they got it back: "They only put ten miles on the clock!" Harry said "So I didn't bill them for it!"

The saddest aspect of this first phase of jungle fighting was that we frequently had no way out for the wounded and, when the Dimapur road was cut, there was no way back to India. In time the little airstrip at Palel would become our lifeline, and Dakota aircraft would be able to come and go, but at first there were very few planes and we survived on parachute drops.

The ambulances collected 250 wounded soldiers from the verges of the Tiddim road and took them back to the tented field hospital near Imphal. We tried desperately to care for our casualties, who must have known that they faced a bleak prospect with little chance of relief from their suffering. In the boxes we laid them in the dust and tried to make them comfortable with a drink or a cigarette as they waited patiently, with little or no cover from the blazing sun or mortar bombs.

Our callous foe did not allow their wounded to be taken prisoner, they preferred to die where they stood, or commit hari-kari from a grenade in the stomach.

Chapter 5

THE SHOW GOES ON

I have forgotten a hundred fights,
But one I shall not forget –
With the raindrops bunging up my sights
And my eyes bunged up with wet;

We were living in a battlefield and we three platoon subalterns of 91 came and went from the officers' mess in rotation, very much like fighter pilots returning to base between sorties. It made us a small elite. Constantly enduring the same hardships and dangers we understood each other intuitively and our cultural and intellectual backgrounds were so similar that we spoke the same language anyway. We developed a code that carried us through the rough passages, playing down rather than dramatizing, yet knowing perfectly well what the other was feeling and saying. We enjoyed a mutual depth of understanding not unlike the intimacy of a good marriage.

Since boyhood and through all my Western training I had been inculcated with the idea that the enemy (always the Germans) and our forces were drawn up in parallel lines and faced each other across No Man's Land. The besieged Imphal Plain was not at all like that and was under attack from concentrated enemy thrusts all around the perimeter. They came out of the hills and jungles from all directions and our fighting units moved to counter these spearheads as they came in.

At the commencement of the siege three infantry divisions and the parachute brigade held the Imphal Plain and within this ellipse there were numerous ancillary support units, IV Corps headquarters and the RAF all disposed in defensive boxes. The Japanese probed between the islands and sent out offensive thrusts and jitter patrols

48

every night to keep them awake. As we moved about in daylight we had the uncomfortable knowledge that the enemy had been racketing over the same ground during the darkness of the night before and that they knew all about us. We were not prepared for the speed with which the enemy cut the Dimapur Road and there were many non-combatant units still in The Plain. For example the Road Roller Company box was jittered one night and started firing outwards, which so alarmed an adjacent Pioneer Unit that they fired back and the two of them belted away all night, long after the Japanese patrol had gone, and consumed a very large amount of valuable ammunition without a single casualty on either side.

Our 91 Company headquarters was always in the Gurkha Brigade headquarters box, because we were there to serve them. Beddowes did not like too many of us being away from HQ at any one time because it weakened his defences, but he dared not voice this too openly because he knew that we had to go wherever the infantry wanted our assistance.

The mess was a dank bunker, a rectangular pit roofed with logs and earth that left a ragged gap around the eaves, through which a dribble of light and air percolated. We joked about making a final stand, in the style of John Wayne, facing outwards through the slit and firing our last rounds at the attacking horde. This was a fantasy because, in the event of a showdown, we would be out with the battalions.

In the gloom of the mess bunker reading or writing was almost impossible in daytime and after dark there was one smoking *butty* (hurricane lamp). We played endless games of Liar Dice, using five dice marked with the court cards, (nine to King) of each suit. This was the Fourteenth Army game, because the little ivory poker dice were weatherproof, portable and visible in poor light. We came to know each other so well that bluffing became impossible and we carried on for longer than the game merited. I had a little pocket chess set that gave us much pleasure. I often beat Bob and explained one day that my father had taught me the game before I could read, to which he retorted, "Five years ago! Is that what you're saying?"

We passed a lot of time in verse and song. I had a good repertoire but I soon discovered that Bob and Harry were more than my equal. Before the war I had learned by heart the whole of W. S. Gilbert's *Bab Ballads* and most of Kipling's *Barrack Room Ballads*. Harry's favourites were the *Para Handy* tales by Neil Munro and he brought them to life in his soft Scottish brogue. Bob knew a great many Irish and English folk ballads.

Some nights we sang by the hour, especially when the monthly liquor ration came up. Taking turns to lead we each sang a song in which the others joined. No repetition was allowed in any one evening. Bob's collection of old ballads included *Where did yon blackbird go?*, *Simon the Cellarer*, and *A man who would a-shooting go*. Harry knew every song that Harry Lauder had ever written. I contributed a raunchy selection of traditional, music hall and bawdy ballads. I could almost bring tears to the eyes with *Suvla Bay* (a gloomy ANZAC ballad about Gallipoli in 1915) or the mournful strains of Dad's grave being moved to build a sewer, or the nostalgic sweetness of *The Hole in the Elephant's Bottom*.

Our remoteness from the rest of the world, the proximity of a vicious foe, the constant noise of shot and shell and the deep understanding that we would probably never see our homes again engendered geniality and fellowship at all levels. Together we had been blooded in battle and one's newness, caste, rank and religion no longer mattered. British officers in Indian Army units were bilingual; we lived with the men and chatted to them off duty and could express ourselves spontaneously in their dialect without working out a translation from English. For all that I could neither understand a word of Bob's Mahrattha speech nor Harry's smooth Punjabi and they could not fathom my coarse Sikh! With HQ staff such as drivers, cooks and clerks we used military Urdu.

After days alone on detachment I talked English to myself, just to hear my mother tongue spoken. In the mess we talked to each other in a polyglot of Indian phrases, schoolboy slang, Glaswegian, Indian Raj, rhyming slang and bits of Irish. An outsider would have wondered what we were saying. My parrot mimicry and travels had given me a repertoire of dialects, Harry sounded like Billy Connolly in his Gorbals accent and Bob could swear in the Gaelic. I can still hear Harry saying in mincing Glaswegian, "Why d'ye call me Jessie when m'names no' Jessie?"

This subaltern merriment never met with approbation from our two senior officers. Major Sahib sniffed and said in his slightly Brummie accent, "Ho! Yes! Very droll, I'm sure!"

Captain Ted often tried to be one of the boys, but lacked our esprit. A sly phrase, a word even and we collapsed into paroxysms of mirth, whilst Ted grinned conspiratorially, pretending that he understood the *double entendre*.

We seemed to be a different caste from them and we sometimes wondered if they realized how near we went to mocking them. The man up the line always has the edge over desk-wallahs and when we were back in Company HQ we were resting whilst they were busy administrating. It was never easy, in such a small cell, to balance between camaraderie and military formality.

It was almost impossible to find skilled medical assistance. There had been a time before the fighting when our field company had a doctor. He was a Bengali called Battercharya and, of course, we called him 'Batterycharger'. He was very black-skinned and my first encounter with him was when I had a touch of fever one day and he poured a creamy liquid into a conical glass and ordered, "Now drinking quickly – *all one go* – please!"

I slugged it back and nearly went through the roof of his bunker. I rushed outside pushing my fingers down my throat, trying desperately to vomit out the burning stuff.

"Very sorry! Wrong bottle!" I heard him calling apologetically after me; he had given me a searing liniment labelled 'For sprains and muscles – external use only'. Bob called our doctor 'Master Quack' and he reminded me of the garish notices in Indian bazaars that advertised 'Doctor Patel MD (Calcutta -failed) – sputum & excreta examined – teeth pulled & spectacles fitted'.

Many of the troops had venereal infections from birth and when one of my men developed a suppurating sore on his shin I recognized hereditary syphilis. I took him to see Batterycharger who gave him two aspirins and 'excused boots for seven days'. I was furious. The man was walking barefoot in the germ-laden dust with an open sore and receiving no treatment. By that time the first anti-bacterial drugs such as Sulphonamide were available.

I ducked into the gloomy interior of the officers' mess bunker and burst into a bitter tirade to Harry and Bob, who were sitting at the table:

"That stupid bloody doctor – talk about M.D. (failed). I don't think he knows a headache from a broken leg!"

I rattled on vituperatively until I saw out of the corner of my eye a small black figure unwind in the dark corner and flee the mess. It was he, of course. I had not seen his dark figure there in the gloom and I had just committed the most awful gaffe of my whole life. Hell hath no fury like a doctor scorned and he stormed off to Beddowes to complain bitterly that either I went or he did. Possibly the O.C. had also been given liniment to drink for his dyspepsia and was as fed up with the doctor as the rest of us, but we never saw Batterycharger again. We decided that it was better to have no doctor at all than a charlatan and there was a good sick room with competent medics at Brigade HQ.

Bob told me that he knew a secret track out of The Plain and that he intended to escape that way if Mutaguchi overran us. I respected his superior map-reading skills and experience from reconnaissance patrols, and he told me about the Silchar Track that snaked south and west between the Dimapur and Tiddim roads and led eventually out on to the Bengal Plain. This was the route by which the first British explorers had reached Manipur, long before the railway reached Dimapur or the road over the mountains through Kohima had been made. I was comforted by the knowledge that there was an escape valve and it buoyed me up throughout the weeks of siege to come. I did not know that the Japanese were across the track in strength and had already established a base depot there!

If we were feeling hot and bothered as we roasted in our grill pan our chef was not. Slim was perfectly content to watch his enemy, without proper LOCs, grinding themselves away against our stubborn resistance and the monsoon rains were imminent. He wrote, "The enemy, by constantly attacking and reinforcing failure, fell into our hands and it was at this period, especially round Imphal, that the process of wearing him out began."

Numerically the Japanese were still superior in fighting troops, and their Generals threw everything into this last throw for India with the reckless abandon of addicted gamblers.

We had only been surrounded for a few weeks when Bill Slim performed what was, and still is, a miracle. In a lightning transfer by air he flew the whole of the 5th Indian Division into Imphal and we welcomed their 'Fire Ball' Div sign to the Corps. To us it was the story of the magic carpet all over again! Dubbed 'The Forgotten Army', cut off and far from home, we had not expected help. We believed that we had been left with the stark choice of cutting our way out or dying with our boots on. Now in one stroke we were reinforced by a whole division and our numbers had risen from 18,000 to 24,000 combatants. We had not been abandoned! This knowledge fell upon our sweating heads like a refreshing shower and confidence in the future blossomed.

"If Orde Wingate could do it, so can we!" We would fight in isolation like the famous Chindits. We would conquer and survive!

We knew for certain that release, clean sheets, Cornish pasties, loving women, cold ale, Chinese suppers and nights at the opera – all the things that soldiers dream about in their foxholes – would not be ours until we had beaten the Jap. It was an attitude that would help Bill Slim a lot and it did Mutaguchi no good at all.

I scribbled a line to my parents on Easter Sunday 1944. Air Mail Letter forms were always in short supply, but, because some of the others were not such regular letter writers, I could always find one. We were also, of course, dependent upon the good will of the Dakota pilots to fly mail in and out. Unable to hint at where I was or that I was surrounded, I wrote:

> "I am writing this under the light of a hurricane lamp on the verandah of a deserted native hut. Looking up I can see the romantic silhouette of an oriental pagoda outlined against a blood-red full moon. Mosquitoes are whining about my head, the noise of crickets is almost deafening and every so often a flying tramcar hits the lamp."

I went on to explain that a 'flying tramcar' was my name for the armour-plated flying beetles, like cockchafers, as big as London sparrows that zoomed out of the night to crash against the glass of my butty.

What really beat the Japanese, long before the atom bombs were dropped, was the steadiness of our men in the face of their mad fanaticism. Men from every corner of the free world – Allahabad, Cheshire, Strathpeffer, Kathmandu, Brixham, Hobart, Brisbane, Rawalpindi, Deccan, Auckland – what a list! These were the men who refused the sons of Nippon any further advance. In the end on the soil of Manipur, man for man, the Japanese were outfought.

Captain Ted Allison, our adjutant, was a strictly raised Baptist boy who had never tasted strong drink, used strong language nor smoked in his life. This suited us because we could acquire his liquor and tobacco rations. Under the stress of active service and seeing the enjoyment we found in consuming his goodies, he had a swift change of heart. Like James Thurber's fabled bear, Ted either leant too far forward or fell over backwards and when he decided to indulge in the sinful pleasures he went for it whole-heartedly. He ordered boxes of one hundred Indian cheroots, three at a time, from Calcutta and from then on was hardly seen without a revolting stogie smouldering in his mouth. Ted tried to drink his monthly ration, a whole bottle of Canadian Rye Whisky, in one evening and he always passed out. On ration night his Sikh orderly waited patiently in the dark outside Ted's bunker to put him to bed and introduced a phrase that became our epithet for complete intoxication. Next morning Arjan Singh would say that his Sahib had finished up in a slit trench: "*Sir nichhe – tang upar!*" (Head down – feet up).

I liked Ted. He was a bit of a clown and a good buffer between Beddowes's acidity and our ebullience. He had the worry of stores, transport and all the administrative work of the Company and he muddled through it without making any attempt at efficiency. If we lost or broke anything Ted could be relied upon to cover for us before the OC found out.

Mutaguchi's 33 Div had come to rest across the Tiddim Road in the south and were held by our Bishenpur defences, and his 15 Div now held the road to complete the encirclement of Imphal. Our policy of aggressive defence was very effective and when they threatened our ring of defences we moved fast. An attack to the north-west by 23 Div was the opening move in the savage Battle of Sangshak. The plan was for 37 Gurkha Brigade to make a frontal attack up the Ukhrul track whilst 1 Brigade made a difficult cross-country circuit on jungle tracks to take them from the rear. It was called a 'hammer-and-anvil' attack. The other brigade of the division was guarding the western side of Imphal town, but was also available to us as reserve.

The battle took place in precipitous mountain jungles, which favoured the defence and we were keen to capture their divisional commander, General Yamuchi, who was nicknamed 'The Rat'. He was reputed to carry a few 'wives' with him in his entourage (our foe was very brothel-minded) and it gave the campaign a spicy flavour. This was the first large-scale jungle battle for our division and we discovered that it was a completely different kind of sport from the flat paddy fighting of the Tiddim Road.

There are still misconceptions about the jungle. Fortunately we

54

never met Errol Flynn, or African lions, or Brazilian anaconda, or chimpanzees eating bananas nor any of the other features of American movies. 'The Green Hell' epithet, coined by the media, fostered an illusion of undergrowth through which we chopped our sweating way step by step. It was not like that, not all the time. We often had to hack thick undergrowth away to make defensive positions or clear fire lanes and the densest jungle clothed the depths of the ravines, but the trees thinned out with altitude, up to the timber line, beyond which no trees grew. The Plain was about 2,000ft above sea level and many of the surrounding mountains soared to another 8,000ft or more above that, so that on the peaks there was only scrub or thin grass, as I had found on my Mombi patrol. Both sides strove for height advantage and at times on the upper slopes we fought in country that resembled European woodland.

The tracks, that the Japanese used so skilfully, were probably initiated by wild beasts and then beaten out by the bare feet of hill tribes. Gradually we widened these narrow pathways for mules and then for Jeeps to pass. Jungle is muddy, wet and thoroughly unpleasant, but after the Tiddim road we came to prefer the forest to open country. We pitied the lads in the Western Desert who had no trees to give cover. We went forward, boots-boots-boots, slogging pace after pace, climbing impossible slopes as we either lifted puffs of dust in the heat or squelched through chocolate-coloured mud. We dug in, filled in, pushed forward, fell back and dug in again. How grateful I was to be in the company of my muscular, phlegmatic Sikhs who took it all as part of their kismet and never grumbled. We were always wet, either with sweat or with rain, usually both. We forgot what clean clothes were and slept for weeks at a time with our boots on. Hot food was a thing of the past.

As we climbed into the mountains the heat was intense and the flies atrocious. To me the Ukhrul road spells bluebottles. A dead soldier in that moist heat turned black and bloated in a day, his skin shiny tight with gases, heaving in a metallic armour of greeny-blue flies and white maggots. I could visualize the history of every fly that crawled up my nostrils, savoured my lips or wiped its feet on my oily bully beef; it had just flown in from a corpse. Even now more than half a century later a bluebottle fills me with loathing and I could never go fishing with maggots for bait.

Working high up on the mountainside, under sporadic mortar fire and whanging bullets on the afternoon of 22 April 1944, I heard a cultured voice behind me say, "Good show, Sapper!"

I spun round to come face to face with my Divisional Commander, Major-General Ouvry Roberts, who had once been a sapper himself.

"You must be Hudson?" He added, taking in my bedraggled state.

It was the first time I had met a general and he was so far forward that I was very impressed. In his head he carried the divisional nominal roll of all his officers and, combined with visual evidence, he had placed me exactly. Blue shoulder lanyard meant Royal Bombay, and 91 was his only RB company. I was with Sikhs so this was No.3 Platoon and my two pips made me the platoon commander. His remarkable memory gave him my name! Such small but vitally important things are the marks of a true leader.

Colossal thunderstorms pressed us into the mud under the sheer weight of water and earth tracks disintegrated into mud slides. I was struggling to keep the track open, to let ammunition and supplies through to the infantry fighting up ahead, when news came through of our other brigade. They had reached their position, their hammer was poised above our anvil, ready to smash into the enemy on the far side. They had a lot of wounded men but Japanese roadblocks on the jungle tracks separated them from us.

There was another circuitous route that could get ambulances and supplies to them, but a bridge would have to be built over a deep valley gorge where the track hairpinned round the inside slopes of a valley in the Litan area. I was picked to do it. It was not on my brigade front but it was known that, as the most recent arrival from Europe, I had probably received the latest training in Bailey Bridge construction

Chapter 6

NOT TO REASON WHY

Me that 'ave followed my trade
In the place where the Lightnin's are made;
'Twixt the Rains and the Sun and the Moon—

The Bailey Bridge, so familiar in Europe, was new to India. Even men of my time who had chosen to do their OCTU in India had never seen one, whereas I had spent many days and nights building them. The one they were asking me to build on the Litan track would be the very first on the Burma Front. It was considered that with my extensive training I would throw it across the gap in no time at all!

No matter that none of my Sikhs had ever seen one before. No matter that the stores list, check list and layout drill would not be observed. (The Bailey bridging drill routines in Europe were as strictly followed as the rituals of High Mass.) No matter that the bridge had come to us across the miles and muddles of India. No matter that the fleet of lorries would be loaded haphazardly and sent forward in the wrong order. Good Ol' Johnnie would do it!

"Good job we've got you, old boy!" Beddowes said obsequiously, proffering a cigarette. Coming from him that was tantamount to receiving a Mention in Despatches before I'd even begun.

That evening I set out with a convoy of mixed trucks and my faithful platoon along an unknown track. Night descended. We came to places on that ghastly road where corduroy surfaces of felled logs sloped greasily outwards to sheer drops over the khud. There really is not an English word for khud, but it filled most of our working lives on those jungle tracks. Cut-and-fill roads round the steep mountain sides meant an excavated vertical wall on one side and on the other a precipitous drop into dense jungle below. The khud on the high side slipped down and blocked the road and the khud on the low side took

57

half the road away with it when it went. It was a constant burden for the sappers.

The bridge had come from our Field Park Company and the drivers were small Madrassi men from Southern India, who were completely out of their element on wet mountain roads and who spoke in a strange guttural tongue. At every difficult section I turned all the drivers out of their cabs and drove each truck myself, one by one, over the hazard. The loss of a single truck would mean a blocked road, no bridge and a lot of wounded soldiers left to die in the jungle. The drivers were only too glad for Sahib to take the responsibility off their shoulders and squatted comfortably by the road to smoke a hand-rolled biddy. Time after time I nursed my nose-to-tail snake over landslides, round hairpins, past obstacles in the darkness and through different dialects to the point of bridge.

I was confident about Bailey bridging. I had personally performed every task myself on training exercises – lifting, hammering, heaving and launching in bright sunshine and night blizzards. I knew the drill like I knew 'Three Blind Mice' and to me it was no more than a big boy's set of Meccano. You put the panels (a six-man load) together, two-by-two on rollers and, as you added more at the back, you rolled it forward over the gap, keeping the tail well down on the home side so that the cantilever nose never dropped disgracefully into the drink. The lightweight launching nose had to soar over the gap and touch down, light as a feather, on the far bank.

A fine drizzle was falling at three o'clock in the morning when we started to bridge; flashes and bangs echoed from the hills on all sides as the infantry fought off the Japanese.

In *The Military Manual* (which all the red-tabbed staff officers back at HQ had carefully read) a case was quoted of a handpicked team of British sappers who, after six months' intensive training on a flat, prepared site in bright sunshine, had 'thrown' a Bailey across a ninety-foot gap in ninety minutes. My gap was about 100ft and Strongbottom probably told someone back at Corps, "A hundred minutes, say about a couple of hours, what? Hrr-umph?"

By the grace of God, as I started work in that diabolically dark corner, I did not know that some publicity-minded idiot at Corps HQ had already given the media the phrase "A foot a minute!"

The site could not have been more difficult. On the narrow road behind me my convoy of fifty vehicles was jammed nose-to-tail in random order and the thousand bits and pieces of Bailey were not loaded to plan. The deep river gorge ran parallel to and between the approach and departure roads, so that the actual bridge itself had to lie in the crook of an acute hairpin. The steeply sloping approach road had the high wall of the cutting on the left side and the drop into the gorge on the other. It was like one of the more difficult sections of the Monte Carlo Rally.

I personally had to do everything. My jemadar was superb and I came to see him in a new light. So were the NCOs, rallying behind him, but completely lost – 'in the dark' might be a better phrase. I had to teach them where each piece went from page 1, paragraph (i), of the Bailey Bridge Manual, which I did not have to hand. What I had once learned in a sunny Nottinghamshire meadow by the River Trent they now had to assimilate in wet blackness under sporadic mortar fire in a muddy gorge.

As they began to get into the building drill my confidence rose.

Beddowes suddenly appeared out of the darkness. I was tempted to ask where the bloody hell he had been, but he was very twitched up, with live Japanese close by and mortar bombs falling and he nervously came out with

"D'you think you'll do it, Johnnie?"

"I might if I'm left alone!" I said rudely; I was extended to full stretch.

"Ah! Well! Keep it up, Laddie!"

God! I didn't need patronizing and I hated the pejorative 'laddie'. I didn't need him, but I would have given ten days of my life right then for ten trained British sappers.

The urgent need for the damned bridge began to build up about me. There was a fleet of ambulances and a full battalion backed up behind my last lorry. The mortar and small arms fire was becoming more and more annoying as the enemy twigged that we were up to something. The bridge was so important that companies of infantry were fanning out over the surrounding slopes to give me cover.

What I could never have allowed for, and what nobody else could understand, was the length of tailback that was needed. A Bailey swaying over the gap is a seesaw and needs more weight behind the rollers than nose in front. We were in the very crook of the hairpin and as the length increased I could not get back far enough because of the wall of rock behind us. Instead of a military drill it was now pure civil engineering. The only solution was to 'drop it in the drink', the worst crime imaginable in bridge training, and then haul it out again by brute force. I let the nose drop into the gorge and the tail went high up the cliff behind me.

Dawn broke and an angry voice behind me shouted, "Christ! Man! You're holding everything up! We were supposed to all have gone through by now!!"

"Split infinitive! You ignorant *twat*!" I spat back viciously at the red-faced red-tabbed staff officer, who I had never seen before.

It was the worst moment. I had tons of heavy metal nose-dived into the muddy river and daylight was growing, but it worked. We manoeuvred it forward as far as it would go and then winched it up the other bank with a team of sweating men and block-and-tackle. My super supermen, my Sikhs, grasped that we were not only under the spotlight but also up the creek, and they performed feats beyond human endurance. As the bridge settled on the far abutments and almost before we could finish laying the decking the column began racing across it on foot.

It was full daylight by the time we finished. We had done it, not in a couple of hours, but in a commendable six hours. I pushed all my own trucks over the khud to clear the narrow road and allowed the ambulances and supporting Bren carriers through. Later we heaved our vehicles back with lorry winches and lined them up for the return journey. Wearily we drove down to Imphal where, to my chagrin, Beddowes greeted me with a vinegar face.

"A bloody foot a bloody minute!!" he chanted sourly "A bloody foot a bloody hour, more like! What were you thinking of?"

No wonder he was acid. Whilst I was up at Litan the BBC (Overseas Forces) News Service had broadcast the announcement that "Last night sappers on the Burma Front threw a Bailey Bridge across a jungle river at the rate of a foot a minute!"

I suppose Beddowes had been castigated by CRE at Corps and then heard the radio bulletin. I myself had never given out this daft statistic, but my men and I had been extended to the limit for 36 hours and the wounded infantry were streaming back to the Field Hospital. I was so proud of my platoon and quite untruthfully told the Jemadar, "Please tell the lads that the Major Sahib is delighted with your wonderful performance last night!" And I added, "And be sure that every NCO and man knows how proud of you all I am as well!"

I turned in all standing and slept for eighteen hours.

Because of the north-south grain of the country our main lines of communication ran parallel to the Burma border and the Japanese front. During the battle on the Ukruhl road documents and a marked map were found in a dead Japanese officer's haversack. These confirmed their overall strategy for the three-pronged attack. Their left hook had already cut the Tiddim road, the central thrust had reached Ukhrul and our lifeline to India was severed. The right hook well up north through the Naga Hills to Kohima was intended to give them a direct route down though Dimapur and open the gate into India. We, of course, had no knowledge of what was happening up north, nor where their 31 Div was, but rumours about the Kohima battle filtered through.

The Battle of Sangshak was a desperate and lengthy struggle. Despite the heavy casualties that the Gurkha battalions inflicted on them Japanese soldiers did not capitulate. They moved or they died, but they never surrendered. At Ukhrul our hammer brigade striking against the unyielding solidity of the anvil brigade had squeezed their invading forces out sideways, but they still presented a serious threat to Imphal. Yamuchi's headquarters was overrun and to our disappointment we found no women.

I returned the empty bridging lorries to the Field Park Company, gave the men a hot meal and a long sleep before we climbed back to join 3/3rd Gurkha. The bridge building had been a refreshing interlude, a bit of real engineering in the routine support tasks of jungle fighting.

On a steep slope one morning, high up under the ridge where the undergrowth was less dense, Lance Havildar Dalip called out excitedly, "*Sahib! Sahib! Idhar ao – tez, tez!*" (Sir! Over here! – quickly, quickly!)

He had come across a smashed Japanese mountain gun, a portable piece, and bits of limbs and dead bodies lay scattered about in the undergrowth; a heavy mortar bomb had made a direct hit. I half-turned and came face to face with a seated Japanese officer, only a pace away. His back was against the bole of a tree and his pebble eyes stared aggressively at me. He was stone dead. Each black whisker on his parchment jowls stood out as though magnified and I remembered having heard that the beard grows on after death. I could smell the nearness of him, sitting at my feet, and it was the first time I had seen a blue-eyed Japanese. His red lips pouted wetly beneath his black moustache as though he was expecting a kiss.

Only a few seconds had passed since Dalip's first shout and, concealing my shock, I spun round to issue orders to search the area thoroughly. His corpse was not cold and the men ripped open the coarse tunic to collect his papers, postcards and a photo of a very pretty Japanese girl.

Now I had not only seen the enemy, shot at the enemy, but I was actually touching one! My frontiers of experience were being pushed forward very rapidly and my curtains of doubt and fear were being drawn back. I was out of the stage fright period and no longer had to worry about what it would be like 'on the night'.

It remains a deeply etched memory.

Up in the mountains chasing Yamuchi's scattered forces I was with a Gurkha company when we were driven out of a Naga village called Yaingangpokpi. We tumbled down from the heights to the battalion HQ position on a saddle below the village. Later that day a runner from 91 HQ found his way up to me from the valley below. He handed me a wafer of squared paper torn from a field notebook with a message scribbled by Beddowes that read:

Lt. Hudson
Have a quick look to see if the road is clear as far as the last house in Yaingangpokpi. Do not let vehicles through until you have had a look.
There is a recovery vehicle coming up to take away the carrier which has blown up. This l/nk will show you where the carrier is.
   (signed)   W. Beddowes Major R.E.   17.4.44

Here it was again! The direct order from my commanding officer to go out and get killed. As usual he was out of touch with the situation forward, well out of date and acting the part of a competent Company Commander. In action you must always obey the last order or be shot. I was going to be shot if I disobeyed his order and I was going to be shot if I did not.

I found Lt Col Chris Pulley commanding 3/3 Gurkha sitting on an ammo box by the door of his dugout. I flung up a parade ground salute and said, "Permission to speak, Sir?" As we were on Christian name terms and very chummy, he guessed I was up to something and nodded agreement.

"SIR!" Clicking my heels, "I have to inform you that I am moving forward with one lance naik to examine the last house in Yaingangpokpi village!" I handed him the message (which I still have) and he replied with a twinkle in his eye, "As I have just ordered the withdrawal of the whole of 'C' Company and all other units from that untenable position I will personally have you shot if you make any attempt to go forward of my leading troops!"

I met Beddowes again a week or more later, after we had retaken the village and were driving the Japanese off the higher ground beyond it. He did not mention his stupid order and neither did I.

The Gurkhas advanced relentlessly and 91 HQ came forward to a position on a saddle lower down. In the fluidity of battle the Japanese overran it one night. It was the usual noisy and confused skirmish in total darkness and probably the enemy were as disorientated as our men. Although Ted hated his office job and was not very good at it, he showed real flair that night. When dawn broke he found the office yakdans that the marauders had thrown about and took all the office files outside and burned them. Nobody ever knew for sure what Ted had destroyed, but from that moment on we did well out of this one thoughtful act by using the magic phrase, "All Company records were lost by enemy action on the night of 26 April 1944, when Japanese forces broke through and overran our position."

For the next year Ted fiddled masses of extra items of equipment and transport because all our stores lists were lost.

The days of fighting grew into weeks and months and we accepted events pragmatically as we grew the hard shell of front-line soldiers. Adaptability is a wondrous thing and we often turned drama into comedy. Lying close to Harry one afternoon under very heavy shell-fire I got my ear near enough to his ear to shout, "Are you bloody terrified, Harry?"

"What me, Jummie?" He slipped into broad Glaswegian "Turrified, didy'a say? O' course no'," adding after a short pause, "Ye have'na' got a wee piece of toilet paper on youse, I s'pose, laddie?"

Our personal needs were surprisingly few and there was no NAAFI shop or canteen. At the end of the dry season in the blinding glare on the plain we longed for sunglasses, which of course we did not get. I shaved with a cut-throat razor, as my father had taught me and needed no razor blades (which were in very short supply). I cleaned my teeth in the manner of the Sikhs using a chewed twig and no dentifrice. The hygienic Indian use of clean water instead of dirty bits of toilet paper at the loo was an improvement and left no litter to give away our presence. When we had no cigarettes, which was most of the time, we smoked what we could scrounge in home-made bamboo pipes.

We discovered the old truism that 'Active service is long periods of intense boredom punctuated by moments of intense fear'. In one of our frantically busy times Bob asked me one day if I would swap one of my periods of intense boredom for ten of his moments of intense fear, as he wanted to sit down and have a smoke.

Our greatest deprivation was reading matter. A tattered paperback was more valuable than gold dust; we could not spend gold dust but we could read a book a dozen times, especially the timeless joy of poetry. Whizzing along in my Jeep one day a paperback blew out of the back into the dust and on my way back a tank man at the side of the road stopped me:

"You dropped this just now, Sapper!" he said, and handed back my book. If I had dropped a one thousand rupee note it would not have mattered, but what selfless integrity to return a book!

Everything had to come in by air. It was like being in an oxygen tent with a foe who could stand on your lifeline at any time. There were now two muddy airstrips, the original one at Palel and a small temporary one near Corps HQ at Imphal. The number of planes and the state of the airfields, especially during the rains, made this a very limited delivery service. When the Dakota transport planes could not land they shovelled the stores out on parachutes. There was a rigid priority list – ammunition, tobacco, food, fuel – and that order was strictly observed. Mail was much further down the list. This reasoning, based on trench warfare, was that Tommy needed bullets first and foremost to shoot the enemy, that he could last longer without food if he had a fag, and if he had no petrol he could walk. Letters from home would only be sent up to him if there were nothing more essential on the load.

They reduced the rations at regular intervals and they were crafty about it. They announced, "There will be a further slight reduction of food rations of just under four per cent as a temporary measure" but we never knew what it was four percent of, nor by how much we had been pruned so far. It was never temporary and there never was an increase. It was the sort of thing that Strongbottom did best and the intention was to confuse us. Eventually we dropped down to 'Seven and a half per cent below half-rations', but below half of what rations, we wondered. We were certainly not overweight and we were always hungry. We were encouraged to smoke and, apart from the Sikhs, everybody did.

To add to our suffering they introduced a square, meatless, skinless block of artificially flavoured soya bean, made in America and called a Soya Link. They were packed in white grease in green tins and later we received the boxes of US Forces 'K' Rations that contained twee packets of dried porridge, sponge pudding and shrivelled apricots. It was a sort of dehydrated attempt at 'food like Momma makes' and we pined for a return to canned bully beef and weevilly biscuits. Whenever I could I scrounged from the men! Food shortage led to a lot of boring conversations about what we would order if we were just sitting down to dinner at Firpo's, the smartest restaurant in Calcutta.

The Imphal airstrip was noticeably close to Corps headquarters, so that, if we were overrun, they would not have far to run to catch a plane out. It was almost impossible for the wounded to leave the beleaguered garrison and return to India. 'Not too badly hit' meant a patching-up job in the Field Hospital at Imphal and then back to the battlefield. 'Severely hit' usually meant being buried on the plain somewhere. 'Very severely hit' and you probably died under an unmarked bush. The limited medical supplies, disease, heat, insects, squalor and doctors like Battery-charger were not conducive to recovery for the sick or wounded. There was a very faint chance of 'Getting a Blighty One' and being airlifted out to India; Blighty itself, of course, was unattainably remote. If you were beyond repair, unfit for further use and refused to die you were consuming valuable rations and were best removed.

In Europe a wounded soldier might be back in an English hospital within the day, surrounded by attentive nurses, but our wounded faced interminable waits under the hot sun, or drenching rain, and a jolting ride to a tented hospital. We were so impossibly remote from home that we stood a very good chance, even after losing a limb, of being given a staff job in the Imphal garrison.

It sounds morbid now, but ghoulishly we discussed our chances. I reasoned that blindness was the perfect 'Blighty One'. I pictured myself sitting at a grand piano in an English drawing room, French windows open to a spring garden, with a pretty girl's arm about my neck as I played Noel Coward tunes and sang to her. Outside would be the neat lawn, yellow clumps of daffodils and the music of song-birds. I could not play a note at that time, but, as a blind hero, surely I would be given free lessons? Harry brought me back to the mud with a jolt, in his mock Glaswegian, "Ye'd see sod-all, much less daffy-dillies if you wus blinded ye daft wee bugger." I hadn't thought of that!

Our folks back home did their best. They had no knowledge of our whereabouts, our situation or that Japanese troops surrounded us. My dear sister sent me 200 Rothman's cigarettes every month, many of which I received, and the parents were always posting books and magazines. We shared everything. Returning from a nasty spell up the line I learnt that a parcel had come for me and found Harry and Bob smoking away and devouring my books.

"We decided," Bob announced, "that while you were off enjoying yourself in the mountains you would not begrudge a few amenities for your poor friends at the front!"

I invented a little chap called 'Morale' who followed me every-where. I entertained the others by holding imaginary conversations with him, and Bob, who was a clever cartoonist, drew two figures on opposite sides of a piece of card. One side showed a jolly Morale laughing and waving the Union Jack as he danced up and down and the reverse was a miserable guy in a bush hat and pouring rain. Each time I entered the mess bunker I could turn my morale card to display my mood at the time. Bob then introduced us to Conscience, a little bowler-hatted apologetic chap who never knew the point at which the line should be drawn. It was escapism, but it helped to preserve our sanity, and both Bob and Harry appreciated my Colonel Strongbottom, who figured frequently in our discussions.

Sitting and talking together we conjured up fanciful pictures of the civilized world outside. When we got out, if ever we did, we imagined taking tea with the vicar's wife, flicking cigarette ash carelessly about, grinding our stub-ends into her Axminster, doing pencilled calcula-tions and sketching maps across her cream wallpaper and throwing the tea dregs out through the door saying, "Damn good drop o' char that, m'am"

When my sister wrote from home that she was going down to Cornwall, Bob said that his mother and sister were down there. Perhaps they would meet. It did not take Harry long to concoct the following imaginary conversation between them:

"Hello! You must be Bob's mother?"

"I am ROBERT's mother yes! Are you Johnnie's sister?"

"Er – JOHN's sister actually. You must be grateful to my brother for the way he dragged Bob to safety out of that blazing bunker under heavy Japanese fire."

"I'm sorry, my dear you seem to have got the wrong end of the stick. Perhaps you should read your letter again; it was Robert who dragged Johnnie to safety."

We had no certainty about anything any more. When the war would end, when the Japanese would be beaten, when we would see our homes again or when we would get a decent hot meal.

Chapter 7

THE BEST IS LIKE THE WORST

The days are sick and cold, and the skies are grey and old,
And the twice-breathed airs blow damp;

Despite Bill Slim's defiance the monsoon hit us savagely on 13 May 1944, but we battled on through mud and drenching rain. The weather was much more to our advantage than it was to the enemy. Our 37 Brigade came down from the Ukhrul road and took over the Shenam Ridge defences from 20 Div. Our job was to bar the gate on the Tamu road and prevent the Japanese entering the Imphal Plain from that direction and gaining an invaluable LOC. We would be living at 5500ft or more above sea level, among mountains that reared up in places to twice that altitude.

From their lofty positions on the surrounding mountains the Japanese could observe stretches of our road snaking round the peaks and they watched inscrutably, without making any attempt to harass us, as we took over. The Japanese could always exhibit a stolid indifference to anything that was not a part of their particular master plan.

Our convoy climbed nose to tail from the paddy fields around Palel airstrip, up the rutted track to the jagged ridge that separated Imphal from the dreaded Kabaw Valley. If Imphal was the doorway to India then we were sitting in the keyhole. General Mutaguchi had to push us off this bastion before he could open the road into Imphal and find everything a little Jap needed to make him happy – food, respite, stores, transport, an airfield and all-weather roads through to Dimapur. His probing spearheads were already running down their reserves and he needed support from the rear. He was losing time in the teeming rain and losing face; no wonder he gave us such an unremitting hammering.

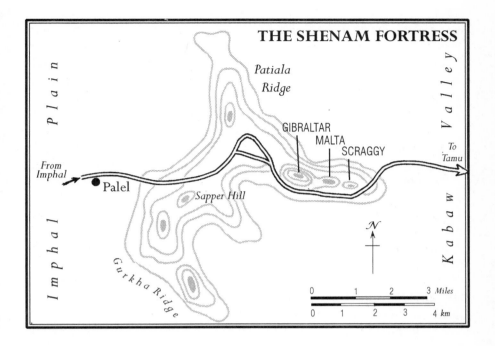

THE SHENAM FORTRESS

Patiala Ridge

GIBRALTAR
MALTA
SCRAGGY

Plain

Valley

From Imphal

Palel

Sapper Hill

To Tamu

Imphal

Kabaw

Gurkha Ridge

N

0   1   2   3 Miles

0   1   2   3   4 km

Our new position was a range of peaks joined by saddles to form the spine of this formidable barrier. Separate units took possession of different hilltops and established their individual boxes. Our company took over Sapper Hill, and there were other prominences with names such as Seaforth, Punjab and Recce. The whole defence depended entirely upon holding the three dominant summits that bounded the road; they were named Gibraltar, Malta and Scraggy.

This was the front line that I had always imagined from the war stories of my youth. No longer free to manoeuvre, amongst paddy or steep jungle, we crouched in deep trenches that followed the contours around the peaks. It was static warfare and we were bogged down in thick mud, or rocky crevices as we looked across the barbed wire to No Man's Land and the enemy beyond. The trees were peeled white by shellfire, their tops blasted away and splintered into grotesque shapes. Around the upper levels the jungle scrub had been burned or cleared away from the torn earth. Human and military debris lay abandoned everywhere.

At this height the mountains had little earth cover, but we never escaped from mud. My dugout was a practical design, a sleeping bench cut into the forward side of the front wall of the trench. The dirt-covered log roof sloped outwards and the fire-slit at ground level faced across barbed wire to the deep valley beyond. At dawn and dusk we stood-to, in readiness for an attack, and I knelt on my shelf and poked my gun through the slit. The monsoon filled every hole that was not drained and the trenches were duckboarded, sloping along their length to discharge rainwater out over the hill. Our dugouts were always awash, which discouraged rats and creepy-crawlies. There were three kinds of rain: drizzle, heavy and torrential. A lot of the time we were shrouded in a white mist that hid us from enemy view and out of which the highest summits projected like islands. It was never dry, never sunny and everything was damp, mildewed or rusty.

Sapper Hill had a guardroom, company office, a tiny mess, and even a First Aid Post, all below ground. Foxholes and bunkers were connected by the trench system that ringed the crest, making it a self-contained position, and we were responsible for our own survival and defence. We lived in our holes like badgers.

The Imphal Plain was like a large volcanic crater, a plateau ringed by jungle mountains, and now cut off from the rest of the world and within the perimeter we built numerous defensive boxes. The Shenam Ridge was an archipelago of mountain peaks and we could only move between our boxes by descending to the road and climbing back up again to the next position.

Along the crest the road was almost level as it wound in and out of the high places. Traffic could move, almost unobserved by enemy eyes, right up to the last high corner, beyond which the Japanese held possession and the road dipped away to the Kabaw Valley. At night the enemy marauded along the road and around our islands, and we sat tight. In daylight there was a lot of movement between the boxes with infantry platoons patrolling defensively. The enemy were extremely close and they covered everywhere they could with machine guns, shell fire, mortars and snipers. When there was no mist we could only move about on the sheltered reverse slopes of our positions or crawl through gullies.

On the few occasions when the clouds lifted and the mist drew aside we had panoramic views across The Plain to the distant ring of mountains. We could see remote glints of water, rice paddy, tree-shrouded villages and forests cloaking the slopes. Manipur looked like an

Arcadian paradise. In those brief interludes we lifted our eyes from the filth of our lives, imbibed clean air and glimpsed beauty. I recalled the front row of the Church choir at home, where young maidens sang 'Stay, Master, stay upon this heavenly hill,' to the tune *Unde et Memores*, except that this hill was more hellish than heavenly. The sweet music of that hymn still conjures up for me those frontier ranges swept by gunfire and monsoon rain.

To our dismay the gunners set up a battery of 5.5s, our biggest gun, in a crook of the road right below Sapper Hill, and we were immediately above their thundering muzzles. We feared that the Japs might retaliate against their sporadic shelling and pepper us with near misses. They could set up their light mountain guns in the most surprising places and one day they dropped a shell or a mortar bomb that must have gone down the muzzle because it destroyed one of the guns completely and to our delight the artillery moved away.

It was never quiet at Shenam. Bursts of mortar and shellfire racketed about our heads all the time. The heart-chilling tacker-tacker-tacker of automatic weapons and the sporadic crackle of rifle fire punctuated by grenade bursts echoed day and night from the valley walls. There was a constant awareness that at any time a shrieking yellow horde might suddenly sweep up from the jungle below. The all-pervading stench of putrefying flesh, excreta and explosives infiltrated our lives. These were the accompaniments to life on our heavenly hills.

It was a brigade position and one Gurkha battalion occupied Gibraltar, another Malta and Scraggy, whilst the third battalion stayed back in reserve at Brigade HQ. The forward troops were in constant close combat with the Japanese and our three sapper platoons rotated with them so that there was always a platoon to defend Sapper Hill. As usual my Sikh platoon was attached to 'turd/turd' (3/3 Gurkha) like a maintenance gang and we dealt with trench repairs, mines, booby traps and any other jobs that the infantry needed.

As mentioned earlier, success or failure on the Shenam Ridge, for both sides, depended upon possession of the three dominant peaks. They were well named. Moving along that last length of road the first and largest peak was Gibraltar, which closely resembled that island rising from a sea of white mist. Malta was forward of it and slightly smaller, and then came Scraggy, the third and last fortress, beyond which the road ran down into the Kabaw Valley. One look at that small shattered hill and the name was obvious.

They were our battle fleet, steaming in line ahead. The big dreadnought Gibraltar looked down on the cruiser Malta under her bows and Scraggy, the little destroyer, was in the van. There was some feeling of security on lofty Gibraltar with its established entrenchments and it was difficult to assail up the steep, bald approach slopes. It was swept by enemy fire from Nippon Hill across the valley and from other vantage points and it was heavily shelled, but it retained an air of loftiness and superiority. Malta was not so high and physically much closer to the enemy and easier for them to approach. It stood directly over the little hell of Scraggy and was responsible for it. There was a path along the connecting saddle between them that was too dangerous to use in daylight.

If Scraggy fell (God forbid!) Malta had to hold, but, if Malta fell, Scraggy was untenable. They were interdependent and to look down on Scraggy from the heights of Malta was like viewing a low aerial photograph of the Somme in 1915. It was an awful place of death with its shattered tree stumps, rocky barricades and bare craters, and life down there was insufferable. Both sides had dug in, right up to and just below the crest until only ten paces of No Man's Land separated the two lines of trenches in some places. The paucity of soil made trenching an arduous task; the rock was hard to move without blasting and we had to build up the parapets and revetments from old ammunition boxes and sandbags. In the very front trench Gurkhas lay or crouched, holding a grenade with pin drawn, or fingers on the Bren gun trigger, unable to relax even for a second. The strain was so severe that they had to be relieved at frequent intervals. They were wrapped in the stench of putrefaction, the most pervasive on earth. I cannot understand why this foetid odour has been described as 'The sweet, sickly smell of death'; it is far from sweet, but once experienced never forgotten. Words cannot convey it.

The men of Yamamoto Force were as fanatical as any in the Nipponese Army and their determination to break into the Imphal Plain had pushed them to this desperate breakpoint where our iron resolve would not let them pass. We were locked like two wrestlers, eyeball to eyeball, neither gaining, neither giving. We had very little ground to yield before we would be tumbling backwards down the

72

precipitous slopes to The Plain. They had very little ground to capture to open the doorway into India.

For the next seventy days and seventy nights at Shenam we were under constant attack. They never relaxed the pressure and hit us from every direction. It was not easy to ignore the monsoon, but at least the chilling rain was falling as heavily on their dirty bristled heads as it was on ours. How strange that such a vast area of mountains and jungle along the frontier between India and Burma lay undisturbed, whilst we beat the hell out of each other on this one small patch.

The steep climb up the track from Palel was in heavy daily use for all our supplies and ammunition, and for evacuating our wounded, and it required constant maintenance. Road repair gangs, non-combatants, tended the lower reaches but around the top it was a sapper responsibility. In contrast the enemy had a poor supply route from Burma, using captured civilian trucks over badly maintained tracks and employing carrying parties or mules to reach the more forward positions. They still clung to the idea of advancing on that little bag of rice at the waist, except that they were no longer capturing villages from which they could replenish it. At that time we did not know that they were so much worse off than we were for supplies and support.

On Sapper Hill we manned listening posts, set out guards, stood-to at dawn and dusk and gazed alertly out over the parapets and wire. We were never subjected to a full attack, but we were jittered most nights. This strange Japanese pastime eventually became farcical. In the darkness they crept as close as they dared, banging off rounds of tracer, tossing grenades about, giving eerie catcalls and shouting stupid slogans in pidgin English, "Hey! Johnnie! You listen Tokyo Rose! She put you right, Johnnie!"

We did not have radios and I had never heard the fifth-rate propaganda of this lady from Tokyo, who was their attempt to emulate Lord Haw-Haw in Europe. Our Indian troops could not understand a word of what she said nor the garbled shouts of the enemy from across the wire. At first it was nerve-racking and we feared a full attack might be coming in, but we grew hardened to it. It was said that jitter raids helped them to plot our positions, but I believe that it was their funny little oriental bloody-minded way of being aggravating. It was something we never did.

I enjoyed marksmanship and calibrated my rifle very carefully by firing tracer across the valley. I once spent a whole day on Malta working on a sniper. After locating his position, which was much nearer than I had expected, I shut him up.

Big ambulances could not get up to us and there were stretcher Jeeps, fitted with a frame to carry two casualties lying fore and aft, one above the other, beside the driver. A lightly injured soldier could sit behind the driver to tend the men on the litters and steady them over the bumps. They ferried the wounded down to Palel where the big ambulances took over; the trip back to the Field Hospital at Imphal took all day. Volunteers of the American Field Service (unarmed non-combatants; many were Quakers) drove the Jeeps and their persistent heroism was a model to us all; we loved them. They arrived at dawn, having driven up from the plain in darkness along a road threatened by marauding enemy patrols.

They were always grateful for battle souvenirs to 'Show mum, one day!' Japanese grenades were unreliable; after striking the firing cap against a rock, or hitting two together, they were thrown with black smoke curling from the tail. They frequently failed and I used to collect the unexploded ones and steam them out for souvenirs. I could always trade them for cigarettes from visitors from the rear areas and a pack of American Chesterfields was beyond price.

Every vehicle that used the road did damage. The continuous rain caused liquid red shale to cascade in landslides from the cutting above to block the road and the khud leached away, making the road narrower. The ruts got deeper and deeper and whole stretches slithered into the valley below; it was like trying to stem a volcanic lava flow with a pitchfork. Shellfire did not help and they could lob shells or mortar bombs into hidden corners. An outside hairpin going round a ridge often disappeared completely and inside corners filled as half a mountain came down from above.

Our road protection works were born of desperation. There was no longer sufficient timber to make corduroy roads and Somerfeld Track came to the rescue. Designed for airstrips, it comprised 25-yard rolls of heavy-duty wire netting reinforced with rods. It worked like magic providing it was stretched taut by pulling lengthways with a truck and securely pegged down, and this made it like a raft over the squelch beneath.

I found Bob one afternoon on a dreadful impasse cutting a hairpin right out and laying Somerfeld across the steep corner. A senior gunner officer arrived at the top of the glistening mud slope, forced past our sentry in his jeep and ran straight down over the unpegged track. It was crass stupidity and a heinous offence against the other trucks and ambulances patiently waiting to pass. The track curled up in a roll behind his wheels as he sank into the slurry and came to a halt.

Bob, tall and autocratic, strode down the middle of the road, swept off his Gurkha bush hat, threw it into the mud, stamped deliberately on it and crammed it back on his head. As a gesture of impotent rage it was electric. The cocoa streams of mud ran down his gaunt cheeks as he methodically told that high-ranking idiot exactly what he thought of him. The sheer magnitude of his rage swept aside any question of insubordination and the red-tabbed, red-faced colonel slunk sheepishly away.

It was not a gunners' war, but as part of any infantry brigade they were always about. There was a length of road along the perimeter of their hill position into which they had cleverly cut a number of garage-like pockets for their Quads (four-wheel-drive gun limbers). I was sweeping porridge off the surface with a mechanical grader 'borrowed' from the road maintenance unit. Traditionally sappers and gunners never got on, it was cat and dog. I hit on the happy idea of cutting the road away from their slots to leave their trucks pigeon-holed about a yard above road level! They could not be driven out and it was not a friendly act. Joyously I went back to tell the others and Bob and Harry slipped off to have a look and a quick gloat, returning in hysterics. The gunners were hopping mad, of course, and our O.C. had a reprimand from Brigade. I had to go back and put things right.

"Bloody kill-joy!" said Bob.

As we worked on the roads we had to drive each vehicle past the worst places ourselves. Not only for the Indian drivers either; you can see British drivers any day accelerating in low gear with spinning wheels on slippery surfaces. We boasted that we could spot a disaster-prone driver by looking at him. It was a pleasant social interlude taking the wheel from an Indian driver, but it was the very devil with a conceited Major Sahib.

Petty discipline ceased to have any meaning. When you are walking hand in hand with death all day reprimands no longer matter. The most important discipline is correct behaviour, man to man, the comradeship of shared suffering. With my own men I always strove to appear calm and masterly (however flustered I was); with the infantry it meant giving helpful consideration; with brother officers it meant being relaxed, cheerful and supportive. The rule was never to do anything that could make life worse, less sustainable or more dangerous for the next man. Never to submit to gloom, rats, shells, lice, filth, Japs, mud, jungle or hunger.

Indian troops eat twice a day. *Roti* was at eleven in the morning and *khana* at six in the evening. This fitted well with active service because we could not light cooking fires during darkness. We had a cup of hot *Chai* (their tea was all milk with a lot of sweetening) after dawn stand-to, worked until roti and again until khana and, apart from routine duties, rested through the twelve hours of darkness.

One night the Jemadar Sahib and others came crashing into my bunker.

"Sahib! Sahib! Wake up! Manna Singh *pagal hogaya!*" (has gone mad)

What a din! So what? Manna going off his rocker was no reason to make so much noise! The Japanese might be patrolling up to our wire and it was essential to maintain blackout and complete silence, yet here they were shouting hysterically and crashing about with typical Sikh boisterousness. I was furious!

They led me round to the forward trench where the poor fellow lay face down with a big man on each leg and two more holding his arms, pressing his nose into the mud. Naik Arjan Singh held the man's long black hair wound round his forearms in a wrestlers hold and he was rhythmically strumming Manna's head against a duckboard. Angrily I made them release him and set him upright before me. They were most reluctant to obey, but I insisted. In a flash the Sikh grabbed a rifle and lunged with fixed bayonet at my gut, burying it in the mud wall of the trench behind me. Only Arjan Singh's speedy reaction and agility saved me. I let them throw him down again; he really was puggled!

"We tried to tell you, Sahib!" The Jemadar was reasonable. "Manna Singh had flipped!"

I remembered having heard tales back at depot about 'puggle'. It meant a man suddenly running amok, going berserk and senselessly slaughtering everyone in sight. It was said that the warlike Sikhs

76

and Gurkhas were most prone to it. There had been an occasion in 3/5 Gurkhas when a sepoy leapt from his bed and decapitated three of his mates with his kukri before he was overpowered.

Manna Singh had been alone, out in a forward listening post and in the darkness things began to get on top of him. He took a little sniff of heroin or possibly a chew of opium (at that time they used such drugs against headaches and fever) and suddenly the few rupees that he owed to the Company Clerk for some loss of kit grew to worrying proportions. He was probably unstable and now he was a mad man. I had him chained, handcuffed and roped to the thick prop that supported the roof of the guardroom and went back to bed.

Next morning Major Beddowes sent for me at dawn. He had his Subedar with him and peevishly looked me up and down, twitching a cigarette between his fingers as he always did when he was angry:

"What the hell's this?" he bawled "Subedar Sahib tells me you have chained one of your men underground in the guard room. Are you mad? Or have you been reading *Frontier Tales*, or what?" He looked at me as though I was the one who was puggled.

The Subedar Sahib could be a thorn in the side of junior officers, in much the same way as the Regimental Sergeant Major was in British units. He was the highest Indian commissioned rank in the Company and enjoyed the CO's confidence. He was a very experienced regular soldier with North-west Frontier ribbons, a haughty Muslim who looked down his nose at Sikhs and new subalterns. He stood behind the CO's chair shaking his head expressively as though to say, "Things have come to a pretty pass!"

I tried in vain to tell them how Manna Singh really was, but they took no notice.

"As far as I am concerned," Beddowes pontificated, "Manna Singh is a soldier – not an animal, but a man – and will be treated . . ." He was emphasizing each word with downward chops of his hand when the unmistakable chukka-chukka-chukka of a Thompson sub-machine gun sounded from very close by.

"I think that might be Manna Singh now, Sir!" I said politely.

My icy tone was completely wasted. A cloud of blue cigarette smoke was all that remained in Company Office of my OC and his Subedar. I had no intention of facing the mad Manna again.

They had ordered his release before speaking with me and he had seized a Tommy gun from the guardroom rack and swept out of the bunker firing madly. Fortunately nobody was killed and after trussing him up like a turkey they despatched him back to the Field Hospital at Imphal. The medics in their turn said, "Tut-tut! Fancy tying the poor chap up like that!" and released him and put him to bed. This time, completely naked (a sure sign that a Sikh had lost his reason) he grabbed a rifle and bayonet from a sentry and killed three patients before they tied him up again

From then on my Commanding Officer always referred to my platoon as 'Johnnie's Bloody Sikhs' and I, of course, added the letters JBS behind my name whenever I signed anything.

We had no time to mope on the Shenam Ridge; we had time to whinge a little, but not to mope. In the forward trenches we could occasionally enjoy a few periods of boredom between the moments of intense fear.

The brigade occupied a small area and we came to know every inch of the position and the road. During daylight hours we could pop up to 'The Front' and back several times a day. I use the Great War word front, but it was all front really, it was just that some parts were more front than others. It was as though we were sitting on a chain of islands, a few of us on each, with Japanese pirates all around, but we could make risky boat trips from one to the other. There were sheltered spots of differing degree; some places were always exposed to small arms fire, some were frequently mortared (we hated mortar bombs, they dropped down so steeply), some were shelled. We learned to discover the safer nooks where a quiet smoke might be enjoyed.

There is always a saddle between two adjoining mountains where the ground goes down and up again longitudinally, but falls away to either side. A saddle is always dangerous to cross because you are silhouetted against the sky and open to fire from both directions. The road across the saddle between Gibraltar and Malta was particularly nasty and called, obviously, 'Hellfire Straight'. It was a short connection but exposed to enemy shellfire and sometimes to machine guns and snipers. The enemy were very accurate and quick on the draw and the ploy was to go like hell, hoping to clear it and get across before they fired.

One dry afternoon, when there was almost a gleam of sunshine, I was nearly caught. I had revved my Jeep up to top speed at the last bend, ready for the mad dash, but when I rounded the corner there was a despatch rider wobbling along on his motorcycle ahead of me. I could neither stop, turn nor overtake. Across the valley, having seen the motorcyclist, the enemy artilleryman had already shouted "Fire One!", or possibly "Get him!" in Japanese. The road in front of me erupted in a cloud of red dust, right under the radiator and I ploughed through it not knowing if I would hit a smashed motorcycle or a crater in the fog. I shot through and, to my relief, there he was wobbling along ahead of me and grinning back over his shoulder.

Each hill had a home side, a sheltered approach. Just before the last bend and the highest point on the road, even Scraggy had a sunken steep path up from the road at the back. Vehicles could motor along under the lee of Malta and into the crook of Scraggy to park within a hundred paces or so of the enemy over the crest. One step round that last corner meant instant death, but surprisingly there were no warning signs and certainly no red-capped Military Police to halt you. There really was nothing to stop an ignoramus, an innocent, a rubber-necker or a puggled person from careering round that bend to eternity. Mind you, by the time you got that far forward there were no more Red-caps nor innocents, and those of us who were there were all a bit puggled anyway.

There was a curfew at night on the whole road. We sat tight, defending our boxes and the enemy could come up out of the valleys anywhere. In darkness they patrolled actively about our islands and we patrolled around theirs. We often found their rubber-soled foot-prints in the mud next day.

"Get up to Gib, Johnnie," Beddowes ordered and, taking some men off I'd go. We collected under the high wall of the cutting on the left of the road just before Hellfire Straight. A long hard climb up the almost vertical back slopes, using pegs and ropes on the steep and slippery places, brought you to the entry trench.

The Gurkhas are mountain men with knotted thigh muscles who could trudge up the steepest slopes, carrying a full box of ammo or a roll of barbed wire. I hung on to the ropes, gasping and slithering. They went plod-plod, legs pumping like pistons, straight up the side of that vicious escarpment, talking casually amongst themselves under their heavy loads, whilst I clawed my way up yard by yard.

Near the top the entry trench led into the defensive positions. The newcomer could turn immediately right into the rear trench system and follow the contour just under the back of the crest. This was a relatively safe retreat where the Gurkhas cooked food, smoked and relaxed as they mended clothes and cleaned weapons. Here I reported to the battalion commander, a lieutenant colonel, in his dugout, where he had telephones, radio, runners and orderlies.

Instead of turning into the rear trench I could have taken a few more steps over the crest and dropped into the forward trenches on the front slope. This was an entirely different world. The trenches still wove their way around the contour but faced down across the barbed wire and punjis, over the cleared fire area of No Man's Land. Officers and men on this side of the hill were deadly serious and strangely quiet and the Japanese kept up a persistent offensive. Snipers' bullets, sprays of machine gun fire, frequent shelling and mortar fire made the adrenalin flow. On any single day Gibraltar might receive over one hundred shells an hour and Malta down below once endured two hundred and fifty in a single hour. The rocky ground and the scraped-out trenches were hard and flinty and death could come by steel or rock splinter. My sappers hauled up sandbags and filled old ammo boxes to improve the trenches and maintenance was a constant chore.

The enemy not only set up mountain guns all around but also found a way to get one of their ugly yellow tanks on to the opposite ridge. They banged away over open sights and it was most unpleasant. Although the direct-line distance was so short they were unreachable down through the dense jungle-filled ravines and up the far side.

The plunging outward facing slope of Gibraltar was hogging, that is to say it curved away from us concavely with increasing steepness to vanish from view in a relatively short distance. The barbed wire was our horizon and it was draped ghoulishly from place to place with enemy corpses in different stages of decomposition. At one time three bodies hung before us, but we had to leave them there. Their accelerated decomposition in the humid heat meant that we had to live with them as they turned slate blue, bloated and stank until they collapsed into skeletons. Irreverently we dubbed them George I, George II and George III for the length of their short and smelly reign.

We set out punjis and booby traps in front of the barbed wire on the steepening slope. This was real sapper work. We spent hours splitting, sharpening and fire-hardening bamboo spears, and then we spent more hours creeping down over the steep hillside to hide them amongst the booby traps. It was doubtful if punjis were effective on such a steep gradient, where the enemy would be clambering rather than running uphill, but the infantry liked them. The main threat to Gib was the night attack and we set out a network of trip wires and tin cans to give early warning of their approach.

I was always canny; a dead sapper is less use than a live one and reinforcements were hard to come by. When we had to work on the bald forward slopes outside the wire I tried to choose misty conditions. We slipped out through the wire and slid about in the eerie silence under shelter of the foggy cloak, pressing ourselves against the mud. Unfortunately at that altitude the swirling winds frequently whipped the cloak aside as quickly as a bullfighter's cape, but without giving us a warning 'Olé!'. On the exposed slope we froze, ran or prayed. Running was not usually a good choice against the steep slope home, through tangled wire and our own booby traps. I preferred freezing and plenty of praying. Lying motionless, face down so that my white skin would not gleam against the mud, was an odd sensation and gave much time for thought. Mostly I thought, "I wonder if some Jap is drawing a bead on my bum right now!"

Then Dalip would whisper in my ear, "*Thik Hai, Sahib!* (O.K.) the mist is down again!" and we would carry on.

White men had an issue of blacking-up cream, but I never used it, not wishing to look foolish nor offend the sensibilities of the men. To us at that time such a thing was unthinkable.

We also worked in darkness. We tried to complete night work early, before the first Japanese attack or patrols came in. After curfew we were prisoners on the hill until dawn, when the reserve battalion sent a company through on the road below us to clear enemy marauders and open the road for the day.

One afternoon on Gib we were visited by a mad gunner, a mountain battery man with what, I presume, was a screw gun. This was the thing they carried round the North-west Frontier on the backs of mules in Kipling's day. He had decided that he and his men could haul it up the precipitous rear slope, screw the bits together and bang away over open sights at the Jap. Our infantry battalion commander went white! The poor suffering infantry in the trenches abhorred Rubber-neckers and Bright Ideas Boys. Banging off pop-guns was not our sort of war and putting a gun on the naked hump of Gib was an invitation for reprisals of the worst sort. In the shallow trenches on that rocky fortress we were very vulnerable to shell-fire.

It was just my rotten luck to be there that day. I was waiting to go over the top to do some tidying up jobs in No Man's Land when he arrived and set up his toy. He banged off about six rounds, probably all he had, and went away again before it got dark. The Japs were so enraged that they added two more tanks to their batteries on the far hill and blasted the hell out of us for more than an hour.

After the gunner had gone home for his tea I was crouched in the forward trench talking to three Sathis. Suddenly *Whhhee-ee . . . crash!* and a shell shattered the parapet. When the dust and smoke cleared three of us were unharmed, but the other Gurkha lay dead at our feet. To my amazement his mates picked up their conversation where it had been interrupted and, while chattering to each other, systematically searched their dead comrade's pockets. They relieved the corpse of cigarettes, knife and ammunition, which they shared and then called up the stretcher-bearers to take him back over the hill for burial.

My civilized Western attitude was not necessarily superior to theirs. Their chum's number had come up at four o'clock that afternoon; it was written in the book of his kismet and now he no longer needed such cherished front-line valuables. They used the phrase '*Likha hua*', meaning 'It is written' and it carried the whole philosophy of fatalism. The few bits taken from the dead soldier's crumpled body were more use to them and he would not have begrudged them.

Chapter 8

FAME NEVER FOUND THEM

Their feats, their fortunes and their fames
Are hidden from their nearest kin;
No eager public backs or blames,
No journal prints the yarn they spin

Malta was much worse than Gibraltar; it was lower, muddier and more frequently under attack. A single battalion occupied Malta and Scraggy so that they could rotate the three companies between the two fortresses and they were completely interdependent. It was not safe nor easy to walk directly between them because, like all saddles, the track was swept by enemy fire from different directions. The only safe route was to go down the back of the hill to the road and walk round.

If I hated Malta I detested Scraggy. It was so bad on Scraggy that the turn-round was cut to two nights on the hill itself and half an hour in the forward trenches, where the men lay in shallow scoops behind earth-filled ammo boxes, smoking incessantly to mask the stench. There was no sleep, no dry place to rest, no hot food and a steadily encroaching chilliness. Although we were almost on the Tropic of Cancer we were also very high in the mountains and the winds and continuous rain bit cold. It was the most awful endurance test of mind, body and soul. Apart from never being dry, the sanitation was non-existent and cover from enemy fire minimal. Dead men and bits of men lay all around and the least movement to assist the circulation could bring a bullet. It was unremitting battle tension and when you looked into the faces of comrades by dawn's first light the grey marks of strain were so noticeable that it was embarrassing. Then you realized that your own face looked the same.

There are numerous stories about Gurkhas and most of them are true. They are the most wonderful men and I would recommend their company to anyone who has to spend a night on Scraggy. What is not always told is the character and superb calibre of the British Officers who served with them. The officers of those three Gurkha battalions that I had the privilege to know intimately were men whose like may never be seen again. They were British, British-born in India, Australian and New Zealanders. Most were regulars, but there were some ECOs from an assortment of civilian backgrounds and they were all men of battle. They were often eccentric, a law unto themselves, with a wild sense of humour, but they were implacable Jap-hunters. Without doubt serving with Gurkhas brings out the best in any man.

When I reported to Malta or crept forward on Scraggy I would find a taut white-faced officer crouched on a box in the mud. His endearing friendliness, encouraging humour and cool mastery of the situation made it all seem not so bad. More often than not he had just come through a night of savage fighting, often hand-to-hand with kukri and grenade, but here he was offering me a damp crummy cigarette and making a joke. They were always so appreciative of anything we could do to alleviate their God-forsaken task that I always felt humble, and proud to be with them.

Front-line trenches do not run in straight lines for any distance, they zigzag all over the place. This guards against a sniper or machine gunner lining himself up to fire along the trench, and it localizes blast from shells or mortars. One quiet morning on Malta I suddenly heard the stutter of one of our machine guns from the next fire bay. Pause . . . then another staccato burst. I peered forward over the parapet expecting to see a Jap attack coming in, but there was none. Again a short sharp burst from next door. Curious, I crept along the trench and peeped round the corner. Two Gurkhas were sitting on boxes in the next fire bay, backs to the front wall of the trench, eating their roti. One of them stretched an arm back over his head, felt for the trigger of the Bren gun, mounted on a tripod above him and loosed off a short burst. The Jap was near enough on that sector to know what time we had food, changed sentries or even used the loo and Sathi was faking vigilance and taking no chances.

Gurkhas became bored in static warfare. The enemy trenches were so close in places that they used to take a grenade and toss it, just for devilment, into the enemy lines. These random lobs always brought

84

1. The author at the wheel of his Jeep, Imphal Plain, 1944.

2. No. 3 Platoon, 91 (Royal Bombay) Field Company, building a pontoon bridge over the Uyu River, 1943.

3. The Sikh Platoon of 91 (Royal Bombay) Field Company starting to launch a Bailey Bridge over the Manipur River, 1944.

4. Sappers constructing a rope crossing over a jungle river, Imphal, 1944.

5. Sikhs wading through paddy in the Imphal Plain during the task of ferrying boats back up the Manipur River, 1944.

6. A Dakota bringing supplies for the beleaguered garrison of Imphal coming in to land on Palel airstrip, 1944.

7. Sarwan Singh or 'Bowunja ('52) doing a bit of make-and-mend at the roadside, Imphal, 1944.

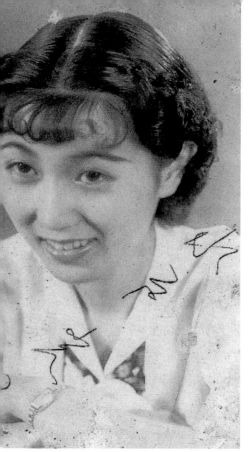

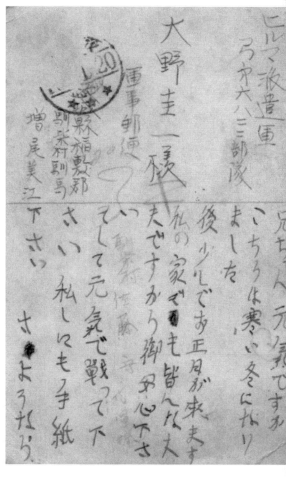

兄ちゃん　元気ですか
こちらは寒い冬になり
ました

後少しでお正月が来ます
私の家で○も皆へな太
夫ですから御安心下さい
○動車佐藤
そして元気で戦って下
さい私しにも手紙
よろしく

ビルマ派遣軍
うや六八三部隊
大野圭一様
軍事郵便
岡県稲敷郡
阿○村○島
増尾美江下さい
さ○よろしく

. Postcard taken from the body of a Japanese officer near Ukhrul, showing both sides.

9. Ordered to go to my death at Yaingangpokpi on the Ukhrul road, April 1944.

10. Sappers of 71 Field Company constructing a corduroy road out of felled timber logs, 1944.

**MORALE is in a
good mood**

**MORALE is morose
and miserable**

**CONSCIENCE butts in
apologetically**

11. Cartoons drawn by Bob Chambers to illustrate our different moods.

12. Mules crossing pontoon bridge over the Manipur River built by 3 Platoon 91 (RB) Field Company, December 1943.

13. Mombi village in the Chin Hills about 6,000ft above sea level where our patrol met the Kuki tribe.

14. Showing the formidable terrain around the Imphal Plain. Note the road zig-zagging up the mountainside to positions on the crest.

15. After the night's fighting volunte of the American Field Service collect wounded in an ambulanc Jeep. Note the mud chains on th wheels.

16. Major Dunkerley and 3/3 Gurkhas mopping up after taking Scraggy Hill, July 1944.

17. The road out of Imphal over Shenam Ridge that took us forward to Tamu in the Kabaw Valley, showing *Gibraltar* and *Malta* hill positions, July 1944.

18. The *Inglis* Bridge, over the Lokchao River, demolished and barring further advance by the tanks. July 1944.

19. Major General Ouvry Roberts CBE, DSO, commanding 23rd Indian Division, later Lieutenant General commanding 34 Corps on the *Zipper* landings in Malaya.

21. Major H.C. Pulley, MC *(Chris)* of 3/3 Gurkhas.

20. Major A. C. Meikle *(Sandy)* who received the MC on Scraggy Hill and later took our troop train to Madras.

22. The author on leave in Bombay after the relief of Imphal.

23. The Mole at Semarang in central Java where we ran into heavy fire from entrenched Japanese when we made our landing. November 1945.

24. The jail in Semarang in central Java where the captured Japanese wrote in their own blood on the whitewashed walls a graphic account of their massacre.

25. The author with 'liberated' Mercedes Benz coupé which was later purloined by a Staff Officer in Buitenzorg.

26. A quiet street in Semarang before the Japanese invasion.

27. A typical native kampong in Semarang, many of which we burnt out when they gave protection to insurgents and snipers.

28. A small boy sniper, about 12 years old, captured in the fighting around Semarang.

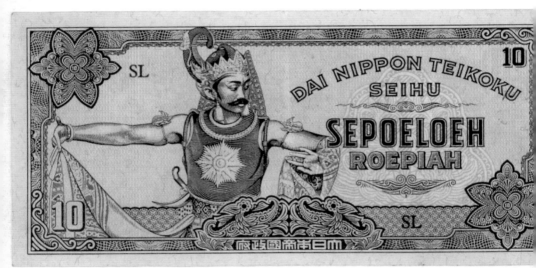

29. Money printed for the Japanese occupation of the Dutch East Indies which had no real value. The one cent note was worth less than the cost of an egg. 1944-46.

a swift riposte, usually of mortar fire, resulting in one or two dead or injured men. Random grenade throwing was stopped and so the incorrigible Sathis took to throwing stones, about the size of grenades, high into the air to fall on enemy heads. Having no sense of humour and, annoyed at losing face over ducking for nothing more than a pebble, the Japanese retaliated just as severely and a few more men were hit. Another order had to be issued forbidding the throwing of grenades and/or stones!

The all-pervading nastiness of using the same small patch of ground over and over again is one of the horrors of trench life. Start to dig and immediately you find a lavatory, a severed hand or a dud grenade. To ease the sanitary problem I installed oil drum latrines, using engine oil floating on a little water, and placed them in recesses in the trench walls as comfort stations. When they were full the lads hit on the happy disposal system of waiting until dark and then rolling them over the crest into the enemy trenches opposite. Did I say the Japanese had no sense of humour? They certainly did not find this at all funny and let rip with everything they'd got. A final order to Johnnie Gurkha had to be issued which, being translated, read:

'In future troops in the forward trenches will not throw random grenades, stones or shit at the enemy unless instructed to do so by an officer.'

On the reverse slope of Scraggy one afternoon, supposed to be the safe side, there were about six Gurkhas hauling up ammunition boxes as I slithered down the muddy path between them. An enemy mortar bomb dropped right amongst us and as the smoke cleared I saw to my horror that I was the only person left standing; all the others had been hit. It was the sort of wild chance that tends to make fatalists of soldiers.

One night I had just come in from No Man's Land on Malta when all hell broke loose on Gibraltar, behind and above us. The noise of battle rolled among the mountains for the whole night. We were accustomed to the exaggerated effects caused by darkness and echoing mountains, but this was no skirmish. When the first light of day greasily felt its way through the wet mist we saw to our horror the Nipponese flag, the red ball on the white background, fluttering audaciously on the peak behind us.

The Japs had seized Gibraltar! The implications of that sight were too awful to contemplate. 3/10 Gurkha had been driven off the heights behind us and therefore our battalion, forward on Malta and Scraggy, was isolated and overlooked. Was the road in enemy hands? The whole of the Shenam position was under threat.

Before we could re-arrange our defences or even make a battle plan of our own we saw 3/5 Gurkha, the reserve battalion, massing on the reverse slope of the captured hill. From our viewpoint they were clearly visible climbing up from the road, silhouetted against the early mist curtain, but out of sight of the victorious Japanese. At least we still held the road. It was like having a very good seat at the theatre! The British Officer stood, blew his whistle and with the traditional sweep of his arm and the battle cry 'Ay-Ay-o Gurkhali' they swept over the crest and surged down into the front line trenches, attacking the Japanese from above and behind. Outlined dramatically against the morning sky we saw small figures firing down, jumping on the heads of the enemy below and slashing furiously at them with drawn kukris.

Then the unbelievable happened. First one, then another, then a small group of enemy soldiers broke over the parapet and started to flee down the slopes. Right under the feet of the savage Gurkhas a yellow scum boiled out of the trenches and frothed over as the terrified Japanese scampered, slithered, tumbled and rolled down the steep slope to the saddle between us.

On Malta we all surged to the trenches on that side. The fleeing mob was running straight towards us and we poured fire into them with everything we had. Our battalion commander, the infantry colonel, was a man of enormous stature and presence and he had been standing on the fire step cleaning his teeth and watching events unfold. I can see him now, toothbrush clamped crossways in his jaw, wrestling with one of his own sepoys for the use of the man's Bren gun!

"Let me have a go!" he was shouting in Gurkhali at the soldier and what is, I believe, the phrase for "Sod off, Colonel sahib!" came the staunch reply.

It was like being on the grouse moors as the beaters drove them towards us. We fired and fired again. I ended up with a blister the size of a rupee coin on my hand from the hot rifle barrel. We could not tell live from dead as they crashed and rolled into the first wall of grassy scrub right in front of us. It ended as suddenly as it had begun; dead bodies lay strewn across the hillside and it was not yet nine o'clock in the morning.

The benefits of that single action stayed with us from that day forward. Would it be an overstatement to suggest that the war against Japan turned in our favour that morning? I think not. We had seen them break and flee; the unstoppable force had met the immovable post of Gurkha infantry! Taking a working party, I dropped down to the road and hurried back to Gibraltar to render assistance and help repair their defences.

Every night there was a disturbance of some sort. Out in the forward positions or back in my bunker on Sapper Hill I sprang awake to the urgent whisper in my ear, "*Sahib! Sahib! Dushman agaya!*" (Enemy attack, Sir!)

I did not know whether it was a jitter raid, a full attack on our position, on another box near by or a false alarm. We stood-to at dawn and sunset, the two favoured times for attack. I went round the men as they stood alertly along the fire step, touching a shoulder here, whispering a nickname there, to give each the assurance of my supportive presence. If out of habit one began a guttural rattle of phlegm as he cleared his tubes; he was rapidly silenced. Dawn broke, daylight grew and the morning came alive until the benison of the call "Stand down!" heralded another day. I lit my first cigarette, sipped the sweet tea that Bowunja always had ready and listened to the crescendo of 'The Song of India' rising around me. It was their morning oratorio and an expression of relief that another black night had ended.

Every morning at first light a body of infantry went along the road, circumnavigating the island positions, to ensure that no lurking enemy remained, and they always took a section of sappers, about twenty men, to clear mines, booby traps and road blocks. When I went with them I rose much earlier to get ready for the dawn patrol. It was a scary job and the early morning mist was chilly wet. The jungle trees dripped, no birds sang, no wild animals moved and we slipped silently round each corner proving the road ahead.

Almost rubbing the backs of our heels as we filed along the edge of the khud came the ambulance jeeps and their brave drivers. Sad little groups of stretcher bearers waited at the foot of the different hill positions and ambulances collected the wounded from them like

87

an early morning milk round. They never returned empty.

After a very noisy night, when the bangs and flashes about our positions had been observed from the plain below, and before the road from Palel had been thoroughly checked, one of these American heroes would arrive and drawl, "Guessed you might need us good an' early this morning?"

"We didn't know the road was open yet!"

"Wa-al!" He grinned his James Stewart grin and drew on his cigarette. "Neither did we, strictly speaking, so we guessed it was time to go and find out!"

The wounded had lain cold and bleeding through the dark hours on the rear of the hills, exposed to falling rain, mortar bombs and surprise enemy attack. They were manhandled down to the road to be stacked, two at a time, on the ambulance racks. Lying on the hard stretchers, open to the weeping sky, gazing up at passers-by with grey faces, they were always grateful for a cigarette, a word or a drink of water. They faced a gut-racking ride down to the plain where they would be put into covered ambulances for a smoother run on level roads to the distant Imphal field hospital.

Grim humour is better than no humour at all. I had a macabre example of this one morning when I was squatting in a trench on Scraggy after a savage night attack. I was scraping a bit of bully beef out of a can when the infantry officer beside me leaned over and with his knife speared a gobbet of human flesh that was plastered against a prop. It bore revolting short black curly hairs on it and as he proffered it to me he said, "Try a bit of the paté, Johnnie!" Very droll, as Beddowes might have said.

One morning Harry shouted across to me from another part of the trenches, "Hey! Johnnie come on over for a cigarette and a wee chat!"

He had been there all morning and I had only just arrived. There was thin patchy mist swirling about, like it does in Hitchcock thrillers. He was round the other side of a narrow valley return, where the trenches wound back in and out again, but only just across the way from my position. He yelled that there was no need to take the long way, it was quiet and safe to pop over the top and cut the corner. As I reached the berm on his side a bullet kicked up the earth right by my boot and, alarmed, I tumbled headfirst into the trench to find Harry and a couple of Gurkhas roaring with mirth.

"You're the third one this morning that bloody sniper has missed!"

Hilarious! What a joke! Until the sudden thought struck home, "He might have killed me!"

"Och! Laddie — I never thought o' that," he confessed, "but you did look awfu' amusin' falling on your tin hat in the mud!"

Perhaps front-line humour is not all that funny, but for us at the time it served to cut the Grim Reaper down to size.

The wetness permeated everything. We never dried out at all. Bowunja struggled to keep me comfortable and well turned out. He dragged the front seat from a burnt-out truck and, with a scrap of blanket over it, installed it in my bunker. He even hung a girlie picture from an Indian magazine and stuck it to the glistening mud wall. I am convinced that he thought I was sexless, or neuter or something. To be my age, unmarried and childless must have seemed very odd to him.

His father had bought him his first wife, on the cheap, when he was about twelve years old. She was much older than him, ugly and more of a harsh shrew than a fond wife and I suspect that she was really a mother substitute. With the good money he earned after joining the forces he bought himself a pleasanter woman, about his own age, good about the house and in bed. Now after long months of active service, spending none of his pay, he had worked out that he had saved enough money to splash out on a third wife, who was going to be a right little dolly-bird. His beady eyes lit up when he talked about it. His wives were also married to his three brothers back home because polygamy and polyandry were customary with Sikhs. In theory the brothers at home protected the lonely wives, but were not encouraged to enjoy full conjugal rights, although, judging from the petitions I received, many attempted it.

Everything deteriorated alarmingly, especially clothing. The thin jungle green cotton material, often from second-rate Indian mills, disintegrated from damp and sweat and would no longer hold repairs. We husbanded as best we could and were never too proud to rob the dead. Gaunt, ragged and Mepacrine sallow, we certainly looked like a forgotten army, but the diligent transport plane pilots managed to keep us going.

It is impossible for men in the trenches to tell those back home what they are enduring. The loved ones have their own lives to lead and could never imagine what front-line conditions are like. In our case they had no information at all, and neither could they imagine it, or even draw upon the experience of returned soldiers. Press reporters never reached our besieged positions and any stories that were printed, after heavy censorship, were bland, late and inaccurate. Wingate's Chindits had enjoyed a few lines after their return in May 1944, but after the Normandy landings we were hardly reported at all. I must not carp about it because obviously the war on the doorstep at home was much more meaningful to the civilian population. We were important to our own kinsfolk and nobody else, but when a bullet struck home we were just as dead as the lads in Europe and we were thankful that they could not see the conditions we had to endure.

The Gurkhas were not inclined to take prisoners and their tally of captured Japs was abysmal. The Japanese themselves preferred death to capture. There were dead ones aplenty everywhere, but healthy ones not at all. The intelligence staff needed prisoners for questioning and a lot of pressure was put on the officers to encourage the men to capture a few. One afternoon there was a vicious air strike by our Hurribombers on a small hill that the Japanese had captured and a Gurkha company went out to take possession and mop up. They were given strict orders to bring back a prisoner or two.

They occupied the hill and found a few bomb-happy enemy wandering about. A short time later a small procession was seen toiling back up the mountain to battalion HQ with a Japanese prisoner. He was carried between two Gurkhas, hanging face down from wrists and ankles tied to a bamboo pole, with his nose rubbing in the mud. They dumped their prisoner, not too gently, at their colonel's feet and announced, "There's your Jap, Sahib!"

The prisoner had a nasty wound in his rump and the officer asked what had happened.

"Those Japs are too cheeky, Sahib! He was propped against a tree and we ordered him to get on his feet. He took no notice. Three times we said 'Get up' but he continued to disobey so we taught him a lesson with a bayonet up his arse!"

How unlucky for the man that he had never learned Gurkhali at school and could not understand a word of what they were saying!

It was announced that there would be a new medal struck called 'The Burma Star' and we discovered that it would also be given to the HQ troops stationed around Calcutta. Men in the firing line are quick to take umbrage and we were bitter that the safely ensconced base-wallahs, the *babus* and the Staff Officers would be sporting it already.

We rechristened it the 'Calcutta Star' to be awarded for 'Gluttony beyond the call of duty' in Firpo's and 'For standing firm in the Howringhee brothels'.

The first gallantry award in 91 Field Company was to perky Lance Havildar Dalip Singh, affectionately known as 'D'leepi-oh'. He was given the Military Medal for working outside the wire on the forward slopes of Malta. A Japanese attack came in and the infantry commander recalled him to the trenches, but he insisted on staying to finish his job, firing intermittently back at the creeping line of enemy as he worked. Having been out in front of the wire with him a time or two myself, I knew only too well his disregard for personal safety.

There was a brilliant *Punch* cartoonist called Fougasse, who also drew many of the famous Second World War posters. He had lost both his legs in the Great War to the device called a fougasse. I decided to make one or two myself to help the defences on Malta. In front of the wire on the steep outward-facing slope I dug deep square pits and packed the bottom with cordite bags from the 25-pounder guns. Cordite is a propellant because it burns much more slowly than the instant detonation of high explosives, and when the gunners were firing at close targets they had surplus to throw away. Over the top of the charge I packed stones, broken glass, bits of iron and other junk and lightly earthed it over for concealment. I laid firing lines back to the trenches and when the enemy approached the wire from below we blew the fougasse straight in their faces. It was most effective and gave the infantry much joy.

Some inventive idiot doodling at his desk in the safety of an Army HQ office hit on a bright idea for knocking out Jap bunkers. Their defensive bunkers were deep, strong and often almost invisible, except for a dark firing slit at ground level, and they were the hardest thing our infantry ever had to face. Why not get a long bamboo pole, stick a chunk of high explosive on the end, poke it through the slit and fire it with a pull-igniter? These small mechanical devices were used on trip wires and other booby traps to fire explosive charges. A man could crawl up to the enemy bunker, poke his curtain rod through their firing slit and pull the wire. Who more qualified for this task than the ubiquitous sapper? Bunkers were very heavily defended and covered by crossfire from cleverly sited neighbouring bunkers. Nobody could explain how one lone sapper, impeded by an awkward bamboo pole with a heavy weight on the end, would climb a slippery mud slope in the face of machine-gun fire and deliver his parcel through the enemy's letter box. Whole companies of infantry had been powerless against deep bunkers.

"Posthumous V.C.!" we told each other, "every time!"

Fauji Singh Beanpole did it. Fauji was the platoon troublemaker. He was as thin as a bamboo pole himself, black as the ace of spades and had a disconcerting habit of muttering behind his hand, so that I always suspected him of insolence. He was against authority and a bit of a joker. On a wet misty day early in June 1944 he went to the very centre of things. He found a muddy gully, carved out by the rains and crawled to within pole distance of a very aggressive bunker, poked his charge through the slit, right into the face of the machine gunner inside, pulled the wire and blew them to pieces. After that he jumped on the only two survivors as they reeled out of the smoking entrance and despatched them with his bayonet.

From that day on it was 'Fauji Singh M.M.' instead of 'That bloody Fauji!' and somehow his impudent grin became a favourite of mine. I tried to promote him to lance naik but he could not hold the job down. He was a loner, I guess.

We had been sleeping below ground with our clothes and boots on for so long that we had become a bit malodorous and could be smelt from yards away. If we got the chance we eased our boots off for a spell, changed our socks from one foot to the other and turned our underpants front to back. Not exactly a full laundry service, but it made us feel better.

Chapter 9

FINAL CURTAIN

That is what we are known as — we are the men that have been
Over a year at the business, smelt it an' felt it an' seen.

From the heights above the Kabaw Valley we heard the far-off battle noises around the arena of the Imphal Plain as the other divisions fought their different corners. We had no news from the outside world, no newspapers and no radio broadcasts, but scraps occasionally reached us.

When the Normandy landings opened the Second Front in Europe in June 1944 I was sitting at the roadside in the rain, up to my knees in mud, looking a bit like my 'Low Morale' cartoon, when Bob roared up in his Jeep, skidded to a halt and shouted, "Our Forces and the Yanks have invaded France!"

"*Shabash!*" (Hooray!) I answered disinterestedly; it was all a long way away from our miserable situation. We had to wait another two weeks for the news that we most wanted to hear. The British 2nd Division had attacked Kohima from the far side and, after a fierce battle, had driven the Japanese off the heights. Our forces had advanced down the road to shake hands with IV Corps at milestone 109 on the Dimapur road. After almost three months the siege was over and we were linked to the rest of the world once more.

Immediately we visualized a big double gate swinging wide open to allow vast convoys to flood into our garrison. They would be loaded down with rich food, strong drink, dry cigarettes, new clothing and assorted luxuries. Fresh divisions would roar in from railhead to take over from us and we would pull out for a rest. Whilst others pushed on into Burma we would be enjoying the fleshpots of Calcutta and the cry went up, "Look out Firpo's here we come" Now we'd show them how real gluttony could win the Burma Star!

Of course no such thing happened. The remoteness, the appalling road conditions, the rain, the worn-out narrow gauge railway and the rear organization were all against us. We stayed put on our mountain range, we continued to battle across the bloody wastes of Gibraltar, Malta and Scraggy; we faced the same relentless foe and the weeks dragged by.

A British tank regiment arrived at Palel on the plain below us. They were there to take part in the final push into the Kabaw Valley and they had to have sappers to work with them. They had driven their General Grant tanks over the twisting mountain road from Dimapur to come to our aid. At last we had heavy armour behind us and Beddowes sent me down to work with them. Sappers make life easier for these monsters, like the little birds that tend the teeth of a crocodile. We disposed of mines, cleared the road, eased them over obstacles and generally waited upon them.

Surajbahn and I took about twenty men down to the tank camp, leaving the Jemadar with the main platoon. When the time came we would roll round that last corner beyond Scraggy, roar on down to Tamu and chase the enemy back across the Chindwin River. My detachment would accompany these magnificent machines at the spearhead of the big push out of the Imphal Plain. It was too thrilling for words, but first I had to learn the new job.

The tank lads taught us all about their tasks in battle, how the machines handled and what their difficulties were. We practised routines and I drove them by the hour. They could not do enough for us and we soon became a perfect team, gaining an understanding of each other's problems. The Tommies and the Sikhs got along together famously. It always astonished me how well the ordinary British soldier can rattle off a mouthful of execrable slang, mixed with odd foreign words, mostly French, and make himself understood. I was bilingual and knew what both sides were saying. Beaming in the friendliest way a Tommy might say, "Nah then! You big black whiskered ape, what abaht it then? Fancy a cuppa char or un more-so de choc-o-latt?"

And back came the Punjabi reply, with a cordial flash of white teeth, "That's good, you red-arsed monkey, try some of our curried goat – it'll make a man of you!"

It was usually much more vulgar than that and Surajbahn acquired a new British swear-word, 'Vladivostok!'

94

It was a holiday for us in the rear areas. I would never have imagined that the sight of a bullock cart could make me murmur "Civilization at last!" The men relished the fresh fruit and vegetables in the bazaar and a saucy flirtation with the little maidens who sold them. In their bright phaneks they flitted around like parrots in the canopy and refreshed our jungle-weary eyes.

I returned to routine duties at Shenam to await the order for the tanks to come forward. When the time came I went down to help them up the mountain track. They heaved their ponderous might up the road with clanking tracks, shrieking sprockets and roaring engines. They came through the night; Strongbottom had decided that this would conceal their arrival from the enemy, but the noise was probably heard in Mandalay! It was difficult enough to get these monsters up a narrow winding road in daylight and the rain and the darkness made the task almost impossible, but we did it. The drivers had a small aperture to look through and we guided them with smouldering pieces of rope, or glowing cigarettes round the narrow hairpins.

General Grant tanks had rotary engines and our special treat was to stand with arms outstretched behind the open steel doors as the driver ran them at fast tick-over to blow warm air through our wet clothing and dry us out.

The push out of Imphal was scheduled for 24 July 1944. The tanks lined up in the lee of Scraggy, ready to advance at dawn, and my team joined them. Somewhere behind us the 2nd British (Cross Keys) and 11th East African (Rhinoceros) Divisions were assembling to come through us when we had reached our objectives.

I have not always been kind about the artillery, I admit it, but that night they came into their own. They lined up their guns, hub to hub along the ridge and all night long the flash and crash of one hundred and twenty guns shook the ground and us. Sleep was impossible, just when we needed it most, and we waited nervously for the dawn.

We were a few short steps away from that last corner where the road dipped away into the Kabaw Valley, beyond which the enemy held sway. We lined up in the exact order that we would have to keep for the whole advance. Once we drove forward on that narrow track there would be no chance to turn or overtake and we had no idea what the road was like ahead. Three tanks led the column, followed by Surajbahn Singh and my men in two Bren carriers, with all their

95

mine-clearing kit and other equipment. The rest of the tank force brought up the rear.

I rode beside the lead tank driver and peered through a narrow slit at the road that unwound ahead of us. I had to look for mines, obstacles and anything that might impede our advance. If I saw anything suspicious I told the driver to stop and I got out and went forward to investigate. If necessary I could call some of my men forward to make a clearance.

Dawn broke, the gunfire stopped and we looked at our watches in the silence. Whistles blew and we moved forward, out of the Imphal fortress at last!

The enemy had few vehicles and very little fuel or oil, and the road had not been maintained nor used much since we had left it months before. The rains had brought down a number of minor landslides and cut deep rivulets in the surface and I had to pop out frequently to check if it was tank-worthy. After each stop I climbed back aboard my tank again and we rumbled on. The Gurkha infantry were moving in parallel with us; sometimes they filed along the road edges at our sides and sometimes they carried out systematic sweeps above and below the road.

I discovered that there was a complete difference between tank men and us. Inside the tank I felt claustrophobic, as though I was under the lid of a roasting dish waiting for the oven to come on. The tank crew were relaxed, joking among themselves and chatting over the intercom. Outside I felt released and free to move and act in my own defence, but when the crew were not in their steel box they felt as naked as a hermit crab out of its shell. They thought I was incredibly brave every time I fell out of the little steel trapdoor on to my head in the muddy road; I never managed to make a dignified exit from the tank. For my part I thought how incredibly brave they were to live all day in a pressure cooker filled with aero spirit!

On the other hand, it was wildly exciting inside the tank when the powerful armament blasted away at enemy hill positions in support of the infantry, or when the Brownings chattered angrily away at dimly-seen moving figures. It was good to sit safely within and hear enemy bullets pinging harmlessly against our steel hide.

We left Scraggy behind and above us, shrouded in mist, and dropped down the valley making a slow but determined progress. The day wore on and we halted by the side of the road at a wider place and we felt pleased with ourselves. We had to pause to allow the infantry accompanying us to consolidate before moving forward again.

Suddenly a Jeep came roaring down the slope behind us wearing the Cross Keys insignia of 2 Div. We were impressed; these were the boys who had cleared the Jap from Kohima and who had received oodles of publicity back home; far more than we Indian units ever had. In the Jeep was a brigadier, red tabs and hatband, bristlingly British as he charged right past us! He never slowed down and were those cries of 'Tally-ho' and 'Yoicks!' that echoed back from the speeding Jeep?

We were at the very forefront of the advance and an unprotected senior officer had just bummed past us into enemy-held territory! He not only had no business to be there at all (his division was not due to come through us for days) but his lunacy was a danger to us all.

As he disappeared round the next corner, speeding on down to where we had not yet been, we heard the familiar chatter of a Japanese machine gun! We had no choice. Tired as we were, with daylight fading and our objectives for that day secured, we had to fire up the lead tank and plunge down the hill after him. Surajbahn leapt into his Bren carrier and followed. We had not far to go. Round the bend the brigadier's Jeep lay on its side with the wheels still spinning. An English soldier, riddled with bullets, hung from it, killed by stupidity.

Of the red-tabbed Brigadier and driver there was no sign. They had been flung out and had scrambled off down the valley to make their way back to safety through the jungle.

"Jolly good show!" I could almost hear the fool's voice, but the poor corpse in the road had nothing to cheer about.

> *'An' the pore dead that look so old*
> *An' was so young an hour ago,'*

There were no Japanese to be seen! As I tumbled out of the tank on to my steel helmet in the mud nothing was moving. Just ahead, on both sides of the road, were gun-pits and under a spread groundsheet some watery gruel was heating over a fire. The Japanese stench hung heavily in the misty air and it was creepily quiet. The deserted machine guns were loaded and pointing up the road, but their owners had fled! It was disconcerting and mysterious to find that Japanese soldiers had actually run away. The red tabs of the brigadier, or his little pennant on the Jeep, must have made them think that their section was overrun and they were left behind.

"Well I'll be buggered! They've scarpered," called the Cockney tank driver.

I brought the Bren carrier forward and the Sikhs heaved the Jeep back on to its punctured wheels, with the shattered windscreen upright and the poor dead English boy propped grotesquely in the back. We coupled it to the Bren carrier with a hawser, dragged it round to face back up the hill and I took the twisted steering wheel. It was not easy to keep the humping vehicle in the churned ruts as we set off. The corpse sat behind me in the cold drizzle and fading light, and my heart wept for grief over that unknown boy.

I visualized his poor mother answering the door in a suburban avenue back in Blighty as she was handed the dreaded note: "We regret to inform you that your son Pte. David Hill died gallantly in the face of the enemy on 24/7/44."

There would be no mention of the idiocy, or the crime committed by a man who should have known better. The tanks could not turn back so the rest of the column had to come forward in support.

I did not steal the commander's pennant, although I coveted it for a souvenir. After all we had done, risking our lives for Big Brigadier Sahib, I half-hoped he might give it to me in gratitude. No such thing; I never saw him again and he probably avoided me in case I might spill the story of his crass behaviour. The Jeep and the dead boy were taken to the rear.

We were unprepared for the state of our enemy. They had seemed so strong up to the last days and now, to our astonishment, we were chasing a sick and dying army. As we drove down the last slopes towards the Lokchao River we found that the spring steel of their resolve had snapped and we were picking up the broken pieces. They had made their last desperate throw.

Mutaguchi's army had become debilitated by hunger, fever and monsoon rain. Their assaults on our fortress and the preposterously long hook round to Kohima had been more than their supply lines and fortitude could stand. Facing them on the ground, we had seen only the ferocity of their aggression, but not the human price they were paying. It explained the uncharacteristic abandonment of their machine-gun pits by the roadside when the mad Brigadier arrived. They had passed from invincible to shattered.

Next day our tanks ground on through the mud and sharp bends as we went on down the road. They were so big and the roads so narrow that every corner was a struggle, but at times we still outran the infantry. Looking through the front slit I spotted the figure of a man pressed back against the high wall of the cutting. I pointed him out to the driver and on his intercom he reported to his officer in the turret.

"Enemy skulking against the cutting, right thirty, sir," he reported.

"I see him!" came the reply, "but he's not making an attack!"

Kamikaze Japanese had been known to jump upon tanks from behind with explosive charges strapped to their bodies.

"He's Japanese, for sure!" I chipped in.

"Japanese, Chinese, Siamese or Stand-at-ease they all looks the bloody same to me, sir!" quipped the driver.

We stopped and I did my falling-out-of-tanks routine. There were no infantry about so I called Surajbahn forward. The man was scared, emaciated, stinking of dysentery and could hardly be nominated for catch of the week. As other Sikhs tumbled out of the carrier they found another one lying face down in the ditch, apparently dead.

"Turn him over, Surajbahn!" I commanded.

"*Thandi kharab hogaya, Sahib!*" This was a common expression for a lorry that would not go, and it meant cold and dead.

"Just do as you're told – turn the *kutta-ka-bachcha* over!" (son of a dog)

None too gently they flung him on his back. He was shamming and he gazed defiantly up at us awaiting the death blow. For a moment I felt such a wave of revulsion against the men of Nippon that I could easily have shot him then and there. Physical nausea rose within me against them and their terrible ways; I thought of their treachery, how they had smashed Pearl Harbor, subjugated and tortured civilians, used our captured boys for bayonet practice and even crucified prisoners; all the atrocities behind them on the long road to where he now lay. The ignominy of capture to him was worse than death. He lay there in the yellow mud, gaunt, almost naked, stinking, a week's stubble on his jowls and glared at us with eyes like glass alleys waiting for us to commit an atrocity on him. After respecting their awesome invincibility for so long, looking down at our prisoners with yellow diarrhoea trickling down their trembling shanks my hatred turned to compassion. Starvation, disease, rain, jungle and the 'vaulting ambition which o'erleaps itself' had brought them to this.

We found another man back in the trees, trouserless, collapsed over his stools and unable to rise to his feet. We left all three in the ditch by the road for the following troops to collect and surged forward; the chase was becoming a rout.

At the bottom of the mountain the road ended at the deep ravine of the Lokchao River, just upstream of its confluence with the River Uyu. Lying askew in the yellow flood was the Inglis Bridge our troops had built a year before. The Bailey now superseded this heavy military bridge and this one was a complete write-off that would take a lot of engineering work to replace it. We could go no further and laagered for the night, with the tanks taking up a defensive position as best they could and the infantry fanning out on the surrounding hills.

It was unpleasant in the gorge. The rain had not paused since we turned that first corner from Scraggy. Persistent, penetrating, unremitting, a constant torrent, a bead screen of water; had there ever been such a downpour? After spending so long on the heights we now felt overlooked and threatened under the surrounding bluffs with the river roaring menacingly between the steep walls.

That night I had an unusual experience. From boyhood I had suffered from a recurring nightmare that undoubtedly originated from the First World War stories I had been told. In the dream I lay on a rutted muddy road sheltering under a vehicle, usually a lorry or an ambulance. The mud was yellow and viscous and we were under heavy shellfire. Sometimes there were horses and other men about, occasionally a Red Cross nurse near by, and I could hear the screams of the wounded. It always ended with a last whistling shell hitting the truck above me that brought me wide awake, soaked in sweat.

The enemy began to shell us; no doubt they had the exact range of the bridge crossing. There was a smashed Japanese lorry against the cutting and I sought shelter beneath it. The lorry above me, the yellow mud, the screaming shells, it was déjà vu, except that I was with Indian troops and there was no English nurse to be seen! We were too deep in the crook of the hairpin to be hit and I never had the dream again.

Exhausted and without kit, I rummaged in the back of the abandoned lorry and found some old blankets. I wrapped one round my

100

wet wrinkled body and collapsed into deep sleep. I woke to the stench from the Japanese bedding. I had been too tired to notice it the night before and now it was crawling down my throat, too awful to describe. I reeled to the edge of the khud and spewed into the blackness of the gorge.

It was the hour before dawn and the rain had stopped. For us it was the end of the battle for Imphal, and for the world it was the end of the Japanese dream of capturing India. The last quarter of the moon drooped over the jungle peaks, stars shone in the indigo sky and the river boiled through the valley. The air was cold and still. Above the flood-song of the Lokchao River a frog croaked, the first wild noise that had been heard for many a day; a cricket stridulated and then a distant animal whooped from the forest, a monkey perhaps? The clamour of battle had died away and nature was reclaiming her own. It was over!

My spirits lifted and a wild happiness coursed through my being. The agonies of recent months, the horrors I had seen, the caged-in feeling of being surrounded, the subconscious awareness of death at one's elbow and the trepidation evaporated. It seemed to me to be like the end of school term, breaking up, going home, taking a rest and having fun again. No matter that I was worn thin and drawn taut like a steel wire, this tattered scarecrow was returning to civilization. I would never be the same again; I knew that.

I stood carelessly exposed on the river bank, drawing hard at my first cigarette of the day, careless of the bright glow as I flicked the butt away in a firework arc just like a base-wallah might do. No longer any cause to fear the sniper's bullet.

I stood at the van of the Fourteenth Army. I was probably the most forward allied soldier and the nearest to Tokyo on the whole Burma Front! And what was I doing? Why, having a drag and urinating into a Burmese river without regard for danger!

I went back to join the Tommies by their tanks for a cup o' char. They had efficient cooking arrangements and good British rations and I breakfasted heartily. My men were stirring themselves, taking their pewter lotas of water into the bushes, chewing tooth sticks and raising the Song of India to the morning sky. My mind went back to all the brave chums I had known – Sikh, Gurkha, British and others with whom I had shared so much and who now lay dead somewhere in the forests behind me. No trim war cemetery for them, no neat rows of white crosses; the jungle had folded them to its bosom and their lonely corpses would never be found again.

Dalip and Surajbhan joined me for a chat and to tap the oracle of my wisdom.

"Where now, Sahib Bahadur?"

"Well we can't get the armour across this gap, it will need a bridging company to do that, so I guess this is where we turn back!"

"*ALL* the way back, Sahib? All the way back to Imphal, to India, to our villages, for leave and women?"

"Could be." I was non-committal in the face of such preposterous suggestions. "This is certainly as far forward as we can go, so I suppose we must go back!"

"Shabash!" they said reverently and rushed away to tell the others.

Strategically we had done our job and the last push had been much easier than we had expected. 37 Gurkha Brigade with left hook, right hook and a punch on the nose had cleared the enemy from the heights, opened the road and driven them headlong into the Kabaw Valley. The other brigades of 23 Div were advancing in parallel with us elsewhere and we were chasing them on all fronts. The swiftness of the enemy collapse was still unbelievable. I guessed that the generals on both sides must have seen it coming, but it was only now dawning upon us, the men in the field, that the myth of Japanese invulnerability was dead.

I was ordered back and said goodbye to my tank chums. I gathered the men together and we rattled back up the hill in the Bren carriers with the lads chattering excitedly like monkeys. Halfway back we encountered an obstruction that came to be known as 'The Slide'. Under our heavy armour and the following traffic one section of the road had avalanched into the valley below. It left a liquid mud toboggan run and Bob was there with his platoon trying to cut a bypass across the corner. He had made a slimy ski slope for vehicles to slither down, but it was impossible to climb back up and it would take a regiment of road builders to restore a two-way road. It was good to see Bob and his Mahratthas again and hear about their recent adventures.

The Bren carriers had their own drivers and so we left them at the bottom for others to commandeer as we walked up to Scraggy to collect our own platoon transport.

We met the fresh troops moving forward to pass through us and take over the push from our division. There were smart Sikh infantry, long-striding Pathans, big East Africans singing musically as they swung along and, of course, the British 2 Div; they were all so well-fed and ready for battle. They looked us over curiously. Was there pity in their eyes? Were they wondering "Is that how I'll look when I come out again?" or were they proud of what we had endured? They gave us dry cigarettes, chocolate bars and other goodies and we fell upon them like ragged beggars.

I fixed an enemy helmet and a skull on the bonnet of my Jeep, and from the wireless mast I flew a captured Japanese personal flag. Their soldiers carried autographed white silk flags with the red rising sun disc and they considered them to be good luck talismans. Back in Cherry Blossom Land their friends and loved ones had randomly scrawled good luck messages in black brush strokes on the silk for the soldiers to carry into battle. My behaviour might seem a bit brash, but I was young and the grinning skull seemed a fun thing at that time.

Ted had our trucks waiting under the back of Scraggy, where the grass had already begun to grow back and the jungle looked less shattered. We made a last brew-up before rolling down the familiar road to the Imphal Plain. Some newly arrived British soldiers stopped to talk. Pointing to the enemy flag flying from my Jeep a Tommy asked me, "What does the writing say, Sir?"

"Ping pong shang, kio-kio fung," I read out solemnly, pointing to the flowing black brush script. "Which means 'Good luck, Kio-kio. – give 'em one for me!'"

I translated other phrases with equal imagination and my reputation rapidly spread. Other Jap oddments were produced.

"And what does this say, Sir?", producing a disc or name plate.

"Ahh!" I looked thoughtful. "That says 'Kalo wong tang sho-sha!' or 'Do not use in wet weather!'"

Fortunately for me they had to press on and we had to go back before I lost my newly won prestige. I shared my subterfuge with the Sikhs and to my embarrassment they kept the joke going interminably. For days they told everybody how clever their officer sahib was at reading the Japanese language and produced all sorts of souvenirs for me to translate. I was worried that Beddowes would hear about it and stop my nonsense, but it was characteristic of our newly shared camaraderie that I could enjoy this sort of fun with the Sikhs.

Back with the whole Field Company in a tented camp on the plain we thought it was all over. Not so! The big boss back at HQ, the CRE, thought that there was still some mileage left in us and enthusiastically volunteered our services again. Beddowes was always glad to be rid of Johnnie's Bloody Sikhs and detailed 3 Platoon to go forward again. This time right down into the dreaded Kabaw to 'do a few jobs' as he called it. Such orders almost always said something like, "Report to Colonel Dung-Fly and follow his instructions!"

Once more we drove round the corner at Scraggy, where the barbed wire was now red-rusty and birds were singing. Down past the abandoned gun pits where Pte Hill had been murdered, over the new Bailey bridge across the Lokchao and into the small township of Tamu. The divisions that had passed through us were now in the next valley to the east and forcing crossings over the Chindwin on the drive to Mandalay. We were demoted to a labouring force, asked to mend roads and perform other menial chores in the rear areas.

In Tamu I saw what was left of the forces of Mutaguchi and Yamamoto. The walls of their base camp hutments had been ripped away to let the air circulate and the raised floors looked like fishmongers' slabs. Cheek by jowl, touching each other, in hut after hut, the rows of dead bodies lay on bamboo platforms. Some may still have been living, but in those stinking charnel houses it was impossible to tell. They had crawled back here from Kohima, Yangangpokpi, Tiddim and Scraggy to die. Many had embraced the proud privilege of suicide and had committed hari-kari with a grenade clasped to the stomach, or had been helped across the divide by their colleagues. All were in advanced stages of disease and starvation. It was the death of an army and decomposition followed death swiftly in the Kabaw Valley.

The name Valley of Death now had a very real meaning; the stench met us before we could see the town. Tough African infantry were gagged and gas-masked as they destroyed the putrefying remains with flamethrowers and bulldozers. Their job was to obliterate the flotsam left along the high-water mark of Japanese aggression as the tide receded.

The insufferable humidity, the torture of giant mosquitoes and the haze of seething bluebottles were the final test of our lowered stamina. We drew in a hundred diseases with every breath. The end of the monsoon was near and there were intervals of steamy sunshine. Protectively I watched over and encouraged my indefatigable and uncomplaining lads in this final torment. We should never have been sent there at all, but we had to accept it as the lot of being a soldier. When we finally got the order to pull out we climbed gratefully into our trucks and left the Kabaw for ever.

It was a long way back to where the rest of 91 was encamped on the far side of the plain, on the road beyond Imphal and at the gateway to Manipur. They were impatiently awaiting our arrival to start the last journey out to a rear area for rest and recuperation.

"Where the bloody 'ell have you been all this time?" Beddowes's formal welcome was like a blessing, and I grinned cheerfully and muttered something very rude.

On my last evening in Imphal I took a bath. Bowunja made a discreet bamboo and grass screen, stretched a ground-sheet over the mud and produced a square ghi tin (the tins in which their cooking fat came up) filled with tepid water and a lota to dip into it. I sloshed water over myself, had a brisk rub down and a close shave before joining my fellow officers for our last supper in Manipur.

A thin steady drizzle was falling as we took to the Dimapur Road after dark with all our headlights blazing. Strongbottom, ever security-minded, thought it wise to move at night in case the enemy spotted us, although they were now at least eighty miles away and still running. More probably it had something to do with single-track working, because the up and the down convoys could only pass at certain places on the long road out.

We ground slowly up gorges, the six-wheeled Studebakers and four-wheel-drive Dodge trucks churning the mud like food mixers, and the little Jeeps fussing to and fro. I was appointed Tail-end Charlie and told to bring up the rear in my Jeep, and gather in any who fell by the wayside. I spent most of the night dealing with '*Thandi kharab hogaya*' vehicles and mending punctures. Stoppages nearly always arose from water in the petrol and I became adept at dealing with them.

Rain no longer mattered, nor hunger, nor sleep, nor any other thing. My mind repeated over and over again, "Out – Out – Out at last!" Out to rejoin the rest of the world, out to eat Firpo's foodless, out to have a sheet on a dry bed, new clothes and to sleep a thousand and one hours.

105

In the middle of the night our column stopped at a staging post to let the down convoy through. Tarpaulins were strung from trees for shelter from the rain and enormous smoky fires lit the night sky as we cooked up. We laughed like kids on bonfire night, no more need for concealment, no more blackout, no more skulking in foxholes! It was a case of 'Light the fires, blaze up, cook up, brew up, drink up and sing up!'

The speed of a convoy is the speed of the slowest member. In the first ten hours we covered forty miles and had still not reached the crest at Kohima. Harry remarked sardonically, "Keep an eye open, Johnnie, in case the mule train wants to come past us."

The mules were walking out and they probably were moving faster than we were. What matter? We were going the right way along the very road that had haunted our dreams so often under wet blankets in our bunkers during the siege. It was a very long night, but we would cheerfully have crawled out on our bellies.

We passed through sad Kohima next morning and looked around us like tourists. The scarred hill station was grimly different from that sunny morning the year before when I had journeyed the other way: the tragic rows of little white crosses over the graves of soldiers, the shattered trees and the ravaged tennis court which no Japanese soldier had managed to cross. This was the scene of the battle that had released us from our siege; if they had not done it we could never have done it. Oh well! They'd done it, we'd done it and now it was ended and we were the lucky ones, alive to face another day. The monument at Kohima declares:

> *When you go home tell them of us and say*
> *For your tomorrow we gave our today.*

We crawled down to Dimapur, and drove on through Assamese valleys, cloaked with rhododendron, heading for Shillong. We came to grassy places, rolling uplands like the Yorkshire Dales, and entered the last one-way road system that led to the capital itself. This beautiful township, adorned with pine trees, had clean and colourful shops and a Victorian atmosphere that was nostalgic and homely. We felt good!

Censorship was still rigidly enforced but I hoped that the newspapers might have possibly, just possibly, made some brief mention

106

of the end of 'The Siege of Imphal' and that my family could work out where I had been.

I looked back over all the things that I had done for the first time in the past year. I had shot rapids, shot a man, seen a wild tiger, learned to think in an Eastern tongue, been mortared, shelled and shot at, driven a tank, captured a prisoner, almost starved – it was quite a list. Surprisingly I did not regret one minute of it. My platoon had lost some men, won three gallantry medals and those of us who were left were much more closely bonded.

Chapter 10

THE INTERVAL

We've rode and fought and ate and drunk as rations come to hand,
Together for a year and more around this stinkin' land:

We came into Shillong like a refugee column. Our clothes hung from us in tatters and our gaunt flesh was stained Mepacrine yellow. Everybody fell ill. In our company there were sixty Indian soldiers to each British officer, but on parade one morning the officers outnumbered the men. Sickness had been an indulgence during the siege when the doctors had so many wounded under care, but now that the men could report sick the floodgates opened. Our bodies succumbed to jaundice, malaria and minor maladies.

Leave was opened and the men went home to their villages, whilst we had to take our break in India. Two infantry officers from our brigade went down to Calcutta, bought a house, installed a couple of compliant Eurasian girls, bought crates of beer and got on with doing what they had dreamt of doing in their foxholes on Scraggy. At the end of their leave they kissed the girls goodbye and gave them the house and everything in it. When you are that glad to be alive, when money no longer has any meaning, you are not far from finding pure happiness!

Harry and I planned to go to Bombay together but I went into hospital with jaundice and malaria. A Welsh Methodist missionary had ministered to the Khasi people and built the cottage hospital. He had tried to put a stop to their headhunting habits, taught them to sing *Cwm Rhondda* and wrote their guttural language in Roman script. He even drew up a Khasi-English dictionary, and translated the Holy Bible and hymn books for them. He must have been a zealot. The chintzy hospital could have been in the Welsh mountains, except that the nurses were petite, dark-skinned wenches with Mongolian features. They fluttered about the wards like a flock of starlings, chattering and giggling as they tossed us about, peeping beneath the bedclothes and touching us mischievously. They spoke no English.

Shillong was paradise. We loved the crystal air, the pine-crowned mountain crests, the billowing slopes of rhododendron and the beauty of the Victorian township. I lived in a small tent, raised on brushwood walls to give me standing height. Between my toes as I lay in bed I could see the distant Himalayas, white-capped, mysterious and infinite in the first light of dawn.

The seasoned planters in the club were most friendly and they understood what we had been through. They knew about our war, they knew the country and knew how vulnerable we all were in this forgotten corner of the world. We stood between them and the end of their existence.

Madness was not unknown. One officer used to draw attention to himself at mess parties by taking out a grenade, inserting the fuse and screwing the base back on. He removed the safety pin and with a flourish released the spring handle. As the tonk of the striker went home we knew that only seven seconds remained before oblivion. We left as one man, through the door, windows and even straight through the flimsy grass walls. Prostrate outside we heard the flat crack of the detonator from inside the mess. Our battle-happy grenade roulette merchant had unscrewed the base and flicked the smoking detonator across the empty room within the seven seconds. As we filed sheepishly back someone asked him what he would have done if the base thread had jammed.

"Chucked the grenade out through the window," he said coolly.

That was where we were lying and the madman said that he was practising with a five-second fuse. He was never very popular at mess parties.

At last I joined Harry on leave. We had chosen Bombay because it was by the sea, we knew it from Poona days and it was the nearest place to Blighty. We were very young and a bit daft with happiness. When I arrived at our seafront hotel Harry had already booked me in, except that he had written 'Australian Aboriginal' for my nationality, so I crossed out the 'Aboriginal'. My brother-in-law on HMS *Kenya* put in to Bombay a few weeks later and traced me to the hotel, but wrote home to say that he had found an Australian of the same name but not me! I had gone again by then.

Harry was crisply dressed in pale khaki and asked me if I had any cigarettes. I handed him a brand new packet of twenty and my matches. He took one and casually threw the lot out of the window of our sixth floor room into the crowded street below. It was a gesture of wanton wastefulness that said all we felt. No longer any need to scrimp, scrounge or husband every scrap of food and tobacco, we were in the land of plenty! Later I took my revenge by lowering all his smart new clothes on to the sunblinds of the floor below.

We lay back and let the music of the waves soothe our ears, we joined the elitist Bombay Yacht Club, probably the most exclusive in the world at that time. We put on a lot of weight. We bought a portable wind-up gramophone and chose a box of 12-inch black 78rpm records of classical music to take back. We chose one symphony, one concerto, one operatic extract and so on until the record case was filled. This choice would last us through many long months to come and the fine music never palled.

My restless kismet sought me out once more. I suffered from a hyperactive CRE at Div HQ who I pictured at some high-level drinks party, surrounded by brass hats and red tabs. Overhearing a remark that there was a shortage of sappers down on the Arakan front he gulped down his Long John Collins and said, "Think nothing of it, ol' boy, I'll send some of mine down there. They're hanging around doing nothing right now. It'll keep 'em out of mischief! What?"

Our company had the order next day and Beddowes seized his chance to rid himself of a few of Johnnie's Bloody Sikhs for a while. I had to go and build a bridge near Cox's Bazar and took a party of about twenty of my best sappers and Surajbahn Singh. In my Jeep I led three Dodge 15cwt trucks out to the rim of the Assamese high country at Cherrapunji. I recalled my geography teacher calling it 'The wettest place in the world', which it was thought to be at that time. Disappointingly it was dusty dry with grim black coalfields. We found the gate to the single track that descended 4,000ft to Sylhet on the plain below, and queued all night for it to open.

Each morning the up convoy took five hours to climb the escarpment and at noon the down convoy was released. The clever trick was to be there very early and be first away to sweep down the crazy twisting road. This avoided the torture of being stuck behind lumbering trucks, or being held up by breakdowns. It took three hours to plunge from the cool mountain climate into the sweltering humidity of the Bengal Plain.

I was not happy about going back to war again so soon, but, once I was on my own, I took my time and savoured the pleasures of the trip. One evening we stopped amongst paddy fields and tufted bamboo groves and discovered a derelict building of enormous size. It must have been a temple or monastery or the palace of a long-dead maharajah. It towered out of the undergrowth, tier upon tier, with erotic carved figures sprawling across the façade. It was inhabited by a busy troupe of monkeys and we explored the lofty rooms and empty courtyards. The horseplay and shouting of my jawans soon exorcised any ghosts, and they made friends with the resident *banda-log* (monkey folk). A naked Bengali boy turned up before we had finished cooking and joined us for a meal, and when his belly was shiny tight he disappeared again.

We spent one night on a tea plantation. The isolation of the planter in his lofty rooms, surrounded by shady verandahs where climbers trailed and the fragrance of jasmine filled the air, was almost frightening. I wondered whether he was in a little paradise, or a little hell. There was no other white man for a day's march or more in any direction. What loneliness! Planters were often Scottish, and talented whisky drinkers. After *tiffin* (lunch) I lay back in a caned chair with a fat cigar between my fingers and a smoky tumbler of malt held in my hand whilst he sharpened thorn needles and played the Beethoven Triple Concerto on his horn gramophone. He was very hospitable and like all lonely men could not stop talking, nor could he do enough for me. It was inferred that he could find me a sleeping partner if I felt so inclined, and there was a dusky lady in the background who waited upon us, and doted upon him.

Our little convoy flogged south, pursued by red billows of dust, across the featureless plain. One morning I sensed through the pinky-beige cloud behind me that one of my trucks was missing. Leading the column I was in clear air, but in the following trucks the men wore dust-chokers over their faces and looked like chalky clowns by the end of the day.

I turned back and travelled almost an hour before finding the missing truck. It was upside down in a paddy field and the men had been tossed out into the squelchy mud. Nobody was hurt and the men

111

were fatalistic about it. We loved the marvellous Dodge 15cwt and travelled with the windscreen down and no canvas tilt so that the steering wheel was the highest point. It was so sturdy that I only had to right it, attend to petrol, water and oil, bash the steering wheel straight and off they went again to join the others.

At Dohazari, on the coast road beyond Cox's Bazar, we had to build a Bailey Bridge over a deep river. This would have been an easy task with a full platoon, but I only had a section and Surajbahn and I went off to the nearest village to round up a large gang of Bengali coolies to lift and carry and make the approach roads. They were undernourished, and stupid. I watched fifteen or twenty of them trying to lift a bridge panel which six sappers normally carried.

As soon as the bridge was done we drove all the way back to Shillong; we had been away about a month. To our surprise The Fighting Cock Division was on the move again, and Beddowes received me with his usual chant: "Where the bloody 'ell have you been all this time?"

We crossed the enormous width of the Indian continent in our trucks, covering the distance from London to Moscow in a blazing heat that burned our throats as we breathed. We came to Madh Island, south of Bombay, where we were about to begin Combined Operations training in preparation for some future beach assault.

Our camp was at the back of a palm-fringed sweep of golden sand where cooling breezes blew, the sun shone, the sea was blue and the plangent murmur of the waves made a homesick sound that reminded me of Cornwall in August. As we drove along the back of the beach I showed my men the ocean, which none of them had ever seen before.

"All that water is salty!" I told them and they began to chuckle and nudge each other; Sahib was talking big again. In a country where salt was so highly valued that it was used as a currency, where could there be enough to season that giant lake?

"Get out!" I slammed on the brakes of the truck "Go down there and taste it for yourselves!"

They never did believe my tide stories. I marked with a stick the precise point to which the sea would rise and told them the exact time it would reach it, but they always believed that the rise and fall was governed by rainfall further 'upstream'. To them the ocean was always a river that was so wide that the far bank was not visible.

"Over there . . ." I pointed to the horizon "If I travelled for many

112

weeks on a big ship I would eventually reach my homeland!" Another of Sahib's stories.

I was now very close to my men. Our shared experiences on the battlefield, followed by leave, good food, healthy sea air and intensive physical training engendered a companionship between us. I spoke their language easily and our mutual respect transcended the relationship between Sahib and sepoy, officer and man. A good British officer was all things to his men – father figure, oracle, judge, even nursemaid at times. Had I not held the hands of shattered Sikhs lying wounded in the mud and sorted out their marital problems? They always had problems at home with other villagers or relatives trying to steal their land or their wives and I had to attend to all things medical, mechanical and social.

In the lines their boisterous behaviour and peccadilloes were tiresome, but part of the game. Which platoon had all the medals, eh? How often had they carried me through? The stews of Bombay were very near to our camp and the traps of the city were a more dangerous threat to them than any Japanese ambush and I was always concerned for their health and safety. There were always loose women about the camp perimeter, which was not securely fenced.

We were being trained for something special and we were reinforced with additional officers. A high caste Muslim officer called Riaz-al-Huq, who had the King's Commission and had been to Sandhurst, joined us. One evening my havildar came into the mess for orders for the next day and we jabbered away to each other in our usual easy way. After he left Riaz turned to me visibly shaken:

"I don't know how to say this, Johnnie, but you speak like an Amritsar guttersnipe! You are fast and fluent, but officers should never use such language!"

I was taken aback.

"What did I say that was so awful?"

"Well when Surajbahn asked what they should do with the rifles you said, 'Stuff them up your grandmother's what's-it!' and you used even filthier phrases!"

I went outside in the cool of the evening to think it over. Riaz was probably right. The lads loved teaching me new colloquialisms and I was a good mimic, but now I felt foolish. Was I dancing to their tune like the organ-grinder's monkey? I relished the rapport I had with my men and they always jumped to obey my commands. It occurred to me, as I walked, that a high caste Muslim officer could not do what I did, any more than a brigadier could bawl out a soldier in broad Geordie using four-letter words. To the Sikhs I was their slightly mad, but loveable, caste-free, white Sahib and in their book I could do no wrong. So I left things as they were and stayed out of earshot of Riaz when I told them where to put things.

We were sent inland to Nasik Lake for training in beach landings, and I came back to the mess one afternoon in my sweat-blackened uniform with a throat like the Gobi desert. Bob and Harry were there, and behaving strangely.

"Here he comes, the wee creep!" Harry said "I reckon he's riddled with some tertiary disease and they want rid of him," and Bob added, "I wouldn't like to make that trip with present shipping and air losses"

Through my weariness I realized that this was different from our usual internecine sniping and I discovered that I had been selected for two weeks' home leave to UK. The war in Europe was entering the last stages and they had decided to test air trooping for the movement of large forces to the East. All of us were months, even years overdue for going home and practically everyone qualified for this break.

Python was the code name for repatriation, but they could not, dared not, release experienced men like us, officers who knew Indian troops and their language, in exchange for rookies from Europe. LIAP was devised, meaning 'Leave in Advance of Python' and it was not only a sop to the electorate but a chance to put air trooping to the test. It meant that a comparatively small number of us could fly home for a fortnight, and then return to our units. Out of three or four thousand eligible men in 23 Div alone only three places had been offered. In the ensuing raffle the sappers had won a place, my Company got it and finally I had drawn the short straw. Bob and Harry continued with their teasing:

"Unfortunately nobody can take this leave unless their jabs are up to date!"

I found my Officer's blue book. Not a single inoculation was valid!

"Get a bottle of whisky!" Harry said, "No, better make that two!" In no time I showered and changed into my best and we tore off in Bob's Jeep. In lieu of a pub-crawl we embarked on a jab-crawl. My blue book had to be stamped up to date before the OC checked it and I knew that he would be meticulous.

We visited medical officers for miles around, plied them with Scotch, and persuaded each one to give me a jab. I was given Small Pox, Tet:tox, Yellow Fever, A.B., Dengue, Plague, Scrub Typhus and whatever other flavours were in vogue that year. We were only supposed to have one inoculation at a time, but I reeled home a couple of hours later with my service book full of new stamps and two empty whisky bottles. I had no ill effects, not even a hangover, such was the power of euphoria.

I flew from Bombay to Karachi and picked up the Dakota that would take me on the first leg home. Our stamina was tested to the limit on the flight; the planes were neither insulated nor pressurized and we were packed into the aluminium tube without proper seating. There was a canvas strip running the length of the plane on both sides, but it was so crowded that we took turns to have a lie down on the cold deck. At Bahrein we cooked at 50° C on the tarmac for nearly an hour and then thirty minutes later we were flying at below zero on the next long hop. It took three days to get home and every time we touched down they gave us egg and chips; we called it 'The meal on which the sun never sets!'

"My parents live in Portland" I told the pilot as we crossed the English Channel. He banked the Dakota over and did a dangerously low circuit over the town, especially for me, and my father ran out into the garden alarmed by the twin-engined transport that was threatening his chimneys.

"Wouldn't it be marvellous, mother," he said, "if John was in that 'plane!"

They did not know I was coming. We landed in Somerset and had to go to London to receive official processing, leave passes, warm khaki uniforms, and money. It was maddening to be so near home after so long and still be in custody.

In defiance of orders that evening two of us slipped out into Marylebone High Street and into the smell of London. We soaked in the sootiness, the plane trees and the low sun carving out shadowed streets. In a back street pub, where the etched glass windows sparkled, we inhaled the nostalgic fumes of old beer and tobacco. I was wearing my Gurkha bush hat, jungle green bush-shirt stained with sweat and egg'n chips and there was a tautness about the way we moved. To the locals we must have looked very strange.

"Christ! Mate!" called a cockney voice. "I don' know where you poor buggars are from but you don' 'ave to pay for your beer in 'ere!"

Foaming tankards of real British ale appeared in our hands. We did not spend a penny all night, which was just as well because we only had a few rupees in our pockets.

Only a soldier who has spent too long in some far-flung land can guess at my emotions as the train ran me down that last leg home. Placid cows grazed the vivid green pastures, engine smoke streamed past the meadows and villages looked like Toy Town models. It was all too lovely to be real, so cool and uncrushed by Nipponese boots. The civilians in my carriage were dressed in drab clothes, worn thin by war and, to their alarm, I kept chuckling out loud at each new vista as I lived my dream.

"Come far, mate?" wheezed the taxi driver at Weymouth station. Little did he know! I flung open our front door, which was never locked, and sent the ringing, singing shout down the hall, that had always presaged my arrivals with "John's home!"

They could not believe it.

My leave was tarnished with the vapours of my recent experiences and the premonition of worse that I knew was yet to come. There was a chasm between my dearest ones and me. In May 1945 the end of the war against Japan seemed a very long way off and I knew we had been groomed for beach landings and further fighting against the powerful foe we knew so well.

Here were linen tablecloths, crisp white sheets on sybaritic beds, cheeky sparrows round the bedroom window, rosy-cheeked, fair-skinned women, unpredictable weather and cakes for tea. There was a lot of whingeing about almost everything: rationing, shortages, prices, the weather, the list was endless and I could not tell them that in a month or two I would be storming up some distant coral strand in the face of enemy fire at H-hour on D-day!

But wasn't I the lucky one? Hadn't I drawn the short straw? Didn't the boys back there envy me? In paradise I could only think of hell. Everywhere I saw youths and lasses, carefree and cosy, home here in Blighty and I was holding a return ticket to evils I could readily imagine. When I asked, "Why me?" there was no answer.

"Little do they know!" I muttered, and added, "nor care!" Which was most unfair of me because they tried desperately to empathize with my dark moods:

"Your orderly?" my mother asked "Bowunja? He sounds a dear! Can I send him back a little something, say a quarter of tea?" This treasured commodity in wartime England was hardly the thing for big Bowunja out there where it was grown!

"I expect you get it a lot hotter than this?" asked my father. I looked at the fresh sou'easter chopping cats' paws out of the blue sea and had a vision of hot, red plains where the dust plastered your sweat and the noon air burned your nostrils:

"Yes! Quite a bit!" How could I explain?

It was an annealing process. The temper was being drawn from mind and body and as the stress relaxed it hurt. Like a diver coming up too quickly I was suffering from emotional bends and knew that my next dive was imminent.

I took my parents down to West Cornwall. I sat in low-ceilinged farm kitchens and listened to their rich speech. Folk who had known me since childhood explained the hardships of their life; there had been three or four bombs on Penzance; it was impossible to get decent skirt of beef for pasties; saffron was unobtainable; the Home Guard took up all one's spare time.

"It's the war, y'know!" they explained to this stranger, this being from outer space. I also met the most beautiful girl, whom I had known since babyhood, and yearned for her. What was the use? Men who live in hard shells and walk in the shadow of death must not give pledges. Little did I guess I had met my future wife!

I climbed back into the aluminium cigar case of the Dakota transport and was borne back East. It took weeks to get back, because the weather was bad and the air-trooping system was not working too well, and there really was cause for anger in my usual welcome.

"Where the bloody hell have you been this time?" said Beddowes. "We thought you had deserted!"

My old mates had decided that I was going to be too late for the next big push and it was flattering to know how much they had missed me. I received a rapturous welcome from the men when I went down to the lines. My guttersnipe Punjabi came back as I exchanged banter with them all and discovered that I had a new jemadar. I had never seen such perfection in a pugree, and I feared that he might be a bit too smart, but he turned out to be a gem. It was a joy to see the silly grins of welcome everywhere and hear Fauji M.M. mutter behind his hand, "Old Chah-chah's come back to us!"

Within the hour I discovered that we were moving, almost immediately, to the coast for embarkation in landing craft. We were going to make an attack on some enemy-held territory! My leave was over and there was sadness in my heart.

Chapter 11

ZIPPED UP

And it all goes into the laundry,
But it never comes out in the wash,
'Ow we're sugared about by the old men

Troop trains are horrid! They carry soldiers to unpleasant places and in India they are even more austere than in Europe. We joined 37 Gurkha Brigade and boarded one of the special trains for Madras, with the men travelling in a string of troop cars, windowless cattle boxes, that were packed to bursting. The officers rode in slightly better compartments of the sort that Rudyard Kipling might have used half a century before, with hard cots and slatted windows.

The train was placed under the charge of one of the toughest infantry officers I have ever known. Sandy Meikle had won the M.C. on Scraggy, but he was not particularly interested nor gifted in bureaucratic administration.

"What the hell does 'OC Train' mean, Johnnie?" he asked me over a stack of typed orders. I did not really know either, but I poured him a Scotch and explained: "I think you have to jump out from time to time, set the points, work the signals and keep us on the move! Don't worry, Sandy, I'll stoke the engine for you!"

Our train ran late. Not a few minutes late. Not a few hours late, but four whole days late. Troopers are an additional burden imposed upon the regular timetable and have to be squeezed in. The single railroad went south across the middle of India for 700 miles or more and we travelled by lines that were tributaries of the main system. We had to hop between passing places, playing a tiresome game of musical chairs with the scheduled trains. An extra ball tossed into the central court during a final at Wimbledon would have been as welcome as we were to the railway officials trying to run their schedule. With the whole of 23 Div on the move there were a lot of troop trains going south and this engendered a lot of chaos.

I have no doubt that a sober and serious OC Train would have blustered and bullied his train through obstructions and officialdom. Not Sandy. We were enjoying it too much to rush things. Out of the reach of staff officers and petty restrictions we waited interminably in remote sidings in the blazing heat. We got out footballs, volleyball kits and hockey sticks and got some very good leagues going. The men went off to distant villages foraging and came back with fresh vegetables, chickens and piglets. Cooking fires blazed up by the rail side, it was like a camping holiday.

On one occasion when the Eurasian railway official pompously told us that our train could proceed down the next stretch of track we had to decline because we had several important fixtures to play off and half our passengers were away over the horizon somewhere.

Madras City station was a vast brown cavern, with wreaths of curling steam ascending through the steep rays of sunlight that pierced the Victorian glass roof. Sandy stood foursquare and unrepentant before a staff officer who was dancing with rage at the lateness of our arrival. Once again those familiar words rang out: "Where the bloody hell have you been?" and mischievously I chipped in with: "Are we late, Sir? We missed our connection at Birmingham Snow Hill. I hope we've not held up the invasion!" I slipped away into the throng of Gurkhas and Sikhs before he could take my name.

We were herded into barbed wire cages like prisoners, which indeed we were; security was rigid and no contact with the outside world was allowed. We knew now that we were heading East to land on some enemy-held beach. The first outline orders gave Phuket as our objective and to this day I'm glad that we avoided that unfortunate name. We were taken to the harbour and put aboard LST (Landing Ships) which had wide opening doors in their bows and ramps down which we would eventually have to plunge. It was a desperate time and it was hard to believe that I had been in Cornwall only the month before and such a long way from this stressful life.

As the vast convoy assembled in the muddy-yellow waters of the Bay of Bengal we lay hove to and the shallow-draft ship pitched and corkscrewed in the rolling waves. It was very stormy and down below my poor men were enduring their first experience of sea travel. The

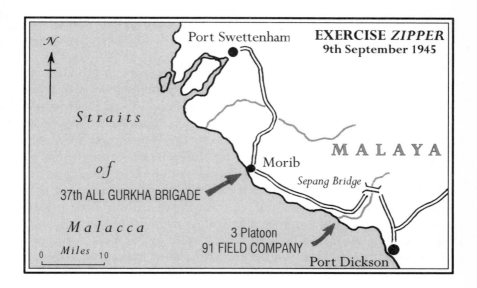

EXERCISE *ZIPPER*
9th September 1945

Port Swettenham

Straits

of

37th ALL GURKHA BRIGADE

Morib

M A L A Y A

Sepang Bridge

Malacca

3 Platoon
91 FIELD COMPANY

Port Dickson

0 *Miles* 10

rich brown of their faces changed to the putty-grey of a wet sweeper's instep. Their half-naked bodies reeled and spewed about the bucketing tin box that held them and their black tresses streamed like horses' tails. They begged me to put an end to the violent motion: "Stop it, sahib, just put a stop to it for a few minutes! Please hold it still until we are all right again!"

I slithered about on the vomit between their bunks, ministering to them until my own senses began to reel and I had to go aloft for a blow of fresh air.

As soon as we got under way I was given my secret orders for 'Exercise Zipper' as the invasion had been named. Our destination had been finalized and was to be the mainland of Malaya. 37 Brigade would spearhead the landings on the west coast, a few miles south of Port Swettenham at Morib beach. D-Day would be 9 September 1945 and H-hour for the main assault was 06.45 hrs, but five hours earlier (H-5 as they put it) my platoon would 'swim off' in amphibious metal boxes called *Alligators*. These tracked craft were manned by the Navy and would transport us up a creek through mangrove swamps to Sepang bridge, that lay on the main road from the landing beach. It looked as though I would be the first British soldier back in Malaya or at least the most forward one. (In fact there had been a guerrilla organization called Force 136 in Malaya throughout the occupation, led by men who knew the country and who recruited effective resistance groups to harass the enemy.)

The orders were ambiguous and left a lot to my initiative. If the bridge was still standing and in use by Japanese troops moving forward to defend the beachhead, I had to demolish it. If, however, the enemy had already blown it themselves, to prevent our forces advancing inland, then I had to repair it. There seemed to be plenty of scope for getting a 'Blighty One', a posthumous gallantry award or a court martial even. I did not like it at all and it felt as though a cool kamikaze wind blew on the back of my neck. It was obvious that 37 Brigade was to be sacrificed, to seize the beach and hold it long enough for waves of fresh troops to follow us in.

It was a long voyage. Too long for our suffering soldiers. A rumour circulated round the ship about a blood-red glow in the East. A bomb to end all bombs had been dropped on the Japanese mainland and it could end the war almost immediately. We very much doubted that; we knew the no-surrender mentality of our enemy. Would a thousand years of *bushido* be wiped out in one August evening?

Our commanders decided to proceed with the invasion of Malaya according to plan and to land on the beaches as though the enemy were resisting us in full strength. It was true that the Japanese were in the throes of capitulation, but it was feared that the belligerent General Ishiguro, commanding their Twenty-ninth army in Malaya, Sumatra and Java would not lay down the sword, but would fight to the death. This was how they had always behaved, and the decision was made to carry out Exercise Zipper as planned.

I stood on the upper deck of our ship that last evening as the elongated convoy formed into line ahead and entered the Straits of Malacca – the flotilla stretched for 40 miles. Was there ever a sunset like it? The welkin flamed in a chromatic chaos of hues, from palest green to blood red, and the flag of Nippon was grotesquely parodied by outspreading rays across the firmament. It was such an awe-inspiring omen that our hearts turned over. In our troubled minds it could portend some dreadful disaster that awaited us on the morrow. Looking back, I realize that we were seeing the pall of atomic dust over Hiroshima and Nagasaki, the dirt of Japan that was screening the backdrop to their demise.

Soon after midnight we mustered below in the dank womb of the ship, where vehicles and men were packed as tightly as the last ferry to hell. We clambered up the caterpillar tracks into our steel boxes and met our Alligator crew. It was a place of dimly lit threat, echoing noises and cold fear. Suddenly a stammer of automatic shots rang out and bullets pinged about the steel bulkheads. Madness! To have travelled so far and survived so much, only to be slaughtered by a trigger-happy sepoy who did not know where his safety catch was!

Engines roared, the sulphurous fug of diesel smoke dimmed the bulkhead lights and we were the first away, skidding down through the jaws into black tropical waters and a velvet night. The musty wet smell of swamps, so close at hand, filled our nostrils and we moved towards the black silhouette of the Malayan shore. Dense primary jungle hung over the slit that was the entrance to our creek. Our craft swam the black waters like real alligators, gliding between walls of mangrove to the music of the dawn chorus from the virgin jungle.

Like many others at the time I believed that the planners had contrived to get the time of high water wrong. Instead of thrusting well inland we grounded on the mud some distance short of our objective. After several changes of date for D-day they had managed to miss the high Spring tides, so that there was less depth at high water. Worst of all there had never been a proper reconnaissance of the inlet, or the landing beaches for that matter. The navy lads were frantic. They did not want to be stranded miles up a creek, in darkest Malaya, defenceless and unable to back away. As the brackish waters drained past on the falling tide they wanted to be rid of us. The first light of dawn showed the slimy black mud of the creek, a slurry that would not sustain our body weight. The grotesque mangrove roots coiled into a formidable barrier between the distant dry land and us, and there were yellow and black striped snakes corkscrewing up and down in the water.

I did the only thing I could. I threw out all our bridge repair timbers and used them to make a primitive causeway over the swamp. Daylight was oozing through the trees as the Alligator crew backed away, shouting, "Good luck, chums! Give 'em one for us!" And they made for the open sea and the safety of their mother ship.

I had no idea where we were. I knew we were some way downstream of the bridge, which I could no longer repair as all my timber was now floating away on the tide. I knew that the road to the landing beach ran parallel to the creek but not how far away it was. We reached firm ground and thin bamboo jungle and moved stealthily forward in fighting order. Suddenly a figure flitted behind a tree ahead. We reacted quickly and pounced on a tiny trembling Chinese girl wearing a black silk shift. In pidgin English, the lingua franca of the whole world, I learned that we were near to a *kampong* (village) and alertly we followed the child into Merbau.

There were no Japs about and the local people were overjoyed to welcome the British *tuans* (sahibs) back! Would we like a cup of tea? I was tempted to ask 'Indian or Chinese?'

The hamlet was little more than a few native huts scattered about the dusty road and our tea was generously laced with a fiery local spirit that was as warming as the friendliness of the village folk. It was almost seven o'clock and the rising sun was opening the new day. Half an hour earlier we had been stalking grimly with fixed bayonets and fixed expressions through the unknown and now we were sipping alcoholic tea with friends, as though we had just dropped by for a visit.

I could hear no distant sounds of battle from the coast. The beach-head was half a day's march behind us to the west and H-hour had long passed. Cautiously we scouted up and down the road and it was deserted. There was nothing else to do but attempt to follow my orders and we set off towards the rising sun to find the bridge. It was undamaged, unguarded and strong enough to carry our armour.

We were relaxed after our morning drink, birds were singing and I knew that there was going to be no war that day. We fell asleep beside the road and the morning wore on. The excitement of heading the thrust into this strange country was tempered by gnawing fears. What was going on? Was this the right bridge? Had I gone up the wrong creek? I heard the two-stroke popping of a motorbike coming from inland and alerted the men. It was a tiny folding bike, such as they dropped by parachute, and a very angry British officer was riding it.

"Who the bloody 'ell are you?" he shouted, "And what the bloody 'ell do you think you're doing?"

We sat side by side on the parapet of the bridge and told each other all we knew. He was a former rubber planter, a member of Force 136, and had been living in the occupied country for some time. The evening before he had dined with the fiery General Itagaki, and had informally accepted his agreement to cease hostilities. He had expected our general to step ashore at Port Dickson and ratify his negotiations, but we were fighting a non-existent enemy somewhere back on the coast.

He puttered off to find the Fourteenth Army and promised to come back and tell me if he found them. When he returned a few hours later he yelled, "Bloody shambles! Good job I made peace with the Japs last night or they'd have decimated your lot! God knows when you'll see them, mate, they've thrown all your trucks into the sea!"

In the late afternoon the first weary lines of infantry reached my bridge on foot, and when Beddowes turned up with the remains of HQ. I was severely tempted to say to him, "Where the bloody hell have you been? Couldn't you find Malaya on your map?" But he looked so dejected that I let him say it first! He even added, "Trust you to miss all the action and keep out of it! It was hell back there!"

I must fill in the background of errors that was Exercise Zipper and explain what happened. In Britain vote-catching had begun and the opposition were making moves to oust Churchill from power. He had wanted to make a fighting return to Singapore, but Attlee and the Secretary for War withdrew from the coalition government. To curry popular favour Sir James Grigg announced schemes to bring the boys home. Python Repatriation would remove one third of all the SEAC forces and all the most experienced men, but there was insufficient transport to carry them home. This meant that they would be stacked up in transit camps in India just when they were needed most.

Faced with a war to win Mountbatten declared, "This is military insanity!"

The investment in an officer such as me was enormous. I knew the men, their customs and their language and had been in action against the Japanese. We ourselves still felt that we had a mission and were resigned to the fact that the enemy would have to be defeated before we would see our homes again.

Rangoon fell earlier than expected and could provide air and sea bases for the invasion of Malaya and so they abandoned the first plans to send 23 Div to capture Phuket Island. Plan II was to send us straight in to the west coast of Malaya, using beaches that were known to be suitable near Port Dickson. Then it was decided that these beaches looked too obvious and the enemy would expect us there, so they changed to Plan III an assault on Morib beaches twenty miles to the north. This procrastination caused us to miss the high Spring tides and the moon.

Experienced Beach Groups from the Normandy invasion failed to arrive and a large number of the small landing craft for the final landings suffered multiple disasters en route for the Far East. The information about Morib beaches was very skimpy. Three two-man survey parties had been put ashore from a submarine, but only one team returned. The surviving two men courageously went back again and reported a bottomless mud ooze below the sandy crust, but their gallant report was pushed aside. A survey in 1928 reported 'more or less sandy' but no low-level aerial photographs were taken in case the Japs might guess our intentions! It was even thought that the unsuitability of Morib beaches was a plus factor because the enemy would not expect us there. This, despite the fact that they knew there was an extensive enemy trench system at the back of the beaches, that large units were stationed strategically inland and that there were sandbanks and ridges offshore in shelving waters. It was a catalogue of folly and we came to believe that Strongbottom himself had been promoted to Army Headquarters to help formulate the plans.

After their withdrawal from Burma the Japanese occupation army in Malaya had swelled from fifty to ninety thousand. It is a military fact that the ratio of three against one is essential for an opposed beach landing to succeed and numerically we were now down to eight against five. They brought the landing date forward from October to 9 September 1944, even though the tides were not so favourable. General Ouvry Roberts, our former 23 Div commander that I had met on the Ukhrul track, had been promoted to command the invasion force and later he said that had the Japanese defended Malaya we would not have survived.

Not unnaturally they chose their best soldiers for the first assault on Morib, who else but 37 All-Gurkha brigade? We were expected to crash across the beaches at great speed and accept large losses. Whilst we were being decimated they would fling a second assault up the better beaches near Port Dickson. My brigade had to secure the Sepang bridge and that was the reason that I was sent inland five hours before the landings. I was not a witness to the shambles on the beach and can only report what my friends told me later. Landing craft had grounded on sand banks some distance out from the shallows so that when the ramps were dropped men and vehicles plunged

126

into deep water. One group of LCTs were two miles out of position and by the time they found the correct place the tide had fallen further, to exacerbate their problems. Instead of driving up the beach at 06.45 a.m., the assault forces were still floundering in the mud when night fell. Seasick little Gurkhas, non-swimmers to a man, laden with heavy packs stepped from the ramps into eight feet of water and many drowned. Vehicles plunged out of sight into deep water and sank through the sandy crust into the ooze. Sunken trucks blocked the egress of those behind, some of which even tried to drive over the top of them only to disappear themselves. The chaos on the beach defies description. Approximately a thousand vehicles, tanks, bulldozers and guns were written off in a single day, together with a large number of LCTs and other vessels, and of course the drowned soldiers.

Every effort was made to hush up this incredible tale of mismanagement. The cover-up was helped by the fact that the Press had landed dry-shod on the quaysides of Port Dickson and Port Swettenham, some miles away, and missed the opportunity to report the most disgraceful cock-up of the whole war.

A senior Officer said later that one sniper at the back of Morib Beach could have shot us all! I can only describe the way it appeared to those of us who took part on that awful day, when men said that it was called 'Zipper' because nothing was buttoned up. Churchill called the fortuitous dropping of the A-bombs on mainland Japan "a miracle of deliverance". It certainly was for us, it saved our lives.

What an evening we spent! The remnants of our Brigade reached the bridge and it became a laager with men cooking over fires and making bivouacs as they told their sad stories. There was no top brass anywhere to be seen.

"Perhaps the staff officers have all committed hari-kari," one Gurkha officer suggested, "or gone to be measured for their bowler hats!" quipped another. With the simple trust of fighting men we expected that heads would roll for this day's work. Not so! The story was not told and this bag full of clangers sank quietly beneath the waters of Cover-up Bay. The Supreme Allied Commander said, "On the 9th September 1945 landings were made as planned for Zipper . . ."

Having lost almost the whole of our transport the official surrender parade in Seremban had to be taken on foot. The shortage of vehicles in the brigade led to a new kind of brigandry. Our unit number was a white 51 on a blue square and I never went anywhere without a brush and two tins of paint. Any unattended vehicle was game and we painted over their insignia with our own. Angry victims tested the paint, and if still wet wiped it out again.

I found Malaya to be a magical country, romanticized in my mind by the stories of W. Somerset Maugham, and names like Raffles, Singapore, Kuala Lumpur and Penang. It was our liberated colony where echoes of the old Imperial Empire lingered and the birth pangs of emancipation were yet to come. To me it was beautiful and peopled by a race of gentle folk who viewed us as liberators from the heel of Japanese oppression. I was not to know that the ignominy of our defeat and rout from the peninsula spelled the end of British rule. The events of the time and our attitudes should be understood and kept within the correct historical context. It was 1944 and the British people were emerging from the bitterest fight of their existence.

I spent an interesting month or so in Malaya. I was sent off on my own, driving a new Jeep because mine had disappeared during the landings, to examine all the road bridges and categorize their suitability for traffic. With Surajbahn and a few men following in a truck I travelled the length and breadth of the whole land, meeting former employees of the Public Works Department. From time to time we came across Japanese depots that insisted on surrendering formally to us. As we entered their lines they struck their detested flag and their soldiers lined up to present arms. Not slow to take advantage of this unusual situation we commandeered anything that took our fancy, which they willingly handed over as long as we signed for them! The following troops who came to take them prisoner officially must have found dockets everywhere signed by *M. Mouse*, or *W.Churchill* or *J. Stalin* and no portable gramophones or other useful souvenirs.

Zipper was not the only piece of incompetent management. In a land of plenty we were short of food and only had skimpy rations. The few Malay Straits Dollars issued to us lasted less than a week in the bazaars, and cigarettes were rationed to eight per man per day. We could get no booze, no writing or toilet paper, and no mail. We had landed in battle order, the absolute minimum, and the rest of our kit was apparently missing. I got some of mine back in the spring of the following year.

Within a short time we were ordered to Java.

I boarded S.S. *Talma*, an ancient steamship of the British India

128

Steam Navigation line. The atmosphere aboard was British pre-war Raj at its best, with Goanese stewards who gave impeccable service in sumptuous teak-lined state rooms. As we wallowed across the Java Sea we wallowed in luxury. Peace had really come!

Little did we know!

Chapter 12

ISLE OF GRIP

*They did not stay to ask
What prize should crown their task—*

Old-timers from the days of Colonial glory called Java 'The Isle of Grip' which may have been a translation from the Dutch or a simple statement that once it seized you it was forever. I was soon infatuated.

The island is about the size of England without Wales and it is an exciting place. It lies just south of the equator and there are three distinct levels. Along the north coast, bordering the Java Sea, there is a steamy coastal plain with sandy beaches, palm trees and tropical growth. Moving inland to the south there is a central plateau at about 6000 ft that the Dutch called The Highlands. The south coast is a lofty spine of volcanic mountains that plunge sheer into the Indian Ocean, with the highest peak at over 12,000ft and lazy drifts of smoke rise from many of the snow-capped craters.

High places on the equator are temperate and sunny, and the Dutch had built their hill station retreats and rich farms in The Highlands. There were dairy herds of Friesian cattle, arable crops, European vegetables, flowers and fruit. On this one small island it seemed that everything was available; from palm-fringed beaches to ski slopes, from tropical delicacies to cold climate foods, from frangipani to tulips and from native *pasars* (bazaars) to company stores. This spice island supplied most of the world's quinine, it had wonderful forests of exotic hardwoods and there was always a magical quality in the air.

The rest of my company had gone inland, up to Bandoeng, but my platoon was detailed to go on detachment with the Gurkha Brigade and occupy the port of Semarang in central Java.

Waiting for my next ship in Batavia I absorbed the exotic mystery

of the land. It was a good example of the colonial strategy of
the Dutch East India Company, being superficially a corner of the
Netherlands, complete with canals, wide tree-lined boulevards, big
cars, trams and all the trappings of a European civilization. Just
beneath this Western veneer the ancient cultures went deep. Smartly
dressed window shoppers drifted from window to window on one
side of the street, whilst in the canal across the way a bevy of topless
local ladies stooped over the murky water, washing their clothes and
attending to the needs of nature.

There was another contrast at that time. The Javanese were well
dressed, well fed and at home in the scene, whereas the few white
Dutch were scrawny, ill clad and on foot. The big limousines had
uniformed Japanese drivers. The word *MERDEKA!* (freedom) was
splashed across hoardings and walls, vividly red and running down
in drips like blood, pulsing with aggressive hatred.

This prolific and fruitful country was harvesting a new crop,
hatred. In place of spices, tapioca, rice, peanuts, quinine, oranges,
tobacco, pepper and rubber the first shoots of revolt were burgeoning
on every hand. Planted wantonly by the occupying forces of Nippon,
watered and fed by Indonesian Nationalism, encouraged by Dutch
intransigence, another war was on our hands. The local population
did not want the Dutch back and as soon as Japan capitulated
numerous factions sprang up ready to take the country over. There
were the Black Buffaloes (led by Soekarno), the Red Buffaloes and the
White Buffaloes, and all three parties were striving for power. They
were united in their opposition to the return of white imperialism.

131

The Konigsplein, Batavia's main street, displayed a mishmash of flags and signs. The Union Jack hung over our navy HQ, the Dutch tricolour over NICA, (Nederlandsch-Indie Civil Administration), Stars and Stripes over ALFSEA, (Allied Land Forces South East Asia), a Rising Sun over the Japanese barracks, our own Fighting Cock sign over 23 Div HQ and the new red and white striped flag of Indonesia everywhere else. Between the Indonesians and us there was a small, but crucial misunderstanding. We thought that we were there to collect and make prisoner the occupying forces from Japan and that we had to do it because the Dutch had no organized forces. The local population saw us as white Imperial colonists, returning to reinstate Dutch dominion over their land. With mainly Indian and Gurkha troops, we regarded ourselves as peacetime soldiers doing a job, and it is unbelievable that the men at the top did not foresee the trouble that was looming.

There were other anomalies. The Japanese had deliberately fermented Nationalism in the native population and trained many of them in modern weapons. Their sudden collapse had placed the ball at the feet of Indonesian freedom fanatics, who were divided and not fully prepared. The Dutch, who did not have our touch in colonial administration, believed that they only had to return, climb back into their big cars and lovely houses and make a lot more money. The Japanese had been ordered to maintain civil order until our troops arrived, but they were either deliberately incompetent or over-whelmed. We walked into this situation like uninformed Christians entering an arena full of lions.

In Indonesia both the Mohammedan and Hindu religions were followed and we arrived with Indian troops from both these faiths. No wonder that the local people saw us as white European Christians employing mercenaries to restore colonial rule. In the eyes of the Dutch we were pro-native, too lenient and too willing to mediate with the insurgents. In Japanese eyes we were the international police force and the victorious enemy. In our own eyes we were triumphant liberators freeing the land from the oppressor's boot, harbingers of the glad news that the war was over and bringers of peace!

We were also battle-hardened veterans facing vastly superior numbers of ill-trained, badly armed and uncoordinated forces.

Evil flourished as vigorously as hatred. White and half-breed adventurers, who had escaped being sent to Japanese prison camps,

132

assumed powers to which they were not entitled and were the first to exploit the situation. Native lawlessness exploded into violence, pillage and rape. We were unprepared for the depth of loathing that existed between Indonesian and Dutch. In our first week the mutilated body of a little native boy was deposited on the doorstep of Div HQ, murdered by a Dutch extremist who believed that this would induce us to start reprisals against the local people.

We had no idea what was happening in the greater part of the country. There were about forty million Javanese inhabitants and, before the occupation, there had been about one million Europeans, Chinese and half-caste people as well. The Dutch men had been sent to the infamous railway prison camps in Siam and their womenfolk incarcerated in local detention camps and it was impossible to estimate the present non-native population.

In the women's prison camps the Japanese had treated them with a contemptuous disregard for three and a half years, leaving them in the utmost degradation and on the edge of starvation. Some of the younger girls had been dragooned into brothels, but the adult women had often been ignored. It was said that the Japanese had an inferiority complex about their inherent smallness and feared derision. Now with marauding bands of freedom fighters everywhere these defenceless women prisoners were in very real danger.

The half-caste population was relatively large, because Dutch colonial policy encouraged their men to take native wives in the belief that this would breed a race that was pro-Dutch with indigenous assets and resistance to disease. Like Bernard Shaw's reply to the famous actress who suggested that a liaison between them might produce perfect children, the half-breeds often displayed the opposite effect. Pedigree animals tend to look down upon mongrels and neither race liked their mixed offspring. The Dutch thought that the Eurasians had shifty native blood and the Indonesians hated their white characteristics.

There was another segregated population that was quiet, self-effacing and very rich. Someone called the Chinese the 'Jews of the Orient' because their merchants were in business everywhere. They were often a great asset to the countries that they had quietly invaded.

The Indonesians had never needed the Europeans and they did not adopt their ways or their artefacts. Houses, bungalows, luxuries and cars were left untouched and, with the Japanese removed, we helped ourselves. It was the land of Dutch wives, Dutch baths and Dutch courage. I soon found myself a Dutch wife, a bolster either of wood or cloth that you slept with, draping an arm and a leg over her to allow free circulation of air and reduce the chances of prickly heat. A Dutch bath meant swilling a pannikin of water over you, and of Dutch courage more anon.

On 26 October 1945 my platoon embarked in an old LCT at Batavia with large amounts of stores, explosives and equipment. These landing craft were like floating horse troughs, steel boxes with a drop down ramp at the bow. They were small and not very seaworthy and 3 Platoon and stores just fitted into one.

I do not know why they only sent one platoon of sappers in support of the whole Gurkha Brigade, who were packed into the other LCTs in the convoy. Instead of reporting to the infantry colonel commanding a battalion I was now responsible to the brigadier for orders and had to advise him when necessary.

We wallowed along the north coast in convoy, a ragged string of steel boxes, nose to tail, making for Semarang. There was a lot of motion in the flat-bottomed craft, but the men were now used to the sea and I let them stay aloft, sleep aloft and do what they liked.

Still travelling east! I had a dream that with peace declared we would just go on picking up Japanese prisoners across the Spice Islands that were strung out ahead of us, Bali, Timor, Borneo, Celebes and even on into the Pacific Ocean and home the other way!

Three Wavy-Navy officers ran the LCT: Skipper, Number One and Subby, who took great pleasure in having a tame 'Pongo' to tease. (Pongo, a species of Orang Outan, was the derogatory name the navy gave to all soldiers.) They wore the wavy stripes of the naval reserve and were, like me, wartime servicemen rather than regulars. In the nicest possible way they tried desperately to make me seasick. Their wretched bathtub rolled frighteningly in the swell as we lay off Batavia waiting for the whole convoy to form. They plied me with Gorgonzola, Guinness, fat pork and cream and I swallowed the lot. They even tried to make me drunk, thinking that strong Naval pink gins would make me roll over with my hobnail boots pointing to the sky. Then they tried to make a sailor out of me.

"Y'know, Johnnie, you'd make a dam' good Navy officer!"

What dizzy heights of flattery! I could be a superior boy in blue instead of a dreary pudden-headed brown job! Their real motive was to enlist an extra officer to share the watches at sea. 'Three watches' with only three officers was very tedious, whereas a fourth watch keeper would ease the watch bill to a more comfortable four-watch routine.

They succeeded in this. I loved driving new things and had already notched up quite a list from steam engines to General Grant tanks; it would be a thrill to con a ship of the line in deep water. The convoy strung out like a line of cygnets behind the pen; the lead vessel had the commodore on board who knew where we were going and how to get there. He had a proper navigator, signaller and charts. We were about fifth back and we rumbled along keeping station to the best of our ability.

As officer of the watch I stood on the bridge, squinting for'ard into the glaring heat, and I controlled our speed by blowing down the voice pipe to the engine room and issuing my orders. If we began to gain on the ship in front I said 'Down five' and if we were falling back I ordered 'Up five', meaning 5 rpm on the diesel engines. If we veered a bit left I called to the helmsman 'Starboard a point' and vice versa. If I got things wrong an angry *Aldis* flashed from the Commodore and my signaller read: "He says England expects you to keep station. At least for some of the time."

If the signaller picked up a message that was too difficult for me to deal with I had to wake up the Skipper or Jimmy-The-One; on no account was I to let it be known that a pongo was running the ship.

In exchange for doing all this work for them I made the skipper promise that they would teach me how to navigate. I believed that all naval officers were superb navigators and it was a science that intrigued me. Skip delegated Jimmy-The-One to be my tutor and he detailed Subby for the job, but lessons could not begin because they could not find the *Admiralty Tables*, without which navigation was out of the question. Being wavy-navy, they did not really know how to navigate themselves. It was such a short voyage that we reached our destination before the missing volume was found propping up the gammy leg of the wardroom table!

It was a wonderful interlude and we became very firm friends and they knew that, like me, they were in reality civilians doing a wartime job. Covertly they regarded me in awe when they knew what I had been through and I admired their courage, pushing this old tub across strange oceans and landing on hostile beaches. They could not understand my easy mastery of sixty bearded ruffians and said that they could never face the mud and shooting of our job. Like the tank crews it was a case of to each his own!

The LCT moored alongside a stone mole that projected well out into the shallow coastal waters from the town of Semarang and it was obviously a long march into the town itself across the raised causeway. We had taken our time unloading stores, glad to have the firm land beneath our feet after days in the rolling ship. The first Gurkha companies began to move off, and in their disciplined way formed platoon files left and right of the exposed causeway as they trudged inland. I left the Jemadar unloading stores with the main platoon and joined the leading infantry with a section of sappers in case we were needed. Secretly I was keen to see what the place was like. Rifles were slung casually over shoulders, and some Gurkhas carried them by the barrel, the wrong way round, in the manner of seasoned soldiers when they do not expect trouble.

The heart-chilling *tacker-tacker* of a machine gun shattered the hot afternoon air. The causeway ran as straight as a ruler across the mangrove swamp to the tree-fringed mainland and then took a sharp right turn into the main street of the town. Facing along the mole was a stone blockhouse and from firing slits in the heavy walls came a steady and accurate hail of small arms fire. The experienced little Gurkhas were down and into position at once and answering with everything they had, which was not much, because we only carried a few rounds in our pouches. There was hardly any cover and we were running out of ammunition, with our dead and wounded crumpled on the embankments. It was unbelievable. We had landed in Malaya a few weeks earlier, with one up the spout and bayonets fixed, with artillery and mortar support and found no enemy; now we had just walked cheerfully up the sunlit road, cracking jokes and singing, and straight into this lot. We had not even brought our artillery to Java.

Face down in the dust with machine-gun bullets rippling along the roadside was unpleasantly similar to the Battle of the Tiddim Road more than a year before. Except that this was supposedly peacetime! It was the feeling that a Formula I driver might experience if told at the end of a gruelling race, "Sorry, chum! We've decided to start the Grand Prix all over again!"

A runner went back to the ships to report and collect a few boxes of ammunition, some grenades and a mortar or two. The six-foot-tall infantry commander, Major Dunkerley, known as Dunk, ruefully showed me a bullet hole in the middle of his Gurkha hat. He towered over me and was always mocking my short stature, but I was quick to point out that if I was a long streak like him I would probably have had one between the eyes by now!

Who the hell were we fighting? Reinforcements came up but we were constricted on the narrow embankment until the mainland was reached. The first thought was that they could be insurgent freedom fighters. With a loud-hailer we tried English, Dutch, Urdu, Javanese and Malay, but they continued to fire on us from their cunningly manned positions. Somebody suggested trying Japanese and, with some difficulty, an interpreter was found and pushed forward behind a tree. Immediately all firing stopped! Ten minutes later a small company of Japanese soldiers emerged from the fort, hissing and bowing apologetically to explain what had happened.

The Black Buffaloes under Soekarno were very strong in central Java and, as soon as they heard about the Japanese surrender, they told them that they would now take over the country and establish their independence. This would give them a lead over other parties anxious to gain power. The Japanese had always given lip service to home rule and they allowed themselves to be disarmed, whereupon the Indonesians collected them in the courtyard of the local jail and massacred them wholesale with their own guns. This was graphically described in sweeping Japanese brush strokes made by a dying man dipping his finger in the river of blood and writing on the white-washed prison wall. We found this grim graffiti when we occupied the town and we also found other Japanese soldiers spread out naked on the *aloon aloon* (grassy town square) riveted to the ground by stakes driven through their navels. Some were still alive, crawling with ants, maggots and blowflies. It was our first encounter with Indonesian cruelty.

Major Kido, a very fine Japanese officer, had been quick to sense the wave of madness that was sweeping the land. He had escaped with a small number of unarmed prisoners and with sticks, stones and anything else they could find they had overpowered armed extremists, repossessed a few guns and begun a systematic reprisal. Their force had grown as they liberated more of their men and these aggressive and highly trained soldiers, calling themselves 'The Kido Butai' (Kido's Battalion), had swept through the town to occupy the blockhouse down by the harbour. Then we arrived. They had thought that our squat troops in jungle green were an organized Indonesian force and had fired upon us.

We moved ashore and occupied Semarang at Brigade strength. We disarmed Major Kido's force and took them prisoner, which was the job we had come to do.

The 23rd Indian Division was now widely dispersed, with their HQ and 1 Brigade occupying Batavia and Bandoeng in the west, 49 Brigade in the east at Soerbaja and 37 Brigade in the centre at Semarang. The indigenous population outnumbered us by a thousand to one and once again we were very thin on the ground.

Without company HQ to service our needs I would now have to do all the administrative work myself. Stores, transport, office, rations, sick parades, punishment, materials and planning all fell to me.

"Sahib! Sahib Bahadur!" came the call day and night. "The truck won't start . . . Ganda Singh has fainted . . . We've run out of . . ." and that could mean Mepacrine, goat meat or bullets. I moved from crisis to crisis without the aid of a handbook. I used my common sense: a broken bone needed a splint, a cold engine needed a spark and a sullen Sikh needed understanding in the same way that a mule did.

The civilized beauty of Semarang at first lulled us into a peaceful attitude of mind. It had an alluring Continental/Oriental atmosphere, being an important port with wide tree-shaded streets, canals and bridges like a slice of old Amsterdam. The glass-fronted shops, night clubs, bars and cafés contrasted with the native pasars and kampongs that invaded the European façade and came right into the town centre. The dwellings of the wealthy Dutch stood among gardens and trees on the low hills just inland of the flat coastal plain.

We took whatever we needed. To soldiers who had been used to jungle and wilderness it was a festival. The local people were not interested in the trappings of their former rulers and, although the Japanese had helped themselves, there was much that they had not coveted or bothered about. We moved into airy bungalows, still well equipped with refrigerators, Venetian blinds, fans and furnishings. There was even a Dutch hospital on the hill with X-ray equipment and all facilities.

What car should I have? After the Zipper débâcle we were still very short of vehicles and we helped ourselves from the civilian pool. The former wealth of the colonists was clear in the pedigree names that abounded: Bugatti, Delahaye, Hispano-Suiza, Mercedes and American makes such as Cadillac, Buick and Pontiac. Before settling on my final choice I chopped and changed a lot, by the simple expedient of leaving the car that I was driving in place of a better one when I came across it. I had a big soft-sprung metallic gold Chevrolet convertible for everyday use, a black Buick Straight-Eight for prestige, and my darling Mercedes-Benz tourer with bright red leather upholstery for pleasure. I found this gem on blocks in a garage and spent a lot of time and effort finding the wheels. It was immaculate and had not been on the road since the owner had been deported.

I chose a comfortable bungalow, hiding amongst ornamental trees on a steep suburban hillside, with distant views across the town to the blue sea beyond. We were defensively grouped around Brigade HQ on a series of hillocks, in a good tactical as well as residential situation. My platoon was around me occupying outhouses, garages and neighbouring properties. Because of the threatening hostility we formed our defensive box with care. I ate Sikh, talked Sikh, thought Sikh and enjoyed their company. From time to time I invited myself to an infantry officer's mess for a British meal.

At least money was plentiful! Somewhere way back, in Downing Street or The Hague perhaps, a wise decision was made to bust the local currency. The Japanese had introduced their own worthless paper money and flooded the country with notes, renaming the unit Roepiah in place of the Dutch Guilder. There was even a 5 cent paper note, about the size of a bus ticket, printed on one side only and not enough to buy a loaf. Dai Nippon had no intention of minting metal coinage for a subjugated country and of course the notes had no financial backing. The whole country was trading in this worthless money and we had expected to reintroduce the guilder, bearing Queen Wilhelmina's head, as part of the reinstatement of Dutch government. We were only an interim force and we had no political axe to grind; what happened between the Indonesians and the Dutch was up to them later, when we had gone.

Summoned to Brigade HQ I took my official car, the big black Buick.

"Ah! There you are, Johnnie!" The brigadier was in a jocular mood. "Got a nice little job for a crook like you!" He pointed through the window to my Al Capone-style limousine and added, "It should go rather well with your gangster image. 'Scarface' Johnnie sounds about right!"

He gave me the task of going through the town and blowing every safe I could find to bring back all the Japanese Roepiah. All the banks, societies, insurance and other empty office premises were lined along Main Street Semarang and off I went with a truck full of explosives and a few men. I started with the Town Hall. Despite my extensive demolition experience this was entirely new to me; I was definitely short on Peter-blowing skills. Like a man who has built himself a reputation as a lion tamer in his local bar would not wish to have a live audience when facing his first big cat, I wanted to be alone as I learned my new trade.

I studied the robust steel doors of the safe in the Mayor's Parlour and began to pack explosive here and there, linking the charges with f.i.d. (fuze instantaneous detonating) to make them all blow together. We withdrew from the room to fire and the result was dramatic. Teak double doors, twice the height of a man, crashed outwards into the corridor, windows blew into the street below and tattered smoking shreds of red and gold velvet drapes, like the curtains at Covent Garden Opera House, hung smouldering in shreds. Plaster dust settled over everything and the only thing that had survived the shattering explosion was the old black safe!

I began to learn by trial and error. In a British unit I might have found a shifty-eyed, experienced safe-cracker to guide me through the principles of the age-old battle between safe-maker and safe-breaker. After my sledgehammer start I came down to shrewdly placed nutcracker charges that blew the interlocking bolts and not the room they were in.

How the money rolled in! I filled three-ton trucks with paper money and delivered my haul to the brigade paymaster. The object was to issue lots of it to the troops, to flood the market with it and thus break the spurious currency. The paymaster, being an accountant, devised proforma acquittance rolls and made every soldier sign for it every week. Files of soldiers plonked their thumbprints against their names and collected considerable sums of worthless money.

As my safe-cracking abilities improved I brought in more and more loads of the stuff and the lads strolled the bazaars like millionaires. The price of an egg rocketed from one cent to a hundred Roepiah within weeks. We organized an inflation that would put a present-day economist to shame!

There was a certain rough justice about it. Collaborators, from whores to spivs, had been stashing the stuff away throughout the occupation and we were now rendering it worthless. The freedom fighters realized that there was more to running a nation than murdering white women and children and shouting 'Merdeka!' We soldiers wearied of too much wealth. We already had enough for our spartan needs and no amount of money would buy a ticket home! We could not amass loads of possessions or take them out with us and the unattended Dutch shops were stocked with free goods for the taking.

I was on a trip through the town centre. The sun blazed down from the blue sky, towering castles of cumulus rose over the Java Sea and I drove a Dodge 15cwt at a cooling pace, with the windscreen down and a section of Sikhs in the back. We admired the innate serenity of the beautiful native girls, carrying their brown bodies proudly under the brilliant colours of their sarongs and tending the market stalls. I was singing to myself and the men were chattering happily in the back. After our task was done we turned back along the flat tree-lined boulevard for home. Above and beyond the town centre I could see the hillside houses among the trees where we lived. The clouds were turning into sulphurous towers of dark nimbus rearing threateningly against the blue and the daily storm was not far off. The sparkle began to die out of the day.

I saw an Indonesian sentry in his paramilitary get-up, a hotchpotch of Japanese and Dutch uniforms, standing guard outside one of their pseudo-government establishments. He might have been Black or Red Buffaloes and he was of schoolboy age. As I drove along he unslung his rifle and deliberately raised the weapon to draw a bead on my head.

"*Hilo mat!*" (Keep still!) I yelled to the lads in the back, as I sensed their aggressive reaction.

Our orders were that we were never to fire unless fired upon. Not a reassuring instruction when you are cruising at a gentle pace in a soft jungle hat across the sights of a loaded rifle that is aimed between your eyes by a child maniac. I could almost read the telepathic message he was sending: "I could drop you stone dead, you white pig!"

141

And if he did it I knew, and he knew, that the most awful bloodshed would start that very day over my dead body. The lowering storm sky and the dark eye of death looking into mine symbolized the tautness of the atmosphere in Java that day. A small spark was all that was needed to explode it.

Not wishing to be that spark I slowed imperceptibly, steered ever so slightly towards the sentry and aggressively locked eyes with him. The incident passed as he sheepishly dropped his rifle, grinning naughtily like the cheeky kid that he was, and the sweat ran down my back. Inflamed by a dogma that he did not fully understand, irresponsible and immature, he burned with illogical hatred and he was a menace.

That night I overheard the men telling the others how old Chha-Chha, cool as ice, had met this threat head on. I loved it!

The very next afternoon a spark exploded the heavy vapour of hatred. It happened a stone's throw from my incident of the previous day. A truck full of Gurkhas came to the pasar at the top of Main Street and, as they drove slowly past the bright stalls, the Sathis were making prurient remarks about the pretty girls. Suddenly the women flung themselves flat on the ground and a row of dark-faced men rose above them and poured automatic fire straight at the truck. With the practised speed of trained infantry the survivors tumbled from the truck to avenge their dead comrades, but the market girls rose again and foiled their line of fire whilst the attackers evaporated into the crowd.

This was war! The Javanese were always a baffling enemy. There was a Japanese-trained nucleus of real soldiers with modern weapons. Young boys, rascals and bandits had rapidly swelled their ranks and some had uniforms, but most did not. We might be attacking a cleverly sited machine-gun nest or a few schoolboys armed with magic symbols and witchcraft and no guns at all. The majority of the population were decent peaceable folk, but they were threatened and blackmailed into aggressive acts by the fire-eaters. Lonely houses were selected to sow mines at random on the roads; we were constantly sniped at from kampongs; a whole platoon of enemy troops could disappear into a village and when we arrived they were sitting in civilian clothes on doorsteps mocking us; the bazaar ladies had been stage-managed. The Buffaloes were capable of atrocious acts of torture to browbeat people into giving support to their cause.

142

For our part we sometimes longed for the bad old days when there really was a war on and we were fighting a recognizable foe that wore a uniform, stayed in it and fought from fixed positions. To this day I feel pangs of conscience over the innocent people that I must have shot in defence against the evil ones.

I wrote home angrily:

'Why does everything happen to me? In the whole wide world there is only one brigade of one allied division that is still fighting! Mine!'

Before that letter had left the island rumours began to come through that there was fighting in the west where 1 Brigade and Div HQ were and that 49 Brigade in Soerbaja at the eastern extremity of the island was under threat.

It had been a short peace for us!

Chapter 13

WAR IN PEACE

Only ourselves remain
To face the naked days

The General Service Medal is greatly coveted by regular soldiers because it is awarded for action when there is no war declared. Palestine after the First World War, and Northern Ireland more recently are examples of campaigns where men could earn this purple and green ribbon. It was one we could have done without and our version bore the clasp 'S.E. Asia 1945–1946' and relatively few were issued. For those of us who were not regulars we would rather have finished the job quietly and gone home. Any active service soldier will agree that insurgency, keeping the peace and such other forms of dirty work are more stressful than real war.

At the end of October 1945 a cruel and unprovoked attack was made on our 49 Brigade group in Soerbaja, and a great number of our boys who had survived the war in Burma perished that night. The Mahratta infantry battalion was nearly wiped out, as was our sister Field Company (71 Bengal Sappers), the men being massacred in the streets by vastly superior numbers of Javanese. This was the characteristic, the hallmark of warfare out there where a very small number of highly trained and experienced troops faced thousands of enemy. We were never defeated in straight conflict, only by overwhelming numbers, treachery or ambush. Brigadier Mallaby was murdered in his car whilst riding under the white flag to discuss a peaceful truce. The mob also slaughtered a great number of Japanese who had been taken prisoner by our forces. The whole country seethed with bloodshed from end to end.

I was given the job of locating a women's prison camp known to be about an hour's run back into The Highlands, near Magellan and just north of Djokjakarta (also spelt Yogyakarta) which became the seat of the Indonesian president. I climbed 2,500 ft from the coastal plain through country of great beauty, past terraced gardens, banana groves, quinine, tea and rubber plantations and a verdant mixture of forest and farmland, with breathtaking vistas back down steep valleys to the blue sea. Far away across the plateau columns of smoke rose from the snowcapped volcanoes.

Java has an ethereal quality that an artist would call aerial perspective. It was November, just before the wet west monsoon, (there are two monsoon seasons) and each afternoon there were thunderstorms that washed the air clean. Every panorama looked as though it had been set in lead crystal, which made the colours sharper, the distances bluer, the skies more dramatic and the picture vibrant.

What a contrast in the women's camp! The loosely wired compound was fenced with bamboo and grass screens and the rickety double gates were clad with woven matting. There were no Japanese guards, no friendly troops, and the 6,500 women lay wide open to marauders. The Indonesians had ignored them up to that time, but hatred of the Dutch colonialists was spreading so rapidly across the country that they were highly vulnerable. The organization called RAPWI (Relief Agency for Prisoners of War and Internees) had been set up across the Far East to help such war victims, but they were overwhelmed and disorganized in Java. There were so many refugees and we were so few. I did not like the look of it at all.

When we arrived in the country there were at least one hundred thousand Dutch and Eurasian women incarcerated in such camps and they were dying at the rate of about thirty a day. Their captors had either ignored them or committed sadistic acts upon them, and they were starving and crippled by tropical diseases. Bill Slim wrote:

> "There can be no excuse for a nation which as a matter of policy treats its prisoners-of-war in this way, and no honour to an army, however brave, which willingly makes itself an instrument of such inhumanity to the helpless."

I stopped my Jeep at the gate and my men came forward cautiously from the trucks behind. We dragged the flimsy double gates open and drove along the dirt road through the middle of the compound. Closely packed bashas, rough bamboo huts with palm leaf roofs and

145

grass walls, were spaced along both sides of the track. There were women and children everywhere, wandering listlessly about in advanced stages of starvation, degradation and undress. What clothes they had were the tattered remnants of their wardrobes of four years before, children had grown and there was a lot of obvious improvisation. Native scraps of material had been scrounged, the borrowed leavings of the dead were not buried with them and most of the women were almost naked and there was no modesty left to them.

An open drain ran through the camp parallel to the road we were on. In the rains it might have been a busy culvert, but now it was a foetid trickle. Over it, without pretence of decorum and, disregarding our gaze, women and children were seen to squat from time to relieve themselves. The stench was awful. Our arrival had provoked no more than an apathetic stir. They were unable to grasp who these swarthy soldiers in battle green were or why they were there; it struck no chord in their tired memories. Weary faces slowly turned our way, loads were set down and backs straightened, stick-like persons with haggard faces gawped at us. They did not see us as the end to their sufferings.

I left my Jeep, hitched my Sten gun nervously into the ready position and stood irresolute, one white man amongst thousands of women, who had not seen my like since their own men had been driven away. Two women, who were somehow more purposeful and dignified than the herd, cautiously approached me from one of the huts. They said something in Dutch and repeated with a Scottish accent, "Who are you?"

In a few seconds I explained that we were the Allied forces and that my bearded soldiers were Indian Army Sikhs and we had come to give them succour.

"Take a wee tip, laddie." The pretty thin face smiled mischievously like a shaft of sunlight across a wintery dawn. "Don't stray too far from your big black soldiers! There's women here who have not seen a clean white man for a very long time!" She inclined her head towards a big-boned blonde lady who was squatting unconcernedly and watering the cabbages "And some of them have slipped back quite a way!"

"Will ye no' take a cup o' coffee?" her friend asked. "Ye'll be all right wi' us!"

I followed them to their shack where forty women were living in a space not much bigger than a railway carriage. The strong odour of immured womankind assailed my nostrils in the closely packed shed and it reminded me strangely of the rows of Japanese dead in Tamu. In a way they were the living dead. It saddened me to see the way so many had reverted almost to animals after the years of deprivation. There were a few males among them, Dutch boys who had reached puberty and matured beyond their years during the long imprisonment. I found them frightening.

I did not want to rob these deprived creatures of one pinch of their valuable coffee, which I did not really need, and yet to them it was their first step back towards civilized behaviour:

"Dinna' bother," the Scottish lady said. "It's only burnt breadcrumbs!"

I sat on the step in the morning sun and took morning coffee with two wonderful women who had not let things slip. They were the wives of Dutch administrators and had lived in Java for years.

"Husbands?" they said, "God knows where they've been taken, but they are in His hands! We may never see them again!" She held an emaciated girl with dark hair against her and looked lost.

"Ye'd best be going!" She nodded towards the growing throng that had begun to gather about their door. "It really could be dangerous for you! There is no telling how they might react, or if they will go berserk when the truth strikes home. We'll prepare them for your return. Off you go and get us help!"

I made a quick assessment of numbers, sickness and food state. What was their most urgent need? They could not say, they had nothing; very little food, even water was in short supply and they were worse off since their Japanese guards had abandoned them. Their most urgent need in my eyes was protection. Their former warders had treated them viciously, imposing savage punishments for minor offences, but what might happen now if a mob of freedom maniacs came amongst them with their corkscrew-bladed *kris*? (Indonesian knives, often poisoned). Tied spread-eagled in the noon sun could be a mild penance compared to what the cruel locals might devise for these hated white women.

I sped back to report and immediately an infantry platoon with a truck laden with fresh food and water went out to protect them until they could be brought back to the comparative safety of the town.

I spent three or four frenetic days in the camp working for my ladies. I set up sanitation, cooking facilities and whatever small comforts I could devise. I found them clothing and utensils. At least I did not have to find sanitary protection for them in their debilitated condition. I had been a little ashamed of their semi-nudity and animal behaviour in front of my Sikh soldiers, but I need not have been. The men were compassionate and full of solicitude for the suffering womenfolk.

Six and a half thousand is an awful lot of women! Talking in Dutch, Javanese, Malay and broken English I listened to them all. The Dutch *mevrouws* all had terrible tales to tell and described how the Japanese had taken their young daughters away to the brothels. They were always trying to corner me, in the hope that I would treat them as a special case and get lorries out more quickly to return them to civilization. It was a task for the Dutch administration, with which we always had trouble. In the early days their authoritarian demeanour gave us a glimpse of how they might have been as colonial administrators. We had felt pity for poor little Holland when the German jackboot fell across their necks, but we often met a jack-booting mentality out there when they advised us to shoot a few Indos and restore the country to normal.

I must not give the wrong impression. The first bureaucrats we encountered were not necessarily who or what they purported to be. It was easy for an impostor or a spurious official to usurp powers to which he had no claim. The real officials were still either in prison camps or too ill to return, and fresh competent staff from Holland were slow to arrive because of shipping shortages.

One thing I could give them was plenty of money. I had my own secret hoard of Japanese Roepiah from my safe-cracking days and this allowed them to trade with nearby pasars. I also did a bit of looting on their behalf and fetched in loads of things ripped from the back of closed shops. Java was always a topsy-turvy land of contrasts and paradoxes. The climate swung from tropical beaches to snow-capped mountains, hot sunshine alternated with threshing rain storms, violent death stalked amidst flawless beauty, rich European commodities were found among native slums and here was I, a soldier, giving fake money and underclothes to pretty women for no favours received!

In the camps the older boys kept a low profile. In four years some of them had reached precocious manhood, but to be seen to be strong meant deportation to the railway. The women had shielded them and they had obviously been of value to the camp, but I did not find them easy to accept. One truculent blonde boy asked me angrily when the useless Englanders were going to do something. They were keen to get a few natives strung up; they were certainly angry young men, waspish and old beyond their years.

I would have gladly exchanged all my grumbling Gretchens for one English girl, be she barmaid or nun, and it was a great relief when they passed out of my care and were taken away to safety. Safety? Nowhere was safe any more in the midst of such hateful and nerve-racking civil disorder. The first two weeks of the west monsoon washed away the sunshine and the overcast of bitterness and fear overshadowed the joy that we had felt when we first saw this place. I never saw the Scottish ladies again, but gradually the half-human scarecrows from the camps began to be seen about town well dressed and bearing no resemblance to the degenerate creatures I had first discovered.

Death was all about us. One afternoon the Sikhs captured five sneak assassins in my bungalow garden. They were squat dark-skinned youths, savage in appearance and truculently aggressive. One carried an American police Colt automatic with a clip of 0.45 dum-dum bullets. I had not seen these ghastly slugs before, cut and nicked so that they spread on impact and tore away half a man's back on exit. We also took from them a superb Luger pistol and two fine kris. The Japanese *Kempei Tai* (Military Police) looked after Indonesian prisoners on our behalf. I passed my party into their hands with the doctored bullets, and they nodded understandingly. They were professional soldiers and knew that such bullets were against International Law, but later I felt ashamed at the cruelties they probably inflicted on the natives. These police were from the force whose men had been massacred in the same courtyard a few weeks earlier and they knew no pity.

The 'wait until fired upon' rule cost the lives of too many officers and our white faces picked us out as we led our Indian troops. To the Indonesians we looked like Dutchmen, even though we had no enthusiasm for the Dutch cause. Before it was over we would lose 1,400 wounded and 400 killed in Java and it was a great strain on young men who had survived the siege of Imphal and welcomed the Japanese surrender. We were greatly relieved when this edict was rescinded and we were allowed to defend ourselves as we thought fit.

Random mine-laying and ambushes on the roads became a nightmare. As the different factions grew in strength and capability they put increased pressure on local people to sow mines indiscriminately, and to form into guerrilla bands and set traps. We used the roads extensively for supplies, ferrying wounded, bringing in female prisoners and for getting sappers to where they were needed. I was always in demand and always vulnerable:

"Get up to Ambarawa, Johnnie!" or "Would you nip down to the docks, Sapper?" Or out to the airfield, or up to Magellan, or report to 3/3rd or go and sort out the electrics at the hospital! I was covering more than a hundred miles a day and I always had to look at each new problem myself before delegating the work to my men. I was the only engineer in town.

I decided that I needed a permanent bodyguard and who better than Fauji Singh M.M.! This rangy character who was so slick with a Sten gun might possibly save me from losing my head. In fact he would have made an American President feel safe; he had a nose like a Pointer for trouble. I was always armed and, even indoors, I kept my Luger to hand, sleeping with my boots on and the lanyard round my wrist.

Sudden death was in the air. My smart clean bungalow, with crisply gravelled drive, pot plants and European comforts, was in reality a death trap. We adopted the 'Al Capone two-step' on entering a room, which meant that we stepped quickly to one side to avoid being silhouetted in the opening. Shutters were invaluable and to snap on the light before closing them was to die. Even at parties or during conversation we automatically dropped to our knees and crawled past uncurtained windows, even in daytime. Many died from taking a turn out into the garden, or taking a Dutch bath.

I slept on the floor in the corner of a room, leaving my Dutch wife deceptively bolstering my image in the bed. I never stood or sat with my back to a window, or in a lighted room without curtains, or moved in silhouette between two opposite windows. Local natives who had been servants in the houses at one time knew every room and cranny. For twenty-four hours a day I concentrated on self-preservation; I grew feral and cat-like and took no risks. We were even more alert than we had been on the Shenam Saddle.

Beddowes and Ted were repatriated and went home, and Bob was now my O.C. but he was 300 miles away in Bandoeng, with Harry as his adjutant. I spoke to them each evening by radio. I was the only one of the three still to be a subaltern and in daily action and I told Bob that I went about "fully loaded and half-cocked day and night." I told them that my motto was *Semper in excretum* . . . meaning "Always in the shit," adding in Latin "Only the depth varies". From overhearing my radio calls the whole division gradually adopted my phrase "Only the depth varies" to describe the mess that we always seemed to be in.

"You're not getting jumpy, are you?" Bob's voice crackled over the air.

"Not really! Except that when a car backfired this morning I poured a clip of bullets into a bullock cart!"

Heavily armed gangs of men moved freely about the town in increasing numbers. Driving back from the docks one afternoon I crossed the town square. The straight main street ended in a small square where the town hall stood and then the road twisted up the hill to the suburban quarter, where we had our billets. It was always a hot spot and I no longer cruised around in my limousines; I had seen too many of my chums lying face down in their own blood as they tried to leave their saloon cars under fire. We rode in Dodge trucks, with no canopy, windscreen flat and an all-round defensive view. Arjan Singh, a laconic lad with an engaging smile, was driving and I was riding shotgun on the front seat. Fauji and several others sat alertly in the back with guns pointing outwards. All of a sudden the chatter of a light Japanese machine gun swept across us. Arjan did a superb skid-turn to face the gunmen and we tumbled out to fire back

We went in with all guns blazing like an old American gangster movie. We were always a lot better than them and we attacked a party of about twenty uniformed Black Buffaloes on the steps and behind the columns of the Episcopal Church. Our guns splattered them as we advanced across the open square and they broke and ran leaving two dead and several wounded in the road. We took their wounded up to the hospital and HQ later questioned them. It turned out that Soekarno himself was leader of the party, the man who would eventually become President of all Indonesia. I often wonder if by missing him that afternoon I missed a chance to change the course of history.

Such street skirmishes were always messy affairs and our superior training always dominated. It was a dirty business all the time and it became dirtier, and in the faeces of sedition we became besmirched. That's how we felt when we found schoolboys, old men and pretty women among the slain. The Repoeblik Indonesie under the red and white flag began with horrific deeds of violence. Ordinary decent folk were made to commit acts that were foreign to the nature of this beautiful and peaceful race of people.

An order came out to say that if shots were fired upon us from a native village, or any quarter of the town, that area had to be burnt to the ground. That same day a sniper fired on our Brigadier from the kampong that lay across the valley from my bungalow. Demolition was a sapper job, but this one I detested – rousting everyone out of their homes, elderly, sick and nursing mothers and setting fire to the settlement.

When we first landed in Semarang, after the little bit of bother with Major Kido's battalion, we thought that we had found a pleasant and easy job. At first in this pretty coastal resort, about the size of Southampton, I was in demand as an engineer to add to the amenities:

"Hey! Sapper! How about getting the town swimming baths working?"

"Let's fix up a dance hall before the fräuleins come out of the prison camps."

"Couldn't we find some dinghies and start holding sailing races?"

These were the kind of jolly jobs that occupation forces sought to enjoy, and it was a peacetime outlook. Thoughts of fun soon evaporated as forty million people told us how much they detested our presence. They cut us off from the docks. They cut us off from the airfield. They cut the roads that came into the port from inland. Once more we were besieged, withdrawn into a tight little ring without any supply routes and dependent upon airdrops. Not only were we surrounded on the hill of Semarang, but we also had infantry out of town at Ambarawa and Magellan who were now cut off from us. It appeared to be much more threatening and dangerous even than Manipur had been.

We were in such deep trouble right across Java and so outnumbered, with losses mounting on every hand, that they sent in our old friends of 5 Div. Once again we were heartened to see their Ball of Fire Div sign, just as we had been when they flew in to reinforce us in the Imphal siege. They went straight to Soerbaja and took over the eastern end of the island and were soon actively engaged in the situation.

The Repoeblik Indonesie Radio Station opened at Magellan and on the night of 17 November 1945 the 'Voice of Free Indonesia' announced:

"Merdeka! This is the last night of peace! By seven o'clock tomorrow morning all European, Eurasian and other non-Indonesians will be dead! Every foreign man, woman and child on the island will be killed tonight, and the British and Indian Forces will flee for their lives!"

There were large Indonesian forces everywhere, some in good uniforms and well equipped, some in paramilitary dress and other mobs armed with knives and cudgels. Mindful of the way our men had been overrun and massacred the week before in Soerbaja and of Brigadier Mallaby's murder, our commander, Brigadier Bethel, had no intention of being caught unawares. He called for his 'O' Group – infantry, sappers, signals and other support units – and he also sent for Major Kido.

We were so hopelessly outnumbered that it was ridiculous to have fighting men guarding Japanese prisoners, who would all be massacred with us if the mobs broke through. We were not only on the point of annihilation ourselves, but we were also responsible for the safety of Dutch, Eurasian, Chinese and Japanese and for all the helpless women and children caught up in this maelstrom. The Brigadier put it to Major Kido, as the senior and most effective Japanese officer, that either we fought together or died together.

He was delighted. He would love to have his sword back, he would love to fight and kill a few more Javanese in the interests of us all. He had seen his countrymen murdered in the jail and crucified on the aloon aloon. Our former detested foe was now a staunch ally! It was a brave decision by the Brigadier and it undoubtedly saved us all. Numerical superiority could only be countered by highly trained troops and our Gurkhas backed by the sons of Nippon were a force to respect.

We could imagine questions being tabled in The House back home: "Is the hon. member aware that British forces in Java have enlisted the aid of our former enemies to reinstate Dutch Imperial Rule?"

It was the very stuff of which newspapers are made and politicians destroyed. Some very fine careers were in jeopardy of ruin and undoubtedly heads would roll. What we did not anticipate was that, after the Brigadier had been dealt with, they would hide the facts and that, even to this day, the event would be cloaked in silence.

It had been thought that the task of collecting prisoners would not need the use of heavy guns and we had left all our artillery behind in Malaya. The Royal Navy sent in the Fifth Cruiser squadron and the two cruisers, HMS *Sussex* and HMS *Norfolk*, stood close inshore to give us support with their 8" guns. This was a new kind of gunfire to us. After the high lobbing of shells by our 25 pounders these flat-trajectory armour-piercing shells parted our hair as they screamed above our heads and their star shells were the brightest and longest-lasting we had ever seen.

We swung into action to establish our hold over the besieged port. Before midnight we took up our positions along the start line. In expectation of the massacre that they had threatened on the radio we stood-to all night and attacked at dawn. This was what we all needed to escape from the tension of recent events, to get down to doing what we did best. No more need to wait until you had a bullet through the eye before you could retaliate. We went in all guns blazing and swept everything before us. The naval guns cracked devastatingly as shells that had been designed to sink a pocket battleship tore into the Buffaloes' HQ. Air strikes swooped low over the besiegers, so close to our own lines that two of Major Kido's men were killed.

"Was my face red?" Sandy Meikle told me later. "I called up our Hurribombers and we knocked a couple of Japs over with our own planes!" He grinned. "But Kido didn't care, he just hissed and bowed, told me not to worry and that it was a risk of war. He also said that our air strike was very good!"

We had tanks and as they rumbled along the pretty boulevards we learned the new art of street fighting. We had not been trained at doorway-hopping and house-clearing, but if we were not very skilled at first our opponents were worse. They had proved to be masters of skulduggery and acts of murder, but could not face hardened troops moving purposefully in a coordinated way. Battle noises echoed about the valleys and hills, across the coastal plain, through streets and kampongs and it went on for two days and nights.

The Kido Butai was very good indeed, but we already knew that. They obeyed every order they were given but refused to make any tactical suggestions of their own.

"How do you think we should take that strong point?" a colonel asked Kido, but all he would say was, "You give orders please!"

We had collected scattered Japanese groups from outlying parts and had a great many more under command than just Kido's original force; we also had their police force and administrative personnel. We used the majority of them for administrative tasks and to guard vulnerable people and places or consolidate our gains. Whatever they were doing they were on our side and valuable allies.

One night we had the dubious pleasure of seeing the Japanese panic when an Indonesian commando got among them whilst they were resting. Our infantry had to go to the rescue and afterwards our former enemies were most complimentary about the Gurkhas.

Our gentle neutrality on arrival had been transformed to a dark hatred by the deeds we had witnessed. We knew only too well the trade marks of these cruel people; babies disembowelled, women ripped open, voodoo murders, torture, plunder, burning and thuggery. Our battalion group that was up in the Highlands south of the town fought their way back, reopening the road to come down to join us. We retook the captured airfield and carved our way down Main Street to repossess the docks. We cleared the European area and withdrew to our hillside bungalows from where we could look down across the smoking town which was now, precariously, in our hands once more.

My lads were jingling with loot when they returned to our lines. After the stringency of jungle warfare it was a new experience for them to move through civilized streets and fight from shops and offices and they had found all sorts of things. They did not go for the artefacts that a British Tommy would collect, but preferred fancy pistols, knives and native baubles. They collected the rude metal badges of the freedom fighters, the trish-trash of equipment that, to them, were battle tokens to take home to their villages to be passed round and admired one day.

In this topsy-turvy land the unexpected always happened. The smart European shops on Main Street stood wide open to all takers with shattered windows and gaping doors, but neither our troops nor the local people appeared to want Western things. There was a large office supplies shop with stacks of new typewriters untouched, dress shops and furniture stores unpillaged. Food shortages were serious across the land because the Japanese had always commandeered

155

whatever they wanted without making any payment and this had discouraged the farmers from growing surplus crops. The rioting and collapse of the currency had made things worse. The local people smashed their way into the dock warehouses and cleared out stores filled with flour, sugar, rice and other staples.

Going back through the town was a hateful experience. The lovely oriental jewel that had been Semarang when we first arrived was now despoiled. Burnt-out shells of buildings, bullet-spattered walls, cars crashed drunkenly into dykes with their dead hanging grotesquely from them and everywhere the stench of death and burning.

I had to clear the road to the docks and make sure that there were no mines on the mole. We were quick to take advantage of our repossession of airfield and docks to get supplies in whilst we could, and the LCTs were coming into harbour as I arrived. There, tying up alongside, were my dear old wavy-navy chums who called a greeting to their tame Pongo and reached for the gin-an-pinkers.

"Is there anything you want?" I asked them and explained the open-shopping arrangements in town. "Just name it and I'll see what I can do!"

They went into a huddle and I heard muttered protestations. "He'll never do that!" and "That's too much to expect!" So I chipped in, "Come on! Out with it, tell Uncle what you want for Christmas!"

They were embarrassed when they admitted that their heart's desire was a three-piece suite: "Y'know – a comfy settee and a couple of armchairs, that sort of thing!"

"Cut or uncut moquette?" I asked airily. "And any particular shade?"

I nipped back along the causeway with my big truck and turned into Main Street where a European furniture store stood wide open with shattered windows. Half an hour later my navy friends were out on the tank deck of their ship laughing for joy and bouncing up and down on a new maroon and gold three-piece!

To the ship's crew it meant that when they were back in a civilized port they could have soft lights and sweet music under a canvas awning over the flat deck and entertain a few pretty girls! When they were at sea their lounge suite was stowed away at the back of the tank deck behind the awning! It was, of course, stuff that nobody else wanted. Nothing for profit or reward, except a smoke and a bit of friendship. Barter was the order of the day.

"I'll give you my car for a portable typewriter!"

"O.K. Done!"

It was no more criminal than my career as a safe cracksman. There was a plethora of goodies everywhere without owners. The local people did not want any of it, the original Dutch owners had gone, we could not ship anything home nor take it out of the island, but at least we could enjoy a few comforts and a bit of fun whilst it lasted. The monetary system had virtually collapsed and there was nothing in its place. The Indonesian Freedom Fighters had split into several factions, all jockeying for power to become the first political leaders of the new country. At the end of the day Soekarno would seize control, but that was by no means determined in those early days and we benefited from their internal disagreements.

Whilst all this was going on all our service pay was building up somewhere in a distant account – we only had to survive until we could draw it.

Chapter 14

MAKESHIFT BOROUGH ENGINEER

This is the midnight – let no star
Delude us – dawn is very far.

We still had responsibilities for inland prison camps and returned in battalion strength to Ambarawa and Magellan in The Highlands where a full-scale battle developed. The fighting troops had to be supplied along the one treacherous road that climbed through the mountains from the coast and then sprawled across the plateau. Running supply convoys through to the forward troops became a nightmare. The whole country was our enemy and civilian house-holders sowed mines indiscriminately wherever they fancied. Clearing a minefield was a routine sapper task and it was child's play compared to finding these sporadic placings. They used old Japanese mines and laid them badly, sometimes even upside down, but the convoys could not go at walking pace for the sappers to sweep every step along the road.

At first I tried to do what we had done when we had driven with the tanks down the Tamu road, by riding in the lead vehicle and keeping a sharp lookout. This turned out to be hopeless. We were constantly stopping for cowpats, fallen leaves and potholes, always with the chilling feeling in the gut that if there was a mine there might also be a machine gun or sniper covering it. This proved to be costly in lives and trucks and I decided to design a special leading vehicle. I purloined civilian and old Japanese trucks and stiffened their floors with welded steel plates and sandbags. The pedals were elongated, with a chain sweep to brush the road projecting on a cantilever out in front and we drove ahead of the convoy at a reasonable pace to detonate random mines. We lost a number of old trucks and a few received splinter wounds, but two more of my men won medals from this sport.

158

When the central Java positions inland became untenable the infantry were ordered to withdraw once more into the Semarang garrison. This was a strategical withdrawal and not a retreat, but going backwards is never pleasant. We extricated 'a large female body' from another prison camp before we left and sent lorry loads of sorry-looking women and children down the hill to the coast. The eight-inch shells of HMS *Norfolk* and HMS *Sussex* flattened the town of Ambarawa and the reek of death fingered my nostrils as we prepared booby traps and carried out the last demolitions. At last the OC of 3/10 Gurkhas said, "O.K. Johnnie! That'll do. Let's get the hell out of here!"

I finished off my sapper tasks and went to the head of the convoy on mine-scouting duty. It was good to be on the road again as we moved across the terrorist-infested farmlands, over the edge of the escarpment and down the steep winding road through dense jungle and steep valleys.

A pretty girl with flaxen hair and blue eyes flagged me down like a student hitchhiker. She did not need to thumb nor lift the hem of her summer frock; lone white civilians were dead civilians up there. She seemed ingenuously unaware of peril and my Dutch was insufficient to talk freely with her. Creeping forward, ever alert for ambush and mines, we collected a number of Eurasian and Chinese refugees from the verges; they dared not stay if we were leaving. This was last bus for Semarang and our trucks were soon packed with an odd assortment of civilians.

A sad Chinese family, obviously people of substance, climbed aboard with a pair of magnificent German Shepherd dogs and six puppies. They were expensive pedigree creatures, probably imported from Germany before the war. To pay their fare the owners insisted on giving me the fluffy puppies.

"Keep them, tuan!" they pleaded. "Please! Oh! Please! With you they will be safe and well fed. We have lost everything!"

It was true. The dogs were unlikely to survive the perils that still faced them and in a few hours I had become a dog owner with a pretty blonde girlfriend. Back in town I left the puppies in the lines and set out for a downtown residential area to return Gretchen to her mother. My active imagination envisaged a romance blossoming on this Javanese dungheap; she was very pretty. She insisted that I go indoors and meet Dad, a dapper little Dutch artisan with a white goatee beard

159

who spoke English, and enthusiastically plied me with *Jenevers* from the square green bottle. A black Ambonesian woman moved silently about, setting the table and keeping in the background. Suddenly a very dark-skinned youth bounced through the door, kissed the black lady and father announced, " This is Hans! My other child! Now you have met us all!"

I was staggered. I knew that Eurasians, especially in tropical sunshine, could be deceptive, but how could such a flaxen little Dutch doll have such a black mother?

A real love affair awaited me back in the billets. The six baby Alsatians tumbled about like woolly balls and they too were a mixture of blonde, black and brown. I was not sure what I was going to do with them, but it turned out to be no problem at all. Every soldier wants a pet and, after picking the best dog for myself, I rapidly placed the other five with officers around the brigade. I could have disposed of twenty!

I named mine 'Sathi', the very special Gurkhali word for my chum, my mate, my pal, my dog for the days to come.

When 5 Div took over the eastern end of the island the remnants of 49 Brigade that had been decimated in Soerbaja came to join us, but their sappers had been almost wiped out. I was still the only engineer officer and indeed the only civil engineer in central Java. I faced a military task that would have occupied two full field companies, say fourteen officers and two hundred men, and, with only sixty Sikhs and a few oddments, I was very overloaded.

I realized that someone above and behind me appreciated my situation when a Scottish technical sergeant turned up at the airfield. Jock was a godsend and took over all the day to day bonnet-lifting, pump-priming, engine-tickling chores to keep things running. Best of all, I now had someone with whom to discuss technicalities and work out problems.

The town services were my biggest concern. Jungle soldiers never had to bother with municipal problems, but here, in this urban situation, I was surrounded by thousands of refugees, female ex-prisoners, Japanese prisoners, and troops all requiring running water, electricity and other services.

I sought the help of anybody I could muster and rounded up some former employees of the public works departments. They were nice, helpful artisans, mostly half-breeds, who would have been invaluable

160

had they survived. As soon as the freedom fighters saw them working for us they either strung them up or knifed them, and those that escaped retribution soon disappeared. I did not blame them for deserting; they had their families living in town and did not want grief.

I went back to the Town Hall, still a little ashamed about the shattered Mayor's Parlour, and found the Engineer's drawing office. My pre-war training came to my aid. Working drawings of the water, electricity and sewerage networks were all neatly filed, exactly like a municipal office back home, and I soon had all the knowledge that I needed.

We were cut off, there was no doubt about that, and we had only a tenuous hold on the airfield and docks. The Indonesian forces had established their HQ at Magellan and they encircled us on the landward side. We were literally between the devils and the deep blue sea. To my astonishment the municipal plans showed that our electricity supply came in on the national grid and that our water supply came through two large pipelines from the Highlands that we had just abandoned.

The Brigadier was taken aback when I put my engineering appraisal before him. Pointing to his electric ceiling fan I said, "You must be the first military commander in history to draw power from the foe!"

"What d'you mean, Johnnie?" He looked at me quizzically.

"This town is fed from the 110 volt Central Java grid and if you go to our forward positions at Oengaren you will see the pylons stretching away into enemy-held territory!"

I offered him a drop of water in his Scotch and raised my own glass: "And this water comes down from reservoirs near Amberawa! We'd better have some Indonesian money ready to pay our bills because they'll cut us off if we try to pay in NICAs!" (This acronym was also used for the new Indonesian Dutch guilders.)

"A toast to sheer ignorance, Sir!"

It was true. We were being supplied by our enemy and I was not sure why. It could have been ignorance, or possibly because there was a very large Indonesian population in town, or because they did not know how to isolate us, or simply because it had not yet occurred to them. Whatever the reason we were very vulnerable.

Water was an essential commodity and came to us through the two 60cm trunk mains that emerged from the hillside just south of the town. My plan was very basic, it had to be. From the Borough

Engineer's plans I had located five or six springs within the perimeter which would have to be developed as water points if they cut us off. I did not anticipate them poisoning the supplies because of their own people in the town.

In the No Man's Land forward of our perimeter defences I discovered two valves with black wheels that controlled the main valves on the trunk mains. Under cover of darkness my jemadar went out and booby-trapped them and laid mines. At the same time Jock and I located the old pre-war town power station that had been the main electricity supply before the grid came. We were occupying offices and houses and the hospital was in constant use and so electricity was important if it could be maintained. Street lighting also deterred night raiders. I left sewage disposal to 'Old Man Gravity' who worked for nothing and continued to take waste out to sea. I decided not to bother about the town gas supply.

The old Power Station was in a very sinister part of town. It was driven by a 1500 hp Sulzer diesel with a direct-coupled alternator on the end of the shaft and it was a thing of beauty. I had the protection of a company of Gurkhas, who took up defensive positions around the plant whilst Jock and I began to figure it all out. It had obviously been well cared for and kept as a stand-by. I worked my way around the switchgear and cables whilst Jock looked the prime mover over. He was a diesel engine man, but this two-storey monster was bigger than anything he had seen before. Surajbahn and I crept about in the tangled undergrowth outside the building locating the exhausts, silencers, fuel lines and cooling-water pipes. There was about half a tank of diesel oil and no reserves.

I opened all the big switches to isolate the alternator from the mains so that we could start up 'off-load' and we levered the giant flywheel round with a crowbar to line up the starting marks. We made another item-by-item check and decided to try to start her.

I climbed the ladder to the gallery round the top of the engine and lifted off the six half-compression levers and Jock was down below on the compressed air starter motor. It was an exciting moment and my heart was thumping as I grasped the shiny steel levers and shouted, "Let her go!"

The engine began to turn and I threw down my levers at the right time and in the right order. I felt her sob, and cough and then she was running sweetly.

162

What a beautiful moment! Out through the windows in the sunlight I saw giant smoke rings soaring from the exhausts and heard the flat bang-bang of the silencer boxes as she steadied her pace and chuffed steadily round firing on all six.

"*The keen unpassioned beauty of a great machine!*" I yelled Rupert Brooke's fine words to the powerhouse roof, and laughed madly! Jock and the Sikhs caught my mood and waltzed around below me.

We had done it and now we could give the garrison power. We were not a day too soon. The grid supply was cut off that evening and during the night there were explosions out by the water valves. In the morning two dead natives were lying near the wheels, killed by our booby traps, and the mains were shut off.

The battle of the valves lasted almost a week. Beginning with a few sappers going out after dark to reopen them it escalated until a whole company of infantry was employed in the attempt to keep the water flowing. I grew to loathe those two large knurled wheels and on the fire-swept end of the water main little Dalip gained a bar to his Imphal M.M.. He had a bullet through his gut but he still wrestled the valves open and staggered back ashen-faced with one finger in his tummy and one in his back to plug both ends of the bullet hole and stop the draught blowing through. What a man!

"*Thik hai! Sahib!*" he reported, "It's all O.K.!" He was back on duty a few weeks later.

Big stupid loveable Nihal Singh, who had been my best naik and served with me since Manipur days, was blown to pieces out there, along with several others killed and wounded. It was too much. I had to call off the water tournament and turn my attention to the natural springs. I made proper water points with pipes and valves to collect the water and lined old trucks with tarpaulins to act as bowsers to supply the units. Now the hospital and civilian quarters had no piped water and there were sanitary problems.

Without the grid electricity I was faced with the staggering burden of running a power station from a dangerous quarter of town, with hardly any fuel. In desperation I turned to the Royal Navy who were so near at hand, wallowing about off shore and giving us artillery support. I approached the destroyer HMS *Caprice* (named 'Charlie Able Price' by sailors). Could they help with emergency water and did they have any spare diesel?

This triggered off a chain reaction. The skipper of *Caprice* whisked me aboard *Sussex* to meet the Admiral of 5 Cruiser Squadron. I was entertained to dinner and even given a cinema show (my first since leaving India) and I was offered the whole of their engineering resources. I spent a few hours out of Java, enjoyed an unforgettable night and was given the support of the world's best technicians.

All sailors love a run ashore and they gave me copious, unstinting help at a time when I needed it most. Petty officers and stokers poured along the mole with boatloads of forty-gallon drums of diesel fuel and handled the Sulzer diesel with reverence and skill.

This freed me to attend to the onerous tasks of a sapper at war. Roads had to be kept opened, mines cleared, booby traps placed and removed, demolitions carried out and even bridges repaired. In the middle of this time of intense stress I had a high-flying visit from the CRE, my boss from 23 Div HQ.

He had heard that there was a water problem. What was I doing about it? Did I understand what I was doing? All the stupid questions that top brass spout when they are proving their superiority. Fortunately Brigadier Bethel took him to one side and said some very nice things about me and how I had taken charge of the whole engineering scene and kept things running. Basically he told the colonel to get off my back.

Suddenly everything did an about-turn and attention was focused on my lonely plight. After having been ignored for so long I began to be showered with encouragement and enthusiasm from above. I even had a congratulatory letter from a very high-up sapper back at XIVth Army HQ!

As soon as I had pressed the button marked 'Royal Navy' I was able to welcome my new engineering team as they streamed ashore. Naval tenders plied busily to and fro, stacking grey steel barrels of fuel oil and water on the quay. An E.R.A (Engine Room Artificer) did a complete assessment of the power station and set up his watches of stokers to run the place.

He came to live with me in my bungalow.

When sailors take 'a run ashore' they have their own ways of behaving. Like my old chums from the tanks they become different men when they come out of their steel shells. Crisply efficient sailors at sea become jolly Jack Tars on dry land. To them Semarang was a wonderful place, filled with civilized comforts and pretty girls and Dutch gin, whereas I knew what a dangerous place it really was. They had to work in a very nasty corner of the old native town, a place where whites were open targets for assassins. I arranged protection for them from the infantry and did my best to instil into them the watchfulness that was inherent in all our movements.

The ERA turned out to be an alcoholic. I noticed it first when my modest liquor stock vanished from the bungalow, and at breakfast one morning found him halfway through a bottle of 'Old Squareface' (Dutch gin, also called 'paint stripper' by some). Late one afternoon I returned to find my little Mercedes coupé upside down in a ditch at the foot of the drive. Then the security forces rang to say that they had arrested him after curfew for trying to shoot his initials out of the Brigade HQ board with a .45 Colt revolver. Apologetically his senior Naval officers explained that he had a Maltese wife who was trouble, that he was very good at his job aboard ship and they replaced him with a more disciplined ERA.

I had to ration electricity very strictly. The Sulzer was a thirsty beast and it was not easy to haul the big drums of diesel across the heaving waves and get them from the docks to the lower end of town. I ran her for about three hours each evening, unless there was a special plea from the hospital or the Brigadier himself.

As 'The First Peacetime Christmas' drew near I suddenly realized how popular I had become. Everybody wanted me at their parties, not for my attractive personality nor my good looks, but for my dinky little power station. When a unit decided to throw a party it was believed that if I were there the lights would stay on a bit longer!

I was too stretched to enjoy partying. By cutting off supplies to all the native quarters I was just contriving to give water and electricity to the 200,000 civilian and military population who depended upon me.

There was always terrorist activity in addition to the daily attacks on our defended perimeter. They sensed the importance of the airfield and docks as well as the services to our beleaguered position. There was no law and order, and marauding bands were everywhere as this beautiful race of gentle people went about killing, looting and pillaging in the streets.

My captured German Luger automatic, which shortly before had been turned on me, had become my best friend. It appeared to accept the standard rimless 9mm Sten gun ammunition, which was plentiful, and I lived with it, worked with it and slept with it always to hand.

In a running street fight one morning I turned a corner almost on top of a mad man pointing a Colt pistol at my head. I fired the Luger straight between his glaring eyes and it whispered 'Click!' when it should have gone 'Bang'. British Sten ammunition was not quite right for it! My impetus had carried me right on top of the man and turning the pistol in my hand I crashed the heavy butt down on his skull.

"Shabash Sahib!" shouted Surajbahn. He despatched my attacker and added, "Mind where you're pointing that thing!"

I looked; the scissor action was delicately poised on half cock over the faulty round and when I turned it round to bang my attacker over the head the jolt might easily have fired it between my own eyes.

'Peace on Earth, Good will to all men' crackled the radios. At battalion headquarters Sandy said, "I found peace this morning – a piece of shrapnel through my windscreen!"

We had to endure the usual commercial American music that they always churn out at Christmas and we joined in with 'I'm dreaming of a white Mistress!'

The returning Dutch must have been saddened when they dragged themselves back from the prison camps to find their proud colony being razed to the ground and all their businesses going up in flames. They expected us as the only international troops to protect their property, shoot at mobs and restore law and order, but our heart was never truly in it.

As we listened to the festive hype from the outside world we wondered where we had gone wrong, especially when the news came through that the dockworkers in UK had gone on strike and we would not be getting anything special for Christmas. We still had not received any mail since leaving India in August. It occurred to us that we were working for the wrong firm! The penalty for strike action out here was death.

We were told that if we went to the airfield there was a surprise awaiting us. I made the hazardous trip and returned with one small tin of 'lost label' variety that turned out to be raw mincemeat. Then we were told that a special liquor ration awaited us and after another sniper-infested trip I received a tot of rum; this in a country flowing with Dutch gin! Finally they sent me a scrawny chicken carcase – chicken was our main food from the pasars and kampongs around town and we were sick of it.

I did have one Christmas treat: I shared two whole days and nights

166

with my men in the lines, my first real break since I had boarded the LST in Madras harbour five months before. We had a make-and-mend, do-as-you-please weekend that was only disturbed by Ganda Singh crashing the Fox-&-Geese board over Bihar Singh's head because he was cheating! I was still Borough Engineer and everyone wanted light but not much water and my sailors brought me plenty of real Navy rum and duty free cigarettes.

The political situation was stabilizing and Soekarno was emerging as a leader. He had once been imprisoned as a dissident, but he was intelligent, shrewd and educated. The Japanese had helped him a lot, expecting him to be a puppet ruler under them, but their sudden demise had thrown the prize he had so long cherished almost out of his grasp. At least we had people with whom we could parley.

Their organization, called the TKR, the murdering devils from Ambarawa whose atrocities had turned our stomachs sick, now agreed to escort some Dutch women and children to the airport. By helping us they were also ridding their land of a few more hated colonials, and it was preferable to slaughter.

Bob, Harry and I had developed an altruistic attitude towards 91 Field Company. It was like an old boy network. All three of us had refused postings and promotions away from the company and we were devoted to our own men. We had seen and done so much together that we resented the very idea of change, but change was everywhere. We had grown old in the Company and in each other's company and the difference in our seniority was slight. They were senior to me in the Indian Army and were therefore promoted first, although I had longer military service than they had because of my previous two years in the UK. Bob had only been Major Sahib, commanding the company, for six months before he was repatriated and Harry as next in line went up to O.C. Naturally as Harry tore off his three pips for a crown my turn came to add another one and I became Captain. In our place green young subalterns were streaming out from the West, men who did not have our knowledge or our innate affection for the jawans.

No.3 Platoon did not know whether to cheer or cry. They threw the biggest party ever to celebrate Chha-Chha's success, even though they hated to see me go. Sikhs do not mince words when it comes to flattery. The good news for me was that Joe Hammett was going to take over. As an ex-boy soldier and a regular, he was as good as one could hope to find. Sikhs appreciate and need a man's man to lead them, to love and care for them and stand no nonsense and Joe was perfect for the job.

Out of Semarang! Out again from a surrounded fortress! Away from the murder and the savagery of central Java! It was like seeing the Imphal road reopened as I left another siege and flew to Bandoeng. Despite all the looting, I was leaving, as I always knew I would, with nothing more than the clothes I stood up in, faithful Bowunja and a gangling German shepherd dog. I was proud of my extra pip and it felt good to be pulling out to do a desk job and to leave front-line heroics to others. At last, I thought, the dangerous work is over! Little did I know!

One thing I coveted more than anything else was my Mercedes Benz coupé. I devised a deep scheme and explained it carefully to the Sikhs. They would soon be returning to Bandoeng when a new brigade took over in Semarang. I told them to pack my car in a three-ton truck, surrounded with boxes of gelignite and fix big red notices all around saying 'Explosives – keep out!' Under no circumstances were they to allow anybody, friend or foe, near that truck, and they must get it back to me. Once more I would sit in the red leather bucket seats, throw in the supercharger booster and speed through the open air! A young man's dream!

Goodbye parties in Java followed a strict routine. We all had shared battle experiences – infantry, sappers, doctors and all – we were on first name terms and knew each other intimately. I had pulled this one's truck out of a ditch on the Tiddim Road, that one had one of my Alsatian puppies, another had sat side-by-side with me on an ammo box on Scraggy . . . memories abounded! I was not leaving in the full sense of the word. The whole brigade was scheduled to move up to Bandoeng and we would soon be reunited, but it was a good excuse for a party. The same applied to my platoon; we would not be parted for long, but my time as their officer was over and their farewell party was very moving.

I climbed into the transport Dakota and we taxied to the end of the rough runway. Sathi was all gangly legs, floppy ears and big feet and he took to flying with his usual enthusiasm for life. He and Bowunja were already firm allies and sat close together on the aluminium deck, both showing their white teeth and pink mouths as the engines roared and dust clouds blew past the open door and the plane pulled sharply up and away. Transport planes always flew with the doors open, often with bored loaders dangling their legs over the edge as the panorama of the most beautiful island in the world unrolled beneath them.

"When I flew home," I yelled in Bowunja's ear, "I rode in one of these for several days and nights!" He smiled politely at my happiness without any comprehension of such vast distances. It was exhilarating to feel the surge of power as the old plane accelerated down the dirt runway and I sang to myself: "Still alive! Alive alive-oh!"

As the wheels left the ground I experienced for the second time the inexpressible feeling of jubilation that comes from escaping from a siege. The pilot stood the plane on its wing tip the minute it cleared the ground to avoid receiving a pan of machine-gun bullets in the soft under-gut from perimeter snipers. The roads and kampongs appeared to gyrate directly below the open door as the plane turned and the grinning loader pointed back at the lazily soaring white tracer from a guerrilla gun behind our tail.

"*Abhi thik hai! Sahib!*" (Now we're OK!) Bowunja yelled, and Sathi gave his brown face an affectionate lick.

In less than two hours we had retraced our outward sea voyage of two days and dropped down on to the tarmac at Batavia. I did not know that I had at last turned back; that I had gone as far East as I would be going and my dreams of Tokyo and going right round the world had ended.

At Batavia there was another transport plane ready to lift off for Bandoeng and we ran over to it.

"Bring the dog and the monkey too, mate, if you want!" shouted the dirty British loader. Thank goodness that Bowunja spoke no English and as we crawled in on top of sacks of flour he said, "Scruffy lot these loaders, Sahib! They'd never make real soldiers!"

In order to climb the steep escarpment from the coast to Bandoeng the pilot followed a steep jungle valley along the line of the road and railway and seemingly brushing forest trees with his wing tips. We were beneath the monsoon cloud blanket as we swerved and soared upwards. I sat up front next to the pilot whilst his Number Two stroked Sathi's ears and tried to talk to Bowunja in the back. He flew as though he was following a well-known footpath, and we roared through the dark cleft of the inverted triangle to burst up through the cloud and reach the sunny plains above. It was very frightening to a soldier's eye as the rain smashed against the windscreen. We passed a fighter making its way down the valley and exchanged cheeky wing waggles.

I was not worried about safety until, after landing, we heard that the Dakota behind us had been shot up and crashed with everybody killed. Harry had been expecting me on it and had heard the news on the radio, so that my premature arrival took him by surprise.

"Och! Well," he said, sounding like Alistair Sim "I had a wee dram in your memory, so it was no bad thing after all!" I was glad that we had made that quick dash across the tarmac; it had saved our lives!

It was officially peacetime and in letters home we were now allowed to say quite openly where we were and what we were doing. One night in Semarang two Indian officers (VCOs) had gone into the town looking for girls and both had been murdered. In the British press next day there was the headline 'Two British officers murdered in central Java' and Semarang was named. My parents knew I was there, but not that the officers were Indians and they had to endure three weeks of trepidation until they received a letter of mine dated after the incident. I was blissfully unaware of any of this because we were out of touch with home.

Chapter 15

TO CROWN IT ALL

Me that lay down an' got up
Three years with the sky for my roof—

It was the return of the prodigal. I not only knew all the Mahrattas, Punjabi Mussulmans, Sikhs, clerks, store-men, drivers, workshop and garage staff in Company HQ, but I was back with my old friend Harry. I had missed the chance to see Bob off but I could not complain because his leaving had given me this promotion. So many things had altered but many were still the same. *Plus ça change, plus c'est la même chose.*

My greatest surprise was the welcome that I received from Subedar Bostan Khan. He who I had so often feared, even mistrusted as he whispered into the O.C's ear against uppity subalterns and their bloody Sikhs, was now a different man. It was a clear statement of my new rank – I was now '*Two-i-c Sahib*' the Captain Sahib, and as much a part of HQ administration as he himself was.

The Subedar was a man that I would have looked up to in any walk of life. He had a gentle and reasonable way of saying things that was precise but never presumptuous and he could put me right, firmly but never insubordinately. Academically he may have been less educated than I was, he was less travelled and below me in rank, but he was a profound and sagacious man. He was deep in the oriental sense of the word, deep as the ocean, and he could make me feel pathetically shallow. He was also a professional soldier and I was a part-timer.

He was my servant – and the better man.

It was now time for me to drop ethnic preferences and treat equally with this mixed company of Hindus, Muslims and Sikhs. In his

171

comfortable quarters on my first evening, over a cup of his special coffee and a cigarette, he began my education, speaking in his faultless Urdu: "We have not always seen eye to eye, Sahib, and that is the proper way for things to be! There have been times when your enthusiasm in support of your brave Sikhs brought a clash between our interests."

Back in the mess with my third pip sewn on a little crookedly (Bowunja had also been celebrating our return) I liked some of the changes less. Through our parents, boarding schools and OCTU training we had developed a rigid set of Victorian principles that might now seem old-fashioned, but it was a code that we could not break. We held women in high regard and were disinclined to risk diseases or shotgun marriages by becoming involved with alien females. We also had a true devotion to the Company and the men under our care. Without Bob one leg of our tripod had gone and only Harry and I remained to uphold the standards as new faces arrived.

The world was in a strange state and we were in a strange situation. The politicians boasted about sending the boys home , but where would they find our replacements? The RBS&M depot in Poona was a very long way from Java, a memo took weeks to reach them and replacements took months to reach us. Young subalterns were coming out from Europe, but, even if they had battle experience, they did not know the troops or the language and they had no enthusiasm for our struggle. They had to do their stint, but they had not the disciplines that were an innate part of our make-up. In the taut atmosphere of hatred from an oriental people it was not easy to tell new arrivals that for us there was still a war on, and a very nasty one too.

Dutch women who had been released from the camps were everywhere and it had become quite common for units to have women in the mess for dancing, drinks and 'snoggery-pokery' (as Harry called it). The women knew only too well that if they married an English soldier they received an immediate one-way ticket to Europe, because our soldiers on active service were not allowed to have wives with them. The Dutch administration was chaotic and it was extremely difficult for a woman to get away by air or sea. Every white woman in Java was in constant danger and many of the self-appointed civilian officials demanded sexual favours in exchange for possible passages out. As commanding officer Bob had been very strict about allowing what he called "a load of fat faced cows who speak no English" into

172

the lines and Harry and I had the same views. I told Harry about the degrading scenes I had witnessed in the camp at Ambarawa before they had been given a wash and clothes to wear.

The flames were spreading west across the island from Soerbaja and Semarang and I knew that it was only a matter of time before Batavia and Bandoeng would be engulfed. My first order as Adjutant forbade women within our perimeter. I was determined that we would be battle-ready when the time came and, above all, I did not want our officers to lose face with the men. They trusted us to keep a firm hand on the reins and not behave like a pack of randy puppy dogs.

The wisdom of this attitude was borne home one day when a new subaltern from the Service Corps came to me for help. He carried the courtesy title Honourable and had an aristocratic family somewhere at home.

"What wotten luck!" he wailed. "I've gawn an' done it now! This girl's Mum and Dad caught me wed-handed in the girl's bed and now they are going to report me to the General unless I mawwy her!" He looked very worried, especially when he added, "and her Mum's as black as a Madwassi's twat!"

It was such a blatant trick and I gave him the obvious advice to brazen it out and go and tell his colonel right away. As I said to Harry later, "Imagine walking up the drive to the honourable home one day and pointing to your pile of kit announcing, 'By the way the little black bit behind my kit bag is your new daughter-in-law!'"

Not for us!

There was even a pay-and-divorce offer. Parents anxious to save the lives of their daughters made special offers. Marry the girl and she was immediately sent home and when you got back you were promised an immediate divorce and a packet of diamonds from Amsterdam.

My old pals were a bit shaken by my appearance; I was gaunt and drawn, with sunken eye sockets, and I was decidedly twitchy after the siege of Semarang. In a new uniform and jaunty Gurkha hat I had a photograph taken to send home. Much later my sister told me that my mother cried all night after receiving that picture of her boy! I was completely unaware of this; we had still received no mail and were completely out of touch with our families.

The Sikh platoon rejoined Company HQ and 23 Div concentrated in the west of the island. They returned by sea to Batavia and on the road up to Bandoeng the 'explosives' wagon, carrying my Mercedes Benz, had a double blow out. The Sikhs had carried out my instructions meticulously and the car was concealed under boxes of explosives. One flat tyre could have been changed quickly, but with two gone the task was very difficult and the convoy was being held up. A bustling staff officer from Buitenzorg came along and made them unload the lorry. When he found my little convertible he decided to have this gem for himself! It was a despicable theft and I swore bloodshed on the head of the perpetrator if ever I caught him! To rob a brother officer on active service was unheard of, but he had only recently come out from UK. I put it around on the grapevine that if I ever caught him I would rip him open. I did meet him too! Three years later at a reunion dinner in the Park Lane Hotel someone said to me, "See that chap over there? He's the one who pinched your Merc!"

By then it did not matter any more and we had a drink together.

I enjoyed being a captain and doing admin work. There is a certain satisfaction in setting out a well-laid table and being prepared for whatever is to come. My experiences in central Java led me to build up reserves of everything. If we were going to be cut off again I wanted to be ready for it. I introduced the word 'liberating' that did not sound quite so bad as looting, and it meant freeing valuable items from destruction by the mob. Dutch and Japanese artefacts, tools, spares and equipment were being destroyed on every side and we rushed to take goods into protection for our own use and the good of the community.

We soon had the most elaborate workshops, garage and stores and I 'won' all the heavy equipment I could lay my hands on. I collected bulldozers, graders, dumpers, compressors, a steamroller and even a large excavator. To such an extent that instead of holding dreary dance parties with old gramophone records and plump fräuleins, I initiated Sapper Sunday lunch parties, which eventually became famous. We provided plenty of drinks and snacks inside the mess and outside all my great machines were lined up with diesel engines knocking, fires lit and steam up for anybody to have a go – after a drink or two! Pushing a giant D8 bulldozer through a mound of earth was said by some to be more fun than pushing a fat blonde down behind the sofa! Well almost!

Our relations with the Dutch were never very good. They had a few troops, mostly Ambonesian mercenaries, but they were always in the wrong place and going in the wrong direction. Several times we fired upon them by mistake. Despite their poor war record the Dutch were often domineering and truculent towards us, especially when they were in authority. I must have spent a considerable part of my last year in the army standing to attention for their interminable National Anthem which seemed as long as a Mahler Symphony. When our anthem was played they shuffled about, coughing, spitting and yawning and seldom stood up.

Queen Wilhelmina's birthday meant a vast parade in Bandoeng, but as there were so few Dutch troops in the country we had to make up the march past. Their few soldiers strutted at the head of the column with their ridiculous Germanic style goose-step whilst our men followed with the mile-eating lope of experienced troops.

Subedar Bostan Khan was infuriated when we were ordered to salute Dutch Officers. Two days before he had suffered the indignity of being called 'a black wog' by an arrogant Hollander. I was so enraged that this calumny should be applied to our brave soldiers that I could have killed the miserable pip-squeak, but the Subedar himself restrained me.

"You see, Sahib," he said in his beautiful Urdu, "I also wanted to strike that oaf between the eyes, but he is not worth it, whereas you are!"

I began to build a new picture of our old enemy, the Japanese, especially after fighting alongside them in Semarang. There were about a quarter of a million in the Dutch East Indies and a thousand or more were killed during the Java troubles (more than they had lost during the original invasion). I paraded nearly six hundred prisoners each morning to organize their work schedules for the day and grew to know them very well. They were conscientious in their care of stores and tools, meticulous timekeepers, clean and very subservient. There was a steep divide between lower and higher ranks. The common soldier was usually a rough peasant, brutish in many ways, whilst the officers were cultured and quick-brained. I discovered their peculiar sense of humour and found that they were often very sentimental.

We had been imbued with the hatred that was essential to the killing game of warfare, but now saw them as soldiers and not so dissimilar to us. It was as though we had walked across No Man's Land to their side of the wire and could see that their view was not that different from ours. I would never forget their hordes sweeping over the Imphal heights, nor their atrocities, but I grew to respect them.

Their fawning servitude verged upon comic opera to our Western eyes as they hissed and bowed and scraped. They were playing the part of a humble and defeated race, but we had met them head on and knew how tough they were. One of their officers told me that although we were the victors at that moment they would be back on top in fifty years time. I laughed at him, but their automobile, electronic and monetary skills have brought it about.

One day Joe Hammett saw a Dutchman laying about a Japanese storekeeper with a pick handle. He lifted the man by his goatee beard and threw him outside into a filthy ditch. It was not for lesser breeds to trample on men who had fought with more courage than they ever knew.

It did not seem to matter what objectives we set our prisoners they never complained and always produced a good result. I tried increasing their daily workload every morning to find at what point they would break, but they would rather have worked all night than admit weakness. We could never excuse their treatment of our p.o.w.s but we learned that this was a race with very different attitudes from ours.

Under Joe my old platoon were doing a bridging job on the steep road down to Buitenzorg and I joined the convoy one morning and went to visit them. To me it was a run out, away from paperwork and I wanted to be back with my old friends for a spell. I was over-awed by the size of my escort. It was not all for me, of course, it was the daily 'Down' convoy that went as far as Buitenzorg at the foot of the mountains to bring back the 'Up' convoy that had crossed the coastal plain from Batavia. The first part of the run across the flat was fast and easy but mines and ambushes abounded on the steep hill road.

That morning we had two armoured cars, several Bren Carriers and a company of about 200 Gurkha infantry. I planned to leave the convoy half way down, spend a few hours with 3 Platoon and then return on the up convoy in the afternoon. I realized at once how flabby I had become and how much my case-hardening had softened behind a desk! I felt like a middle-aged father going to play football with his sons.

We took to the road and within an hour we were ambushed. Once

176

again I was among the angry chatter of machine guns, thumps from mortar bombs and grenades as we beat our way through a relatively light road block, but my heart was thumping. Nonchalantly the convoy commander told me that it was nothing and that the day before they had lost six men in two hours of bitter fighting.

Astonishingly we drove unprovoked past an Indonesian parade ground further down the road. Their paramilitary troops were drilling in threes on a village green with bamboo poles for imitation rifles and they gave us a mock salute as we swept past. Life in Java was always unbelievable. Whilst our general was holding talks with Soekarno the Buffaloes were ambushing one of our convoys; whilst the TKR were escorting women prisoners to safety another of their units was attacking our positions. It depended upon who you met and where you were – shooting one minute, saluting the next. It was nerve-racking, especially to time-expired men who should have been on their way home.

I was thrilled to see what a good job Joe was doing with my old platoon. Like me he had been in the ranks himself and he was as strict as he was fair, just what Sikhs appreciate most. I almost felt a pang of envy! There was a lot of backchat when Chha-Chha arrived on that wild jungle stretch of road.

"Not often you see a Captain-Sahib as near the enemy as this!"

"Hope he won't disgrace himself when the shooting starts!"

"We've got Babu-jis in the front line now!"

"*Chup! Chup karo!*" (Shut up!) Surajbahn shouted his warning with a twinkle in his eye. "They're not so well behaved since you left us!"

As the familiar Sikh humour flew about I knew how much I missed them all.

Back at HQ I built a rest room in the lines and painted the mural myself. It was a map of the east with all our travels and battles marked upon it, our medals and losses, and little pictures and the men loved it.

Sathi's brothers and sisters were now scattered around the Gurkha brigade, but to me he was still the pick of the litter. He had grown rapidly and I dosed him with calcium and vitamin tablets scrounged from the medicos.

Young subalterns were always coming and going. One turned out to be a gem because he had been in action on the Western Front and he was the first experienced soldier we received from Europe. A young English officer who had not been out East more than six months met and married a local girl. She was Eurasian, tarty and dramatically beautiful, and was known to have collaborated with the Japanese. We went to all three weddings: the first in Dutch, the second C of E in English and finally the official military marriage. They hardly spoke a word of each other's language and within two days she flew out to Holland, although she had no contacts there, and his real 'Dutch Wife' was no more use to him than the bolster in my bed.

The railway line that divided the town of Bandoeng separated the Dutch residential area from the business and native quarters and two of our men wandered along it one evening and were never seen again. They had almost certainly been enticed across the tracks by a local girl and then robbed and murdered.

A whisper was put about that Muslim troops in the Indian Army were being seduced into the Indonesian cause. This was something that experienced Indian Army men had never dreamed possible. We took for granted the loyalty, courage and devotion of our men, but undoubtedly we were employing Muslim troops against Muslim nationalists to reinstate European colonialism.

Harry's father was taken dangerously ill and he was suddenly sent home. Like all of us, he was overdue for repatriation and would never return. Hurriedly I seized the reins and to my surprise I was promoted immediately to Field Rank, Major Sahib! I had only been a captain for sixty-three days! After three years without promotion I never dreamed that I would one day command my own Field Company, much less dear old Ninety-One!

I knew that I had been commended for my work in Semarang and later I was told that the Dutch had put Jock, my Scottish sergeant and my Jemadar and me forward for the Order of the Orange of Nassau. In fact I was shown the memo, but the decorations never materialized.

Five years to the day from pulling on my first pair of Army Issue underpants I was sewing on my crown! In fact the authorities had little choice. A new Major from Poona would have taken weeks, even months, to reach Java, if they could find one. I knew the Company, the men, and the country and, above all, I was there. Although else-where men were flooding home and I myself was well overdue for repatriation and demobilization I was D.O.V. (Delayed Operationally Vital). Eventually my replacement would have to be a regular Indian Army Officer.

I took a stroll round the lines late that night and joined the Sikhs as they were singing and chattering together and told them in my guttersnipe Amritsar, "Now listen you 'orrid lot! There's a new Major-Sahib starting 'ere tomorrow! From what I 'ear he's a proper bastard and 'ates the guts of Sikhs . . . so just watch your step!" That is a free translation, but Surajbhan picked it up and started embellishing and exaggerating impossibly, with hefty winks and nudges until even the dimmest jawan realized that old Chha-Chha was now their new O.C. Then the celebrations began and I wallowed in their genuine delight at my promotion.

I was on the spot and I had to get on with it. I put up my crown and contrived to have Joe made up to Captain as my 'Two i/c'. His promotion had been much faster than mine and as a regular it meant a lot more to him. He was from Devonshire and as an ex-boy soldier was probably an old soldier by the time he was sixteen. I never met a better scrounger, which was an enormous asset to have in an adjutant. He had a lanky, loose-limbed way of moving, a bluntness of manner that overrode rank, race or creed and he was a wonderful friend to have – or an awesome foe!

The Fighting Cock Division was fully engaged in West Java and the remnants of 71 Field Company after the Soerbaja massacre were attached to me. After the war they held a dinner in London called Darmo Night in remembrance of that awful event and I attended. My company was the only engineering force in the area, everybody was in a bad way for replacements and it was getting worse.

"Serves us right," said Joe, "for insisting on carrying on fighting when the rest of the world is at peace!"

The Division itself had been an 'emergency only' formation to face the threat in Burma and was marked down for disbandment. As we lost men in action, or to repatriation and demobilization, the powers back at Army HQ were probably pleased to see how well we were running down. Unfortunately we still had a job to do and far more work than we could handle.

In my first two weeks as OC I lost two subalterns: one to Class B Release (on compassionate grounds) and the other to a sniper. I managed to find two replacements, but one of them was so good that

179

the CRE immediately stole him for his staff at Div HQ. The other was sent to help the Field Park Company, "because," the CRE told me, "they haven't got an experienced CO like you!"

It was flattering to be called experienced after only a fortnight in the job. Two more subalterns arrived from Sumatra, where the occupation forces were having a quiet time. As soon as they reported they told me that they headed the repatriation list! Their CO had taken the chance to off-load them on to me. It was dog eat dog.

As adjutant I had been able to recharge my batteries behind an office desk, but I soon found that I needed all my powers in my new job. Things were different now; unlike Beddowes who could keep well back out of the nasty stuff and issue orders, I was back in the field again, not only as commanding officer, but, without a consistent quota of subalterns, I frequently had to manage the platoons myself. On the credit side I had a strong and happy Indian company who got on with me very well. Three-quarters of them had been through the Imphal battles and as regulars did not want to leave the army. Jock had been promoted to sergeant major in charge of all the workshops and I had a new British sergeant to run the garage and vehicle fleet. I could take some small comfort in a report that we were the only unit in the Division to be completely free of venereal diseases. Otherwise things looked bleak.

Once again we were under siege. From the docks beyond Batavia the road ran for about forty miles across the flat to Buitenzorg and then climbed to Bandoeng sixty miles further on, and it was always under attack. Those Indonesians who had received military training from the Japanese were well able to establish a pattern of roadblocks such as we had first encountered on the road to Tiddim. The airfield runways were being lengthened and strengthened by the Japanese prisoners to accept the heavy impact of the transport planes, but the bulk of our supplies still came in by road.

In this topsy-turvy land the railway was a complete paradox. For most of the time it operated as normally as though the year was 1938 and in the same old-fashioned way. The pre-war Javanese and Eurasian staff managed it as they always had, from station to station, from Batavia to Buitenzorg to Bandoeng, and all intermediate stops. Imagine a child's toy train crossing the pitch at Twickenham during an international rugby match. It was as incongruous as that and it belonged more to them than to us. We could be fighting to the death at a roadblock and see the steam train chug past us, with a cheeky whistle, as it ran along the valley.

It was not unknown for them to call for reinforcements and commandeer a train to rush men up to the action. They would unload the train and, after using it, reload the goods and send it on its way. On one occasion after they had committed a massacre they filled the train with dead bodies and sent them down to Batavia for a proper burial.

Anti-Dutch, anti-White propaganda flamed from every hoarding and wall and the population showed a more united antagonism than before. Everybody was hostile to a degree; every man woman and child had to be regarded as our enemy. A young girl walking to morning market with a basket of fruit on her head was found to be carrying mines and grenades under the paw-paw. The old lady collecting cowpats for her fire was scratching a hole in the road for a mine. Indar Singh seized a small boy who was behaving strangely and the lad turned and blew half his face away with a carbine. Young men lounging in the sun on doorsteps could be a dangerous commando hiding from us. Arms and ammunition were hidden in cooking pots or under piles of grain.

I was sent on a perilous aerial reconnaissance of downtown Bandoeng in an Auster spotter 'plane. Possibly there were not enough officers at HQ capable of making this appraisal, but, if I was too 'operationally vital' to go home, why risk me on such a dangerous mission? We occupied the salubrious north side of town, but across the railway track there were closely packed native quarters, factories and businesses. It was a large town and the ratio of indigenous population to white colonials was about forty to one.

This was a new kind of flying for me. The high-wing monoplane was made of wood and canvas and was very frail and the toy wheels were sprung with rubber bands. The engine frame carried two canvas seats side by side for the pilot and me and the overhead wing gave us a clear view of the countryside beneath. We hovered in mid-air, so slowly and so low down that I expected a bullet up my bum at any moment and I could see several pot-the-plane snipers firing up at us.

"Lousy bloody shots these Indos!" called out the British pilot and his cool bravado served to steady my nerves. Despite the obvious truth about their inaccuracy, so far, I wished that he would not tempt them so much. He not only floated, as low and slow as a buzzard, over the

181

interesting places but insisted cheerily, "I'll just go over that bit again, but a bit lower. It looked as though there was a machine-gun emplacement in that pile of rubbish!"

For my part I thought I saw the fillings in the back teeth of one Indonesian as he gazed open-mouthed at us. What was more frightening was what I saw disposed below me. Their troops were everywhere, aggressively active and very numerous, and they appeared to be forming up for an attack across the tracks at any moment. A Dutch rubber factory was a blazing inferno and we circled the black column of smoke like a gnat over a bonfire. My task was to report upon their defences and readiness for action, and to assess the sapper tasks needed to get our infantry forward. Tank obstacles, dykes, canals, bridges, fortifications and minefields speckled the pale earth like measles and I plotted them all on my kneepad.

It was like snorkelling in pellucid waters looking down on the strange life of the seabed below except that the creatures below me carried guns.

At Div HQ plans were well advanced for an immediate attack. If there was the slightest provocation or threat we were ready to seize the initiative and take the whole town. Back in my own lines I planned our requirements and drew up a battle plan in readiness.

Suddenly there was a disturbance outside. A shattered party of Mahrattas from 1 Platoon came into camp. The day before the down convoy to Buitenzorg had taken an NCO and twelve men as sapper support. They had got safely down to the plain, stayed the night and come back on the morning convoy. On the return run they had encountered a massive roadblock.

This would later be known as 'The Big Battle of the Convoy' on 10 March 1946. I had lost seven Mahrattas and two more were lightly wounded; there were considerable infantry losses with the destruction of many supply lorries. It had almost been a wipe-out and oddments of troops and trucks were left behind in isolated pockets down the road. We were in dire straits, and really cut off again.

As the Mahratthas were reporting events to me my phone rang. 'Immediate O-Group at Div HQ!' We were ordered to be ready at once. The strength of their forces north of us on the road and the troops massing across the tracks to the south meant that we were sandwiched between a hammer-and-anvil attack, and this time we were on the block. The night was spent in frantic preparation; an armoured column formed up with full infantry support and air cover for a dawn attack back down the road. I said goodbye to Sathi and Joe and joined the column in my Jeep with all the men and equipment I could muster. We knew that we had to make this a brutal success and we had murder in our hearts that morning. I had radio contact up and down the column with my platoons and could direct them strategically to deal with obstacles, roadblocks, mines and bunkers.

As first light broke over the smouldering volcanoes on the skyline behind us we went in. There was a thin drizzle falling as we crept down the thread of tarmac. I never felt less heroic and pined for a joke with Bob or a wee cigarette with Harry, but those days were gone and I was left to face this ordeal alone. It was not entirely due to dawn nerves and empty stomach, the usual accompaniments to an attack, nor to my new responsibility in command of a much larger force. One of my best friends, a Company Commander in 3/3rd Gurkhas, had been killed the day before on this very stretch of road as the convoy fought its way back. The senselessness of his death a few weeks before he was due to go home bit deep.

It was a long, long day. Halt and fight, move and halt, advance and retreat until by nightfall we had cleared the road to a point halfway down the mountain. We liberated the isolated boxes of resistance from the day before, which were still fighting, and sent the wounded back up to Bandoeng in the 'soft' vehicles we had liberated.

We had to laager when night fell. On a suitable shelf we formed a box around the column. Sturdy little Gurkhas after the long day of fighting, marching and counter-marching walked straight up the steep slopes and dug defensive positions around us. Little fires began to twinkle everywhere, mostly tins of sand and petrol, but enough for a brew.

"*Chai Chhaina?*" from the Gurkhas or "*Char mangta, Sahib?*" from Indian troops or "Want a wet, Sir?" from the British tank men – the welcome enquiries from all sides as hot, sweet mugs of tea, sticky with condensed milk were passed round.

I went among my men. I joked with them, listened to their stories, checked that they had supplies and drank mug after mug of tea. Cold snack rations appeared, dry as dust but welcome to hungry mouths. Darkness cloaked the deep gorge, the rain stopped and a full orange moon rose over the black silhouette of forested peaks.

I felt good. Really good. This was the other side of the coin of battle.

The dawn chill of fear was now forgotten and I revelled in shared comradeship, the great outdoor breath of life sweet in my lungs, the joy of weariness after the day of campaigning and above all the pleasant glow that victory brings. We were the victors too; after desperate fighting our disciplined force was conquering.

I tried to sleep in my Jeep. The ground outside was very wet, except on the hard tarmac under the trucks where men were already roosting. As I said to a Gurkha officer next morning, "Have you ever slept across the two front seats of a Jeep?"

"Can't say I have!"

"Neither have I!" I replied with feeling.

I was up at 04.30 to go round my platoons and give them their orders. I scraped my chin with a razor in the dark, wetting the brush from my tea dregs amidst the acrid fumes and roar of starting engines. A wan glint of first light appeared in the east, fires were stamped out and The Song of India in all its nasal beastliness rose to the heavens. I swallowed the last tea dregs, had a spit and a smoke and a squirting spray over the khud and we moved forward again.

Our advance was governed by the speed of the walking infantry. The convoy moved, stopped and moved again, like Bank Holiday traffic on the Exeter Bypass. The troops had to divert on our flanks to deal with enemy threats as they occurred. We were the lads who had thrashed the Japs and a few crude Indos were not going to stop us and we whistled and sang as we swung along. The rain had cleared, the white cumulus towered against the blue of the sky and the air was like crystal as I walked with the column in the glory of the morning. Fruit abounded by the road as we dropped through the last foothills and entered the plain. There were prickly red lychee, (the local name sounded like 'Rumplestiltskin'), big stinking-sweet durian, bananas, plantains, oranges, mangoes and strawberries. Along the verges pineapples grew like weeds and flowers tumbled in profusion. The horrors of the day before evaporated and the men gathered orchids, bougainvillaea and other exotic flowers to make garlands as we entered Buitenzorg like a carnival procession.

It reminded me of Provence: the hot sunshine, the tree-shaded roads and the restful air. Food was brought and more tea, men rinsed off the white dust of the day in the tepid dykes, we collected the 'Up' convoy from Batavia and set off on the return journey.

We had proved the road; it was completely clear and we ran

cautiously back up the hill at a steady pace. We laagered again on the same shelf that we had occupied the night before, but this time the rain fell all night as only Javanese rain can fall, blinding, steaming, hissing down like an exaggerated Hitchcock film set. I proved once and for all that it really was impossible to sleep across the two front seats of a Jeep and rose stiff and wet to face another dawn. By the time we reached the plateau the infantry were riding on the trucks and armour and we motored into the welcoming sanctuary of our own lines.

Men shouted silly obscenities to each other, thrilling to the joy of still being alive after the ordeal. It had taken us fifty-three hours to cover a round trip of about 125 miles but it was a decisive victory.

Sathi was so delighted to see me back that he leapt right through my Jeep, from one side to the other, before returning to lick me and whimper with pleasure. It was like a message that there was still love and goodness somewhere in the world. I thought that he would soon be big enough to go with me on my sorties.

We only had time for a quick wash and shave before orders came from Div HQ that the attack on the other half of Bandoeng was imminent. The General had been provoked too far and he had decided that it was time to throw them right out of the town. If they wanted trouble we were ready to give it to them. We did not care, our tails were up after the successful road clearing and we were ready for anything.

We moved up to the start line during the night in readiness for a dawn attack. We were strung along the railway embankment. Joe had exercised his ingenuity to build me a command vehicle; it was a six-wheel Studebaker with radio, stationery, typewriter, maps, sleeping bunks and everything a commanding officer could possibly need to run a campaign. It would have been invaluable to a General and it was certainly a bit grand for a minor officer like me, but I loved it.

This time we were the ones issuing warnings over the airwaves. We had captured their radio station and announced: "We are coming! Be sure that non-combatants are out of the battle area!"

Soon after midnight fires were springing up right across the old town to the south of us as they scorched what Dutch earth they could find and singed quite a lot of Indonesian bits as well. Explosions punctuated the red glow in the sky and I retired to my command truck and tried to sleep. A dawn attack always follows hours of sleeplessness; it was the same the night we broke out of Imphal and the morning we landed in Malaya and it is the same wherever there is war.

Before dawn their machine guns were rattling aimlessly away, firing burst upon burst in our direction and high over our heads. To our experienced ears it was the sound of an untrained operator, a magazine-at-a-time man, but nasty all the same. In the darkness you lie still and analyze the noise: Theirs or ours? Near or far? Before, behind or on the flank? That's a Japanese machine gun. That's an enemy mortar bomb. That sounds like one of our grenades. You draw upon experience to make accurate assessments. Their orchestra rose to a crescendo just before dawn when we added our own military accompaniment. The controlled short phrases of automatic fire, the tympani beat of hand grenades and mortars as our infantry began their remorseless advance across the tracks as we advanced.

Almost beneath our noses there was a tremendous explosion. We came to a smoking crater in the road that told of some enemy attempt to halt us or blow us up. It was by the level crossing gate and was not a very professional job because several of their own men had been blown to pulp. The revolting stench of shattered men and pieces of steaming human meat adhering to the walls told the story.

Street fighting again! It was like a newsreel as our tanks rumbled down the middle of the main road, the infantry skipped from doorway to doorway and the sappers removed mines and barricades. In the event, it was a short and very victorious day's work and it was a satisfying straight fight after so much hole-and-corner work.

We now held the whole town of Bandoeng and made good our perimeter defences. Our precarious hold on the road meant that we were virtually encircled, but at least we were in a good box and knew where we stood. Above all we felt a lot safer in our beds now that the constant threat of sneaking terrorist assassins was practically removed.

Chapter 16

GLOOMY SUNDAY

Revenge that knows no rein—

The convict nearing the end of his sentence, the sailor approaching the home channel, the schoolboy at the end of term, the last week of pregnancy and the soldier on the eve of armistice all have the same emotions. Think of the tragic man who was the last to die at 11 a.m. on 11 November 1918; to be so near to release before that last shot! My feelings were the same; I was long overdue for going home and for demobilization and threatened in a cause that I did not support.

In Java the murderous month of April 1946 took its toll. Good friends of many a long day fell beside my soldiers, my companions and me. My end was near, one way or the other. However much I wanted to change Major for Mister I still did not want to leave 91 Company in the lurch. Men with later demobilization numbers than mine were already passing through the sheds in Britain to collect their pinstripes and trilby hats, but because of my D.O.V. status I was still on the opposite side of the world and at war.

Pressure mounted. I was even offered an enticing regular Indian Army commission which, for a few moments, tempted me. The pay was excellent and I visualized myself with two rows of medal ribbons ordering a 'Long John Collins' in the Poona mess like any other koi-hai. Common sense told me not to trust them. How right I was! I did not know at that time that the Indian Army itself was nearing the end of its life and that 23 Div and 91 Field Company would soon be disbanded. Five years later the unemployment offices in England would be flooded with those who had accepted regular Indian Army posts.

I was not the only one suffering. Like that night long ago on Shenam

187

Ridge a Sikh went puggled. I was working in my office one afternoon when I saw an unkempt Sikh run past the open window, followed by another with fixed bayonet and Surajbahn shouting excitedly. The buildings were arranged in a closed square and he was being chased around the inside of the courtyard. I rushed out and nearly bumped into him on his second chukka. Eventually the poor lad was over-powered, heavily roped and led away to the guardroom.

Two days later a Mahrattha committed suicide. If only Bob had been there to fathom it out for me; he understood them far better than I ever could. A few days after that three PMs disappeared completely, and we never knew where they had gone. Bostan Khan was deeply disturbed, being the leader of the Muslim faction, but still unable to find an answer. It was becoming very sinister.

A newly arrived subaltern, straight from U.K., fell madly in love with a half-caste girl. She was ravishing, the most incredibly beautiful girl with copper-coloured skin, slanting green eyes, long black hair and enough to turn any man's head. She turned the head of this twenty-two year old Englishman and he pursued her diligently. She bestowed upon him the favours that our prurient imaginations saw in her. Eventually he asked her to marry him but she told him she already had a lover. When our tall, blue-eyed, cultured English lad found that his rival was a squat Ambonesian private in the Dutch forces his injured pride descended like an axe and split his personality with schizophrenic accuracy. He had to be shipped home.

Parties became frenetic. Death walked so closely beside us and we were all getting near to the end of our service and our tether. Parties with the Medical Corps, who had a capacity for earthy fun that was like a tonic, gradually replaced my Sunday bulldozer parties. They were a whiff of laughing gas and we needed all the laughs we could get by that time. At one party, listening to Artie Shaw's haunting 'Frenesi' I asked an attractive half-caste lady if she had any NICAs – meaning the new official paper currency.

"Oh! No!" She lifted her skirt as high as her belly button. "I never wear them, but I carry a pair in my handbag!"

Convoy operations were a detested chore every day. The Indonesians did not have the Japanese tenacity or skill in making roadblocks but they continued to harass us. With grim pride and often a bloody nose, we continued to punch our way up and down that wretched road.

In the workshops Joe developed my Semarang mine-buster trucks to a high degree and the two British sergeants brought much ingenuity to their design. They fabricated cantilevered chain flails to thresh the road ahead and heavy rollers to detonate randomly scattered mines. We had plenty of old civilian lorries that were on their last legs after years of Japanese misuse. It was a kamikaze operation because we lost the lead vehicles frequently; on some days we lost two lead vehicles and very few survived three trips.

After the wet west monsoon in Java there is a showery, sparkling spell before the relatively dry east monsoon blows up. At that height above sea level on the equator we enjoyed the most perfect climate in the whole world. The hues of morning and evening, the vaporous mists about the volcanic peaks, blue-magic vistas of spacious distance and the sheer breathtaking glory of Java mocked man's evil ways.

Sathi's ears were now erect and he had the alert watchfulness of the champion dog that he undoubtedly was. One evening I heard him out in the court growling threateningly and I rushed out with my Luger. He was standing foursquare above a supine sneak thief, his bared fangs almost touching the man's face, holding him imprisoned. He was so intelligent and well trained that I knew I only had to give him the command 'On!' and he would have killed the dacoit. Instead I murmured, "Stay" and left the intruder cringing beneath the dog whilst I fetched some troops to take him away to the guardroom.

Sathi loved to go out with me and stood on his hind legs in the passenger well of my Jeep with his long body and front legs stretched out along the bonnet. We always had the windscreen down, both for defence reasons and also for what we called 'A bit of coolth!' I loved and depended upon that wonderful dog and I began to make arrangements to ship him home with me when the time came.

There was a song about at that time called '*Gloomy Sunday*'. It had been banned in Europe because it became a cult anthem for suicide parties. For me Gloomy Sunday was Easter Day 1946. At the end of a week of disasters I wondered if one of the evil spirits of that enchanted land had singled me out for treatment. My dear Sathi was stricken with a distemper that turned him into a gaunt grinning wreck, slobbering, rigid and not knowing my voice. My doctor friends rallied round, but to no avail. At least it was not rabies, but they advocated putting him to sleep and, with the Luger that had saved my life so often, I took the life of my dearest love. The doctors also insisted

189

that I should take a course of anti-rabies injections 'just in case'. It was a lengthy and painful treatment of countless injections in the stomach.

Joe, my greatest ally and supporter, had been ill for a while. He never complained but, visiting his room one evening, I saw him unclothed and he looked like an inmate of Belsen. He was gaunt and shrivelled, his bones stuck out and every rib was visible. I rushed him round to the hospital and eventually they diagnosed tropical Sprue. I had never heard of this rare disease but it took Joe away from me. The only cure was to leave the tropics for ever, to go home and stay there. The perfect old soldier's disease for malingerers, except that Joe was a dedicated regular, who did not want to go home, nor be invalided out of his chosen career.

I was now virtually alone in a company of over three hundred Indian sappers, with only two greenhorn subalterns who could hardly say 'Yes' or 'No' in Urdu. My plight was such that the CRE, in a well-meaning way, suggested that he demote me back to Captain in order to give him a stronger case to demand a regular Indian Army Major from Poona immediately.

"It would give me a bigger cudgel to batter them with!" he asserted. "No offence to you, Johnnie, of course, but it would get us out of this mess and you could stay on as Two-i/c. They'd have to send me a regular major, and you'll soon be off home any way. Eh?"

I could see his point, but it did very little for my shattered morale. One good thing it did for me: it demonstrated how vulnerable life was in the army and it killed for ever any thoughts I might have entertained of signing up as a regular. Before this idea could be implemented another cruel blow fell. I had a mutiny!

This emotive word was a reminder of Oudh in 1857, when the native troops rose up against their British Officers. It was also a word that always ended in savage retribution and bloodshed. The Indonesians had been putting out a lot of clever propaganda about our use of Muslims against Muslims. We believed so deeply in the loyalty and devotion of our men that we never thought their allegiance would waver, but there had been disquieting rumours about deserters in other units.

Bostan Khan came to me in distress to say that the PMs of 2 Platoon had refused to go out on the next convoy. This proud high caste Mussulman, whose lip had often curved derisively at the escapades of

190

Johnnie's Bloody Sikhs, and even Bob's Mahratthas, now had to report the defection of his very own people.

After an exhausting round trip to Buitenzorg and back the Mahrattha platoon had dragged themselves back into the lines that evening, the Sikh platoon were resting and it was the PMs turn for the next day's convoy.

"They refuse to go! Sahib!" The Subedar was near to tears. "They will not even listen to me!" I put a hand on his shoulder:

"Come now, old friend," I said gently. "Gather them together in the rest room and I will talk to them!" The old Indian Army regular, with his Waziristan Medal and fifteen years' service, was shattered and a mere ECO like me had to gather up the pieces. Whilst he mustered the mutineers I took a turn round the camp in the gloaming. 'What would you do, Bob?' I asked the evening sky, 'or you, Harry?' But they were half a world away and I had to confront this one on my own.

The merest whisper of mutiny could bring disaster down upon us. My demotion and probable court martial were unimportant compared to the loss of pride for the Company. The VCOs, NCOs and men were all regular soldiers and the good name they had earned in so many campaigns would be besmirched and all would suffer to some degree.

I entered the hall and faced the seventy or more grim faces of the Muslim Platoon. Informally I waved them down and they squatted on the floor beneath the map I had so lovingly painted. Some looked aggressive, some angry and some frightened. They too knew about firing squads. I asked the VCO and all the NCOs to leave the hall before beginning to speak, which they, fearing for my safety, unwillingly did. I stood for some time without speaking, looking from one to the other and gazing into the eyes of men I had known for more than three years.

One thing was clear, it was an explosive situation and I had to draw the detonator. It had to be done in their language, too. The adrenalin flow made my mind run smoothly and, although my Punjabi may have had a slight Sikh accent, at least it was their own tongue and not formal Urdu. I sat casually on the edge of the platform at the end of the hall, swinging my legs and smoking a cigarette. I began to chat inconsequentially.

I bestowed flowery phrases of approbation upon the PMs, saying

191

how often I had wished that they had been my platoon through Imphal and Semarang, but my kismet had led me to the Sikhs. A translation would have sounded obsequious to Western ears, but it was in the idiom of all Indian discussions and it served to lower the temperature. I threw in a casual observation about not knowing why this had happened on this particular day and said that I had no intention of forcing the issue here and now. I dropped a hint of menace with the phrase that "I did not wish to see anybody flogged at the wheel" a slanting reference to the army punishment for cowardice, desertion or mutiny, that portended the firing squad. We were old companions and deserved each other's respect. I was sure that we could solve the problem together and not lose the brotherly friendship that had been forged in battle. I prized their affection too highly to risk losing it in a moment of heat. I had my orders and I had a job to do and I knew that the Sikhs, tired and exhausted as they were, would not fail me and would turn out again at dawn if I asked them.

The speech was shrewdly aimed and at the mention of the trustworthiness of my old platoon they began to shuffle about and mutter amongst themselves. I held up my hand: "It's not a question of guilt or cowardice. I don't know what the trouble is but I should be pleased to hear your feelings."

They all began to talk at once, three or four at a time, and then I noticed a spokesman emerging. I knew him as a high caste Muslim who had the shifty ways of a barrack room lawyer. I called him out to the front and asked him to speak for everybody.

A Gurkha had been seen, during a house-to-house search in the town, kicking over a box on which lay a copy of *The Koran*, their holy book. Possibly he had desecrated other religious artefacts. Did I think it right for a Hindu to trample on the sacred words of the prophet in the course of reinstating white supremacy in a Muslim country? (In fact Java was part Hindu and part Muslim.)

It was a sharp question. It was all there, festering away, the pus of enemy propaganda affecting the loyalty of our own men. As the murmuring rose again I knew, deep in my heart, that I was approaching the core. There was a lot of justification in their argument and the last thing I wanted was a political discussion. Alternately I gave way and pushed back, and allowed them to blow off steam.

"*Thik hai*, lads!" I said eventually "We understand each other. I have no intention of ordering you out on the convoy in your present mood and I'll ask the Sikhs to go again! They are very tired but they'll do it for me!"

The murmuring began to die away and their native pride overruled their qualms. They would go! Nobody could call them cowardly! The mutiny was over!

I drooped over a cup of very sweet tea in the Subedar's quarters as I gave him the full story. He was unstinting in his praise for the way I had handled things and pleased to have the names of the ones I thought might have been the troublemakers. They were the very ones that he had suspected! One way or another, I thought, there will not be any more trouble, at least not for the time being.

It was still not the end of my problems. One dark night a young and rather stupid PM, out on listening post duty in front of our wire, was tricked into losing his rifle. It was so soon after the mutiny that I feared more sinister overtones, but it turned out to be nothing worse than sex and stupidity. We guarded our defensive boxes rigorously and he had been alone in a foxhole out in No Man's Land; a local houri approached him and whilst she kept him occupied her boyfriend stole his rifle.

Unfortunately this too was very high on the schedule of heinous military crimes. To lose a rifle on sentry duty was even worse than sleeping:

Faithless the watch that I kept: now I have none to keep.
I was slain because I slept: now I am slain I sleep.

Any of us might have been slain because our sentry was not vigilant.

In the Indian Army there was a special kind of Court Martial called a 'Summary General Field Court Martial' that gave enhanced powers of punishment to a commanding officer in the field. I only had to sit a subaltern on one side and the Subedar on the other, and I became a Court of Law. It was not a tribunal because I was not required to consult with, nor allow the others to speak, unless I wished. It gave me the power to impose flogging, dishonourable discharge or even the death sentence in certain circumstances. After the trial and sentencing the proceedings went back to Army HQ to be scrutinized and ratified by the Judge Advocate General, who would check that I had conducted a proper trial, fair but not too lenient.

Abdul Samih was a clown, a joker, and normally a very cheerful

193

but silly man to have around. His defence was farcical. Shortly after I opened the Summary Court Martial he became stone deaf! His plea was that a sudden attack of deafness had rendered him unable to hear the approach of a large band of rifle thieves who had sneaked up on him in the darkness. Whilst taking a pee he had put his rifle down and they had cunningly whipped it away.

With a heavy heart I sentenced him to 12 months imprisonment and discharge from the Army. The maximum sentence for this offence was death and I dared not be too lenient in case the JAG overrode my judgement and enforced the heavier penalty.

To my astonishment when the time came for Samih to be taken away he insisted on seeing me to say goodbye. The thought occurred to me that he might want to commit one last mad act of retribution and knife me for giving him such a heavy sentence. I even had my trusty Luger in the top drawer of the desk as they brought him in. He wept and clasped both my hands in his, he said what a good and fair officer sahib I was, like a mother-and-father to him and he gave me a trinket as a parting gift.

I felt awful, but the Subedar explained to me, like a father talking to his son, that Samih had committed a very serious crime, and he knew it, and moreover he had been caught. That was his kismet. As his commanding officer I had tried him and sentenced him fairly and that was my kismet. It was all written in the book of fate. There was no undertone of anger and the lad just wanted to say goodbye to a good officer and a friend. Indeed he thought I had been most lenient. On the North-west Frontier he would certainly have been shot. Bostan Khan had fought there himself and knew!

In all this gloom I hunted through the repatriation lists daily but my name was still not there. How I wanted to get away from it all!

I made my way to the medico's Sunday party to sink my sorrows and one of my doctor friends said, "My God! Johnnie, you look awful!"

They diagnosed 'Tertiary Javanese Twitch' and prescribed Gin-and-Benzedrine. This was before the days of serious drug addiction, but new formulae were coming on the scene all the time and Benzedrine had been prescribed for the armed forces as a pep pill to give them extra gusto on beach and parachute landings.

I shook off my blues. I was twenty-six, resilient and too busy to mope. Farewell parties became more and more frequent as the names of long-serving officers came up on the lists. Sandy from 3/10 Gurkhas was granted home leave; he was a New Zealander and a regular who had not seen his home for seven years. I had depended many a time upon his sagacity and cool strength to see us through. I had helped him with the netball fixtures list on the troop train to Madras and he had brought us back to Semarang from Ambarawa.

The Gurkha mess was open house for his protracted farewell party. It went on and on, through the first night, all next day and on into the second night. People dropped in, crashed out, had a pick-me-up, did some work and then came back again. Busy as I was I popped in from time to time; I was going to miss Sandy. Eventually we all trooped down to the airfield, carrying jugs and flasks filled with a mixture of all the left-over drinks, to give a fitting send-off to a great man.

There were always women about in the messes, half-caste and Dutch, hoping for a ticket out. The very next day Sandy was back at Bandoeng airport! He was more than a little hung-over and rather embarrassed about his surprise return. He had discovered a willing and enthusiastic Dutch girl sitting next to him on the plane out and as he hazily came round, over the Java Zee en route for Singapore, she greeted him, "'Allo! Darling! Are you feeling bettaire?"

"Who the bloody 'ell are you?" He asked muzzily.

In the next half hour she told him that sometime during the previous night, possibly in bed, he had asked her to be his wife! Apparently he was taking his new fiancée home to meet his mother! He still did not know her name. Being a resourceful jungle soldier, who had been in tighter spots than this one, he did the only sensible thing when they touched down on the tarmac at Singapore.

"Excuse me, my liebschen," he said politely, hoping he had used the right endearment for his new bride-to-be, "I must attend to the dog!" And before she could reply he slipped out of the aircraft door, ducked under the wing, crossed the scorching tarmac and climbed aboard another Dakota that was about to taxi out.

"Where are we going?" he asked the loader

"Bandoeng, mate! er . . . Sir!"

"But where's Gretchen now?" we wanted to know.

"Buggered if I know" He gave his old endearing grin, "but she's off my back and probably where she wants to be!" His last sight of her had been a plump and rather stupid face gazing vacantly from the window of the plane where he had left her.

"She's saddled us with another farewell party, Sandy!" We kept the second one a bit quieter and got him away before officialdom could sort out his papers.

"I'll come to all your farewell parties from now on!" I told him, but I never saw him again.

Chapter 17

LAST BRIDGE OUT

We're goin' 'ome, we're goin' 'ome,
Our ship is at the shore,

Because of the losses of officers and men across the board I was now reporting direct to Divisional Headquarters, instead of Brigade, and carrying responsibilities well above my (acting) rank. In the eyes of the army I was still only a lieutenant; this was my war substantive rank and if I had volunteered for regular service I would have reverted to subaltern. Moreover, whilst I was hobnobbing with the top brass I also had to do the work of junior officers because there were so few about.

A new wave of administrators was coming in from Holland and they were completely different from the ones we had tried to deal with so far. We had been plagued by trash, opportunists who had acquired titles and uniforms to match. It was a relief to see competent Dutch officials who would have to sort out their own affairs, and we hoped that this heralded our release.

A tactical panic called for a very large Bailey Bridge, 290ft in length and weighing over 100 tons at launch. It would be the biggest that any of us had seen in the East before and it fell to me to do the job. Recalling the little one I had dropped in the drink at Litan I now had the opportunity to drop a really big one into the river on the Buitenzorg road. How I wished that I could be a real CO, to stand back and carp at the subalterns and say, perhaps. "A foot a bloody minute! More like a foot an hour!"

It went like a dream. The men were brisk and careful, and a young lieutenant just out from UK knew more about Bailey Bridging of this size than I did. By the time we got back to camp we were tired out but happy, and praise flowed freely for the job we had done. I slept through until early afternoon and then remembered that I had not been in to Company Office to check the day's mail.

My chief clerk, Nawab Khan, was a plump and educated babu-ji. He was a delightful character and I leaned heavily upon him to handle all the administrative complexities. He greeted me with a sheaf of paper and in a manner of such solemnity and grave portent that my heart fell. Obediently I perused the daily returns, the VD figures, the ration state and the other routine paper work. I knew that he was baiting me and enjoying himself whilst he did it.

"Come on, Nawab!" I asked in desperation. "What's going on? I know you are up to something!"

"Ah! Ji, Major Sahib! There is still one chitthi that you have not seen!" And with a flourish he handed me a message from HQ congratulating us on our bridging job. I turned away a trifle disappointed, it was good to have a pat on the back but I had thought from his manner that there was something more crucial.

"Right!" I yawned, "I'm off to take a shower and get smartened up for dinner."

"Oh! By the way Sahib I have just remembered, there is another message, I almost forgot!"

He handed me an instruction from Corps HQ to say that if I was ready and willing to go and if I was available, I was now cleared for repatriation and demobilization. All I had to do was check my inoculations, documentation and go! I stood like a man in a dream holding the paper in a trembling hand and the world swam about me. Nawab Khan stood there with glowing eyes, savouring my pleasure and the success of his little subterfuge.

"Many will be sad, Sahib, to see you go! This is good kismet for you and bad kismet for us!" I could have hugged him.

I was by no means out of the tunnel, but at least the end was in sight. The important word in the memorandum was 'available'. I had been DOV for long enough and I now wondered if they had found a replacement for me.

I went over to the Mess in the evening light. My new 2 i/c was taking the daily Mepacrine parade and I put Chopin's 2nd Piano Concerto on the old wind-up gramophone. I recalled the day Harry and I had bought it and the time when Bob had thrown some subaltern's pop records into the fan. I had built my last bridge – from the day I had carried my first Bailey panel to the enormous one just completed.

198

From the first shot I had fired in anger to the fierce fighting in Indonesia it had been a long road. Now I had another 8,000 miles left to do, through Singapore, Suez and the Mediterranean to take me home at last!

In the last few weeks the tension within me screwed up so tightly that a friend told me that I twanged when I walked. My replacement, a regular Major, had left Poona and would arrive any day. My new adjutant was also a regular Captain, and very competent, and I could leave the company in his charge if the new OC was delayed en route.

I began my farewells. So many of my old chums had gone, either as casualties or to other units, or to their homeland, but there were still a surprising number left who wanted to take a final drink with me. The hardest farewell of all was in my own Company lines.

Bright-eyed Mahratthas with nodding heads, teeth gleaming, whispered 'Ram Ram', their hands clasped prayer-like before them; fair-skinned and sophisticated PMs with solemn flattery; HQ personnel, cooks, clerks and drivers; each and every one a friend and a memory. Some I had punished, on some I had pinned gallantry medals, but regardless of rank or creed they were all my comrades. Finally I came to my old platoon.

The Sikhs regarded me as the carrier of good kismet. I had been lucky to journey with, like a ship's captain who has a reputation for taking prizes and getting his crew safely home. They showered me with gifts: a gold ring, an engraved pocket watch, a walking stick, and packets of sweetmeats galore. Each, according to his purse, pressed a present upon me. They squeezed a Kara on my wrist to remember them by. Bedecked with garlands I ate my last meal with them and stood up to give my farewell speech. It was my longest and most emotional speech in their tongue, and the last time I would speak it.

Next morning a convoy of trucks escorted me to the airfield, where even the Japanese prisoners were lined up for a last ceremonial salute. Once again I sat on my kit, suspended over the wide open door of the old Dakota looking down on a stationary Javanese house that was the centre of the spinning scenery as I pulled out of my last box. We even did a couple of air drops as we ran north to the coast and when we swept across the coastal plain to Batavia I saw the blue sea ahead. I was on my last road home.

I lay on a charpoy in dusty dockland, already a nobody with no responsibilities, a time-expired man and a mere passenger. The thousand and one worries of recent days evaporated; there was nothing to do but wait. Nobody depended upon me and nobody knew or cared. Even the chance of a bullet in the back had gone and for the first time in recent memory I was relaxed with nothing to face but the boredom of a transit camp.

O leave the dead be'ind us, for they cannot come away
To where the ship's a-coalin' up that takes us 'ome today.

The ship that would carry me away was S.S. *Plancius*, an old coal-fired tub, a dirty Dutchman, a Far East coaster. I looked at her rusty plates and black smoke stack and I loved her. The ship's officers spoke the pidgin English of oriental docks, and had women in their cabins from flaxen Zuyder Zee to dusky Java Zee. She only carried a few passengers, the food was awful and in my cabin the cockroaches were holding hands. The mooring ropes splashed into the filthy water, she gave a throaty hoot and we steamed north for Singapore. I did not care how long it took, nor how I travelled and I kept singing to myself 'Going home! I'm going home! At last I'm going the right way!' There was one other British officer on the ship, a major from 2 Kumaoni, which was one of the infantry battalions of 23 Div. He was a Scot going back to Greenock and we became firm friends. It was pleasant to lie back and let others do the work, fire the boilers, steer the ship and take us out of Indonesia.

"Goodbye! Isle of Grip!"

I lay in the sun and dreamed the dreams I had been afraid to indulge in before. I'd get another dog, a Golden Retriever I thought, and call him Sathi too. I'd buy a red sports car, an MG (T) probably or, if the money would not stretch to that, a big 500cc motorcycle. I'd have a week in London, see some opera and dine at Pinoli's. Perhaps I would go back to complete my schooling and finish my university degree, if I could rouse my brain to academic levels again. I'd certainly have a few weeks in Cornwall and look up that lovely golden-skinned girl I remembered so well. I hoped that she was not already married and wished we had written to each other.

Singapore transit camp was as frugal as any I had yet seen and it was packed to bursting with time-expired soldiers and bureaucratic embuggerance. It was contained in a huge dusty barracks. We were no longer active service material and we were treated as returned empties, demob trash, not wanted on voyage or anywhere else. Which is exactly what we were. The quarters were crowded, dirty and lice-infested, the food was execrable.

Despite the fact that I knew how to look after myself, to keep myself clean and alert, physically and morally, I did something so stupid in Singapore that I cringe when I remember it. Jock and I did the rounds of downtown Singapore, but soon ran out of cash, and resigned ourselves to loitering about the depot waiting for our ship. One dreary evening, not wanting to sit and soak at the bar, nor having the money for it, we wandered down into the basement and found an old table tennis set up. Idly we began to play and in the hot, windowless cellar we stripped to the waist.

A very inebriated old major with bristling moustaches burst in. He reminded me of Fred Emney and was obviously a koi-hai, a blimp and a base wallah. Drink and incompetence had denied him promotion because he was no higher in rank than we were. He was the very opposite of us and all we stood for. He started in an aggravating way and quickly became aggressive, as drunks will.

"What are you doing down here?"

"Playing ping-pong!"

"Have you the authority?"

"Bags of it!"

"Did you know that this table is reserved for officers?"

"Hoo-bloody-ray!" We were not being rude but we resented his interference and we were mocking the old fool. Without our tunics he did not know our rank.

"I shall report you for being drunk and disorderly!" he shouted

"We're not as drunk as you are, old man!"

He fumbled in his tunic pocket and produced a tatty wallet from which he withdrew a dog-eared document that said something to the effect that:

"This is to certify that Major Bloodknock has an infinite capacity for alcohol and can never become inebriated.
(signed) J. Soap Medical Practitioner"

"Why are you improperly dressed?" he demanded.

"This is our games kit!" Batting the ball to and fro we patiently humoured the old sod, who would not stop annoying us. Finally he grabbed our ball and pocketed it. He said he was empowered to have our names struck from 'The Lists' and that really went home. The Lists, the nominal rolls posted on the notice boards each day, determined when you were going to board ship for home. That morning Jock and I had found our names listed for SS *Empress of Australia* in a few days time.

"You!" He poked a chubby finger in my chest "Rank, name and number!

"2143939!" My old ranks number tripped off my tongue. "Gunner Snitswitch."

"Regiment?" he bawled

"2nd Kumaoni First of Foot!" I quipped

"Spell that, man!"

"K – M – Y – . . ." I pretended to spell Kumaoni, but switched to nonsense "X – W – Z" He wrote it out, letter by letter. Jock also told him a lot of rubbish and we walked away out of the gloomy basement and left him.

"Halt! You two are under arrest!" We dodged round him and went off to bed laughing.

The next morning a runner found us and said that the Camp Commandant wanted to see us at once. It was a long and dusty walk through the heat, across the camp enclosure to the HQ block, and we reported in our sweat-stained uniforms, looking puzzled. The adjutant looked us up and down, wrote down our names and ushered us into the presence of the Brigadier who commanded the transit camp.

"Now then!" He sounded angry. "What's all this I hear?"

He told us that one of his senior officers, Major Bloodknock, wished to press charges against us for being drunk, disorderly and insubordinate. We had drunk nothing the night before, and could hardly be subordinate to a man of the same rank, but the inebriated old pig had tracked us down and was out for revenge. His report stated that we had been improperly dressed, resisted arrest, unable to spell the names of our units, and listed numerous other charges.

Unfortunately we were as vulnerable as a couple of whores in Bow Street magistrates court. We were Emergency Only officers, running back to civilian life, and it was not seemly to insult regular old-timers or staff officers. Fortunately for us the Brigadier was an active service soldier and had once commanded a battalion in Manipur. He did not remove us from the coveted lists, but gave us a dressing down with a twinkle in his eye. We crept back to our bunks and behaved circumspectly for the rest of our stay.

A week later we went aboard SS *Empress of Australia*. She was a First World War German liner that had been taken as part of the reparations in 1920 and renamed. She had reached the knacker's yard by 1939 and, being well and truly clapped out, she was ideal for service as a troopship. I personally did not care how seedy the old lady was and, so long as she took me back to Blighty, I was prepared to love her.

On the outward trip from England she had carried a load of important dignitaries, British and Dutch diplomats, bureaucrats and administrators returning to take their place in the colonial halls of power. Angrily they had complained about the old *Empress*, elaborating to the press on the poor conditions aboard, and how badly it compared with the halcyon pre-war days when they had travelled on crack P & O liners. As we lined the rails that sunny morning the paper boys on the dockside down below us were displaying boards which said: "3,000 leave on Hell Ship!"

That was us! She now carried 2,900 troops in place of the 500 civilians, who had made the outward trip, but to us she was our ferryboat to Paradise and we were not complaining. We were leaving behind a life far worse than anything a 'Hell Ship' could provide.

The *Empress* could be difficult. Her 22,000 tons of old iron stood on end in a storm as we crossed the Indian Ocean, and the steady force of the monsoon wind against her high sides caused her to list over at a steep angle all the way from Singapore to the Red Sea. Our ankles swelled up from walking the tilted decks all day. She was also a dry ship, which was the usual rule for returning troopers. One alcoholic old koi-hai had a medical dispensation allowing him to enjoy one bottle of Scotch a day, half his usual intake.

The permitted speed through the Suez canal was lower than the speed at which the old liner would steer and we cannoned from bank to bank, still listing in the hot desert wind. Our time-expired passengers savoured the pleasure of shouting rude epithets at a heavily loaded troop ship that passed us on its way east: "Hey! You're going the wrong bloo-oody way!"

"Git yer knees brown!"

Souvenir sellers and the clever gully-gully conjurors in Port Said besieged us before we slipped into the beautiful blue waters of the Mediterranean and left the Far East behind us.

I passed an uneventful twenty-sixth birthday and when we entered the mouth of the Mersey in the last week of July the old Liver birds did not look down – we were obviously not virgin soldiers. The ship's Tannoy speakers implored us not to rush all together to the port rails or she would develop such a dangerous list that they could not warp her alongside. It seemed strange that this enormous four-funnel liner could be so uncontrollable, but she had been made almost half a century before to do a straight Atlantic run carrying far fewer passengers.

It was Sunday in Britain as we tied up and were told that we could not disembark because the dockers were on strike! Apparently a porter at Paddington station had been sacked for bursting open a crate of tomatoes; this was serious stuff and out came the railway workers, the miners and the dockers! We had seen a lot more anguish than a broken crate of tomatoes and the dockside pickets fell back in the face of three thousand angry men streaming down the gangplanks. It did not take us long to find, amongst the military men on board, those who could man cranes, open hatches, get the donkey engines started and offload our kit on to the quay.

I was carrying an odd assortment of loot. I had a shot gun, a ciné camera of sorts, engineering tools, taps and dies, a typewriter, a gold ring, a walking stick and a lot of other rubbish that had seemed valuable to me when I was in Java. It really was not worth much but it was all dutiable. Just ahead of me in the customs queue was a smart young staff officer returning from a short post-war fact-finding mission in the Far East. Condescendingly he said to me, "Don't worry, old boy, just watch the way I handle these chappies!"

He went forward, smiled at the customs officer ingratiatingly, flashed his silver cigarette case and offered him one before declaring his small haul.

"Twenty-five pounds!" the official said. That was a small fortune in those days and far more than I could afford. It looked as though I was in for a caning. Unlike the young officer in front of me I was poorly dressed, gaunt and Mepacrine yellow and even a bit awkward in English after speaking Indian tongues for so long.

"Anything to declare?" The customs man turned to me.

I produced my lengthy, but strictly honest schedule of goodies.

"Been out long?" He seemed genuinely interested.

"Three and a half years or so!"

"Whereabouts?"

"India, Burma, Assam, Malaya, Java . . ." He cut me off

"Quite a trip!" He gave me a friendly grin and called, "Next please!"

At least somebody appreciated us.

It was all over!

ALPHABETICAL INDEX

MILITARY FORMATIONS INDEX

Allied Forces

Fourteenth Army,
 4,8,15,35,46,91,101,125, 164
 IV Corps, , 45, 46, 47, 48, 58, 64, 65,
 93, 198
 5 Indian Div *(Ball of Fire)*, 52, 152,
 160
 17 Indian Div *(Black Cat)*, 3, 5, 26,
 35, 42, 45, 46, 47
 20 Indian Div *(Mailed Fist)*, 46, 48,
 68
 23 Indian Div *(Fighting Cock)*, 4, 17,
 45, 46,47, 54, 102,112,114, 120,
 125, 126, 132, 138, 143, 164, 173,
 179,187,200,
  1 Brigade, 54, 138, 143
  49 Brigade, 47, 138, 143, 144, 160
  37 *(All Gurkha)* Brigade, 2, 20, 45,
 47, 49, 54, 68, 102, 119, 121, 122,
 126, 130, 134, 138, 177,
   3/3rd Bn, 21, 37, 45, 61, 62, 71,
 150, 183

3/5th (Royal), Bn, 37, 47, 77, 86,
 3/10th, Bn, 37, 86, 159, 195
 15 Parachute Brigade *(Snarling Tiger)*, 46, 47

OTHER FORMATIONS
2 British Div *(Cross Keys)*, 93, 95, 97,
 103
2 Kumaoni, , 200
6 Mahrattha L.I, 144
11 E African Div *(Rhinoceros)*, 95, 103
Force 136 (Malaya), 122, 124

ROYAL NAVY
5th Cruiser Squadron, 154, 164
ENGINEERS
91 (RB) Fd Coy, 12, 14, 17, 42, 43, 48,
 49, 63, 91,105,167, 178, 187, 205
71 (Bengal) Fd Coy, 144, 179

Japanese Forces

15th Army, 3, 46
 15th Division, 46, 54
 31st Division, 46, 61

33rd Division, 3, 42, 43, 44, 45, 46, 54
29th Army (Malaya), 122

INDEX OF QUOTATIONS

NOTE: All quotations are from Rudyard Kipling